GRAND CRU

REMINGTON NORMAN

GRAND CRU

THE GREAT WINES OF BURGUNDY THROUGH THE PERSPECTIVE OF ITS FINEST VINEYARDS

REMINGTON NORMAN

WITH A FOREWORD BY AUBERT DE VILLAINE

STERLING EPICURE
New York

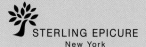

STERLING EPICURE
New York

An Imprint of Sterling Publishing
387 Park Avenue South
New York, NY 10016

STERLING EPICURE is a trademark of Sterling Publishing Co., Inc.
The distinctive Sterling logo is a registered trademark of Sterling
Publishing Co., Inc.

Published 2011 by Sterling Publishing Co., Inc.
First published in Great Britain in 2010 by Kyle Cathie Limited,
23 Howland Street, London, England W1T 4AY www.kylecathie.com

Text © 2010 by Remington Norman
Design © 2010 by Kyle Cathie Limited
Photography © 2010 by Jon Wyand*
Designer: Geoff Hayes; Project Editor: Sophie Allen; Copyeditor: Stephanie
Evans; Proofreader: Francois Gaignet; Indexer: Isobel Mclean

ISBN 978-1-4027-8548-1 (hardcover)

Distributed in Canada by Sterling Publishing
c/o Canadian Manda Group, 165 Dufferin Street
Toronto, Ontario, Canada M6K 3H6

For information about custom editions, special sales, and premium and
corporate purchases, please contact Sterling Special Sales at 800-805-5489
or specialsales@sterlingpublishing.com.

Manufactured in China

2 4 6 8 10 9 7 5 3 1

www.sterlingpublishing.com

* All photography by **Jon Wyand** except:
pp. 7, 10, 16, 24, 25, 27, 32, 33, 34, 35, 36, 52, 60, 63, 69, 110, 114, 119, 123,
141, 152, 154, 169, 171, 173, 182, 191, 201, 202, 214, 223, 224, 226, 227
by **Geraldine Norman**; pp. 29, 41, 86, 96, 117, 128, 149, 156, 157, 172,
176 bottom, 221 by **Mick Rock/Cephas Images**; pp. 30, 103, 137, 143,147,
162, 166, 167, 176 top, 177, 206 by **Ian Shaw/Cephas Images**; pp. 178-9,
213 by **Tim Winter**; pp. 218, 225 by **Kevin Judd/Cephas Images**; p. 49 by
Diana Mews/Cephas Images; p. 205 by **Shaffer Smith/Stockfood UK**; pp.
210-211 by **Herbert Lehmann/Cephas Images**; p. 217 by **Bruce Jenkins/
Cephas Images**

Page 81: The Clos de Vougeot ownership table is published with the kind
permission of the magazine *Bourgogne Aujourd'hui*, number 92

The maps on pages 50, 64, 72, 79, 82, 100, 102, 106, 108, 111, 112, 118,
122 were supplied by Géoportail with the overlaying map text design by
Eugene Fleury.

CONTENTS

Foreword
by Aubert de Villaine

Anyone who steps into a specialist bookshop, such as the famous Athenaeum in Beaune, will find the profusion of titles on winemaking, wine history and wine drinking – particularly relating to the wines of Burgundy – a veritable jungle in its range and diversity. In this fertile environment where obsolescence is rapid, there are fortunately some books that are both essential and enduring.

The Great Domaines of Burgundy was in its time an essential work and remains so – a completely new edition has recently been published – because the writer revealed clearly and in fine detail the history, practice and philosophy of the great domaines of the Côte d'Or, the jewel in Burgundy's crown.

The purpose of *The Great Domaines of Burgundy* was to observe and describe vineyards in, as one might say, 'horizontal' fashion: at a given moment in their history, providing an inventory of the various activities of the profiled domaines, describing Burgundy from all its visible and evident aspects.

With *Grand Cru* – a natural follow-up to *Great Domaines* and just as essential – Remington Norman delves 'vertically' into the core of the concept of *terroir*, as defined and developed in Burgundy. Here his task is not to describe but to understand the secret of the 2,000-year-old adventure of a remarkable wine region – divided and classified to the extreme – one where the determination to link wine to its birthplace, to identify it by its origin, has been pushed further and in a more detailed and refined way than anywhere else in the world.

At a time when the notion of *terroir* is either looked upon as the Holy Grail by the world's viticulturists, or simply denied, it was natural that such a connoisseur of all things burgundian as Remington Norman would want to reveal to us the secrets of this unique wine region where *terroir* is king.

What is it that brought worldwide renown to this hillside, some fifty kilometres long and barely one kilometre wide? And renown to such a degree that the viticulture man has evolved there is acknowledged as a model of its type, worthy of consideration as a UNESCO world heritage site? What is the key to the region's continuity and prestige?

The answers are varied and complex because they integrate the physical aspects of the site and interweave them like organs, each dependent on the others for the survival of the whole. To conceptualise the complexity and uniqueness of viticulture in Burgundy, the word *climat* (not to be confused with climate) was coined, whose meaning, as you will discover throughout the book, goes much further than *terroir*.

To approach and understand the *climats* of the Côte d'Or, Remington Norman considers the well-rehearsed debate on the importance of both physical constraints and human volition on the birth and make up of the *climats*. Was the Côte an obvious choice as a suitable site to plant vineyards and craft great wines? Or was it human endeavour and expertise that succeeded in creating these great wines from a site no more favourable than any other?

The author recognises that the physical aspects of the Côte – in particular its climate – impose great constraints, but also that the Côte has a privileged ecosystem, situated as it is at the extreme margin of ripening both Pinot Noir and Chardonnay without transgressing it. He notes the unifying factors of vineyards that are mostly on clay and limestone soils and face due east/south-east. But within this apparent façade of unity, if I may so express it, he observes the great diversity of soils and microclimates creating different growing conditions more or less favourable according to their altitude and exposure.

What can man do with this raw material offered by Nature? Well, instead of looking for ways to free himself from these climatic constraints and extreme diversity, he uses them to his advantage, exalting the multiplicity of *crus* and vintages, to form the basis of an unrivalled and supremely successful viticulture that has stood the test of time. This is the fascinating, 2,000-year-old history of the relationship between man and the Côte that has culminated in the identification and classification of the *climats* in space (delimitation and appellation) and time (vintage).

Some of those *climats* are recognised and celebrated as consistently yielding sublime and sought-after wines, year-on-year. Located on the most privileged sites of the slopes, where soils and microclimates are at their most favourable, they bring their crop of grapes to full and harmonious ripeness better than any surrounding vineyard. These are the *Grands Crus* (such as Le Chambertin, Le Clos de Vougeot or Le Montrachet) and the finest *Premiers Crus* (Les Rugiens of Pommard, Les Saint Georges of Nuits or Les Pucelles of Puligny…).

These exceptional vineyards command the greatest respect. Their role is to express at the highest level the potential of the *climats*. The *Grands Crus*, red and white, amount to just over 1% of the vineyard area and less than 1% of the wine production of Burgundy. They are at the heart of the notion of *terroir* and are in fact its culmination. Within the wider compass of the commune, a *Grand* or *Premier Cru* is a *climat* identified and defined for centuries, whose product has very specific qualities dictated by the natural attributes of its site that, year after year, place it above its neighbours, always assuming that the winemaker is capable of extracting this potential to its maximum. We winemakers working within the ecosystem of the Côte know that without this extraordinary natural potential unveiled by the genius of man, our desire to produce great wine could not be realised.

Across these privileged sites, Remington Norman portrays the birth, the construction and the exceptional destiny of the *climats*, substantiates the reality of the *terroir* concept and reveals the living natural and human heritage they have created. 'There are no vineyards predestined to greatness, only the stubbornness of man,' wrote Pierre Veilletet. 'Both inherited from nature and shaped by man, the *climats* are a historical legacy, witness of past human communities to be handed over to future generations' (Jean-Pierre Garcia).

But even more importantly, Remington Norman shows that this viticulture, nourished by tradition and the teachings of history, is not from a bygone age, but is both modern and progressive. Every day, science vindicates the age-old traditional vine-growing practices, and especially the fact that in the context of a joint venture between man and nature – so typified by Burgundy – man alone cannot achieve his aim without optimising the natural conditions and protecting them from chemical and technological aggression. This ethos adheres to the principles of caring for the environment and maintaining a sustainable agriculture that have at last been universally recognised.

Climat viticulture can even be portrayed as doubly modern as it demonstrates the success of a universality based on diversity. Diversity is quintessential to the vineyards of the Côte. In a world that is regrettably becoming increasingly uniform, the Côte offers the community of nations the example of a human activity where diversity merges into a unity that surpasses it – '*l'aventure des climats*'.

I must pay tribute to Remington Norman for having understood and presented these ideas in a book whose brilliant writing illuminates in a passionate and inspiring way the 'hidden aspects' that make up the mystery of the Burgundian adventure.

Aubert de Villaine
Domaine de la Romanée-Conti
Vosne-Romanée, Côte d'Or

INTRODUCTION

Burgundy is diverse and complex. At its best it produces ethereal wines of sublime delicacy, silkiness and energy that suffuse the senses leaving the impression of an indefinable touch of magic. It is also capable of maddening inconsistency. For those struggling to fathom its intricacies, the mosaic of vineyards, a convoluted pattern of multiple-ownership and seemingly illogical classification make for abiding frustration; for devotees these very idiosyncrasies merely increase the fascination. Disentangling the complexities requires effort, but once past the intellectual plateau the rewards are tremendous.

There are two keys: the Domaines and the vineyards. For the consumer interested in buying decent quality the Domaines provide the most secure route; if a good bottle is the sole aim, no deeper analysis of the region's workings is necessary. While *The Great Domaines of Burgundy* explores the Côte d'Or through its finest producers, their vineyard holdings and individual philosophies, *Grand Cru* takes the tale a stage further, extending the reach to the vineyards. It profiles each major vineyard and discusses the concept of *Grand Cru* itself, the factors driving quality in modern Burgundy, what makes one wine fine and another pedestrian, why one plot is designated *Premier Cru* while its neighbour is *Grand Cru* at several times the price; what defines *terroir* and whether it is really the key to understanding Burgundy's wines; the role of the media; how one sets about buying and tasting Burgundy intelligently; how vineyards are managed to maximise quality and what considerations should concern the conscientious winemaker. If the producers are the interface between the consumer and the land, the conduit through which Pinot Noir and Chardonnay find expression, the vineyards are Burgundy's source of that potential – its true essence. This book analyses this 'essence' in depth and equips those who can't understand what the fuss is about with the tools to find out.

In many vintages, the finest *Premiers Crus* come close in quality to the *Grands Crus*. This energises the perennial debate as to the validity of the current classification and whether it is time to consider changes. It is now widely accepted that there are vineyards (or, more accurately, parts of them) which do not merit their *Grand Cru* status and equally *Premiers Crus* which are strong candidates for promotion. This book reflects that reality with profiles of the finest *Premiers Crus*. Contem-plating the tortuous bureaucratic process involved in elevating or demoting a vineyard and the local political foment this would unleash, significant revision is unthinkable. In truth, classifi-cation has limited relevance for the consumer: in Burgundy a useful guide perhaps, certainly not an absolute demarcation of quality. What matters is what ends up in your glass; unless you are an irredeemable snob you drink the wine not the classifi-cation.

Buying Burgundy is bedevilled by the fact that much indifferent wine still finds its way through the perfunctory screening system, signifying that the contents are deemed worthy of their respective appellations by those charged with upholding standards. As well as inflicting derivative harm from those who treat themselves to an expensive bottle, are disillusioned and vow never to trust Burgundy again, mediocre stuff at fine wine prices damages the region's reputation and makes life more difficult for producers and resellers striving to do an honest job. There seems no political appetite to tackle this chronic problem (as has been so effectively done with *Vendange Tardive* in Alsace). Forget the haphazard controlling of yields, vineyard inspection panels and the rest of the regulatory rigmarole which any wily *vigneron* can circumvent if he puts his mind to it. What is needed is simple: enforcement of the existing regulations with rigorous, independent tasting for AC certification (*agrément*) with no compunction about declassifying sub-standard wine. Give the egregious lack of effective quality control it is hardly surprising that international markets have done the authorities' job for them with differential pricing for the best *Premiers Crus* and lesser *Grands Crus*.

This book is not, however, written as an ode to political ineptitude or bureaucratic defalcation, rather as a paean to the exhilaration and excitement that Burgundy is uniquely capable of generating. Its greatest wines are incomparable: as intellec-tually stimulating as they are sensuous with a core of internal energy which far transcends mere varietal expression. Hours of friendly disputation may be spent over a bottle or two arguing the relative merits of this or that producer, vintage or vineyard in a way which it would be difficult to envisage for most other grapes or regions. A dedicated coterie of specialist importers, tasting groups, websites and blogs devoted to its wines, history, culture and food, provides an invaluable resource for the consumer and attests the extraordinary degree of international interest in

Facing Page: Chambolle-Musigny from Premier Cru Les Fuées

The magnificent saddle of Corton

modern Burgundy. Indeed, as *Great Domaines* argues, choosing a good source matters more than nuances of vineyard, vintage or appellation. Fortunately, the best producers are well-known and widely followed.

Burgundy's infectious appeal has spread. Its noble grapes, Pinot Noir and Chardonnay, are now planted in many countries where talented producers offer excellent examples in a range of styles, many as flagship bottlings. Great strides in know-how have powered the fine-tuning of grape-growing and vinification; quality is constantly improving with site-specific wines

and premium selections becoming more common. Chapter 16 explores the challenges of burgundian varieties outside France.

Writing about Burgundy raises more general questions on how we think about wine. Efforts to turn wine appreciation into a quasi-academic subject have led to some pretentious posturings on the 'philosophy of wine'. Consumers need taste, discrimination and honesty to back their passion for wine. Writers, whose job is to communicate understanding independent of influence and without favour, need experience and above all integrity. This neither requires nor amounts to a philosophy. There is a genuine, albeit recondite, debate to be had on the contribution of individual experience to taste – on absolutes of quality and to what extent taste is intrinsic rather than influenced by extrinsic factors. Although extending the long-standing philosophical problems of perception and of the existence of an external world beyond individual sensation, these are of marginal interest outside expert circles and of negligible relevance to wine appreciation. The trite observation that it is people not machines who taste and that knowledge and accumulated experience alter taste in more or less subtle ways merely restates the reality of individual differences in perception and preference.

Rarity and high prices have inevitably attracted trophy hunters to Burgundy. Whereas genuine wine lovers appreciate that there is pleasure and value to be found at every level and drink across the board, 'cash connoisseurs' don't seem content unless they are drinking highly rated Bordeaux or *Grand Cru* Burgundy. While not endorsing Clive Coates' ruthless prescription that 'those who only drink first growths because it is beneath their dignity to drink anything else… are idiots and should be lined up and shot', one cannot but feel it truly disheartening to find vinous treasures in the hands of people whose limit of appreciation barely transcends knowing their rarity and cost. All too often, this 'only the best' attitude reflects insecurity and ignorance rather than deep appreciation. Drinking by classification provides but limited protection against an inability to discern true quality. In the universe of quality assessment, appreciating what is at the top is only possible by contrast with what is at the bottom. Being helicoptered on to the summit of Everest can bear no relation whatever to the experience of climbing it. Those who mix Romanée-Conti with Dom Pérignon (a Dom-Pinky is apparently a fashionable cocktail among the ultrawealthy in some Far Eastern countries) or, worse still, with diet lemonade, destroy a work of incomparable beauty and their own self-perception as civilised people in equal measure.

It is more than a cursory observation that a person's approach to wine tends to reflect their approach to life in general. Those who hurry from one fine wine to the next or line up an excess of grand bottles, betray a desire to impress rather than a genuine interest in what they are drinking. There is no law of nature linking enjoyment directly with either quantity or price although in an impatient, materialistic world one might be forgiven for thinking the opposite. In my experience, a few good bottles intelligently shared provide infinitely more satisfaction than a table groaning with rarities.

These pages are not written for those in search of specific recommendations or assessments of individual wines; nor will they trivialise great wine with scores where half a point seems to make the difference between 'must buy' and 'leave alone'. The reader will perhaps also be relieved to be spared the mind-numbing litany of tasting notes which passes for expertise in some quarters. Fine wine is emphatically not defined by 'gobs' of super-ripe fruit, 'decadent' alcohol, 'lashings' of new wood or anything that such crude epithets might suggest. Too many published tasting notes are little more than lists of aromas and flavours, set forth presumably in the belief that this amounts to some kind of understanding. Clotted nonsense, of course; strings of descriptors do not equate to any kind of discernment. In any case, it is facile to assume that a description, however complete, or a numerical score convey anything that is truly important about great wine. Genuine understanding transcends such banalities. Chapter 12 attempts to refocus tasting on the real fundamentals of quality and the media are discussed in Chapter 15.

Fine Burgundy stimulates both senses and intellect but not by the fashionable route of contrived opulence or crude power. Here, rather, one finds refined elegance and discreet dignity; German high Baroque replaces the voluptuous fleshiness of the Italian Romantics; the almost painful intensity of *Ich Habe Genug* rather than the bombinating blast of *Nessun Dorma*. Burgundy's emotions are not obvious or showy but being concealed beneath subtlety and restraint are thereby the more impressive and profound. There are Burgundies for every occasion – from simple suppers to grand banquets and everything in between. Their collective message is that those expecting easy approachability are likely to be disappointed while those prepared to work a little for their enjoyment will be amply rewarded. Such civilising pleasures are independent of classifications, decrees, regulations, pH, canopy management, fermentation technology, polyphenols, resveratrol and the rest. This is not to diminish the value of background knowledge in refining the palate, rather to affirm that in the pursuit of pleasure, technicalities take second place to good food and congenial company. Pinot Noir and Chardonnay from noble vineyards and skilled *vignerons* make for memorable meals and a richly enhanced quality of life. With the greatest, the pleasures transcend the wine itself, making Burgundy a source of deep satisfaction and abiding fascination.

PART 1

EXCELLENCE & PROGRESS: THE EVOLUTION OF THE CÔTE D'OR

CHAPTER 1
THE CÔTE IN THE CONTEXT OF HISTORY

Even the most casual or impatient visitor cannot fail to notice that Burgundy is saturated with history. The merest glimpse within the walls of the splendid old town of Beaune, with its magnificent Hospice and runs of atmospheric subterranean cellars, is enough to imbue the most disinterested of tourists with a sense of antiquity and tradition. Venturing further afield yields a plethora of riches – the Cistercian Château du Clos de Vougeot, fine ecclesiastical buildings, old wash-houses, stone crosses and a wealth of architectural heritage – often tucked away in the most unlikely places. Ancient history beckons from almost every chimney, shutter and wall to attest centuries of activity and civilisation. Vine growing has a long pedigree here. Although there is evidence for the existence of wild vines in Burgundy in Neolithic times (8000 BC), the best archaeological evidence supports the conclusion that viticulture started in earnest in the first century AD, probably with the arrival of the Burgondes in 436. Columella, writing in Latin in the first century, described several vine plants found in 'Gaule septentrionale' – that is Burgundy. Carbon dating from remains found at Vosne-Romanée confirms some eight centuries of viticulture and recent excavations on the plains of Gevrey-Chambertin have unearthed Gallo-Roman vine remains from the end of the first century and the first half of the second. It was the expansion of viticulture to the hillsides during this period, as their superior quality became recognised, which necessitated measures to limit soil erosion and delimit individual parcels. It was from these retaining walls and other forms of enclosure that today's vineyard pattern evolved.

From the 12th century, the powerful religious and monastic establishments – bishops and monks from Cluny, Cîteaux, Bèze and Langres – drove progress, establishing guidelines for viticulture and winemaking and initiating the search for the best sites. Indeed, the broad areas of Beaune, Nuits and Dijon were already identified by the 14th century. Between 600 and 1200 AD Cistercian monks planted vines to ensure supplies of wine for religious offices which included Mass several times a day. They also researched with zeal the best sites and most appropriate grapes. Their idea of adapting grape-type to site and soil was a crucial step towards the modern concept of *terroir*. There would have undoubtedly been some excellent wines made, especially during the medieval warming period – a well-documented era that climate-change apologists have expediently sought to expunge from the record.

Autumn vines in Pernand-Vergelesses

The pre-Revolution sociological history of Burgundy is essentially one of monastic hegemony and royal and ducal patronage. The Abbey of Bèze already had vines in the Côte in 640 and the monastery at St-Vivant (-sous-Vergy), near Vosne founded in 890 was ceded vines in what is now Romanée-St-Vivant in 1232 by Alix de Vergy. The two great monastic orders of the Middle Ages – Cîteaux (Cistercians) and Cluny (Benedictines) had cellars in Burgundy; indeed both were born there. The Benedictines, daughters of Cluny, came first, from the Abbey of St-Vivant in the 10th century, followed by the Cistercians in the 12th century. According to the archives at Cîteaux, the monks of St-Vivant also owned vineyards in Flagey-Echézeaux in the 12th century. The 18th century saw further refinement of the idea of *Cru* – recognition of site typicities and that one vineyard is of higher quality potential than another. Thus on to vintage as the sole index of quality a vineyard hierarchy was progressively superimposed. The 1789 Revolution brought the sale of monastic lands which, for most Burgundians, merely replaced one employer with another. It was not until the arrival of the deadly phylloxera in the late 19th century that large estates were finally dismembered and ordinary citizens enabled to acquire good land affordably.

Burgundy's history reflects a continuing struggle for supremacy between quality and quantity punctuated by occasional but devastating natural disasters. At the end of the 14th century, an outbreak of *Latinea uvella* larvae decimated the vines during flowering; in the 15th century pests ravaged Burgundy prompting the Church to issue a proscription against profanity in 1460. This didn't work, and more drastic measures were taken in 1533 by the Vicar-General of Langres who ordered priests to publish a sentence of malediction and anathema on 'flies, grasshoppers and caterpillars and all their posterity' in the hope that they would forsake the vineyards and retire to the woods. Between July 1878 and 1879 phylloxera devastated Burgundy's vineyards, progressing northwards from Meursault to Gevrey; this was followed in 1910 by mildew which attacked the regrafted vines.

Until relatively recently the focus was firmly on quantity. In the 14th century the Seigneur of Gamay (near Meursault) decided that Pinot Noir be replaced by the more resistant and prolific Gamay. Plantings were mainly on flatter, more productive land and the slopes were then largely abandoned. In 1365 the King's son, Philippe le Hardi, ordered the removal of the 'bad and disloyal Gamay' and that it be mandatorily replaced on the Côte

Vines in the Clos de l'Arlot with the Domaine beyond

with '*Pinot Noir à jus blanc*'. This decision was reinforced by the Grands Ducs of Burgundy under whose aegis no manure or rotten matter was allowed in the vineyards; those who disobeyed had their chariots and animals confiscated.

Nonetheless, by the time of Dr Jean Lavalle's 1855 *Histoire et Statistique de la Vigne et des Grands Vins de la Côte d'Or*, of the 26,500 ha of vines recorded on the Côte d'Or – an extent that suggests massive plantings on the rich soils of the plains – a mere 2,500 ha were Pinot, 23,000 ha being the inferior Gamay. Pinot therefore played a relatively small part in wine production, despite its prominence in villages such as Vosne-Romanée. It was universally considered as a premium variety, its primacy defended by growers, and was thus much sought-after by those seeking quality. Then (as indeed in recent times) Gamay was fraudulently mixed with Pinot Noir to bulk up wine. Nowadays its appearance on the Côte is confined to participation in the Gamay–Pinot blend Passe-Tout-Grains. It was not until the establishment of Appellation d'Origine Contrôlée (AOC) in 1936/7 that Gamay and Aligoté disappeared for good from the Côte's better sites, although a few patches of ancient Aligoté still

exist and indeed produce excellent wine (most notably Ponsot's plot above Clos de la Roche, the source of the fascinating Clos des Monts Luisants). It is also noteworthy that pre-AOC yields were no more than 18–20 hl/ha in the better *climats*, up to 24 hl/ha in the less propitious (about half those of today). Hardly industrial production, but largely ascribable to *provignage* (= hedge formation), viticulture and untreated diseases reducing yields. The arrival of the first commercial plant selections in the 1960s did nothing for quality either, as most were selected for disease resistance and healthy productivity to assist *vignerons* after the years of wartime income famine. Modern clones are selected for quality not fruitfulness.

Up to the late 1970s, the market was dominated by the powerful négociant houses who mainly bought in fruit or wine from small producers. Some were scrupulous about quality, others 'label sellers' were not. In recent times, Burgundy's commercial structure has been marked by two seismic changes. First, the better smaller grape growers have abandoned their links with the négoce to make and bottle their own wines, a process which created today's plethora of small- to medium-sized Domaines.

Although many continue to sell a little in bulk, supplies of good wine for the négoce have become severely restricted which has led them to buy vineyards or even entire Domaines to secure their requirements. The second small but nonetheless significant trend has been the arrival in Burgundy of multinationals with large budgets and deep pockets buying estates or underperforming négociants (Arlot bought by AXA, Bouchard Père by Henriot, Domaine Engel by the Pinault group). This, coupled with established négociants buying land to secure supply, has helped restore a significant vineyard area to conscientious, well-funded hands and thereby increased the supply of quality wine at every level. Top négociants (among them Bouchard Père, Drouhin, Faiveley and Jadot) operate as overgrown Domaines, with an uncompromising focus on quality offering a Domaine as well as a négociant range to their clientele. There remain a slew of medium to large producers who continue to turn out respectable wine but without that obsessive passion which transforms a consumer-oriented approach into one producing wines of character and distinction.

The common ground between Domaines and the négoce is the battle to acquire good land. Fixed supply and insatiable demand, especially at *Premier* and *Grand Cru* level, mean that what little does come on offer finds ready buyers. The market is imperfect in that a government organisation, SAFER (Société d'Aménagement Foncier et d'Etablissement Rural), has the right to first refusal on land sales with a remit to ensure that young *vignerons* have access to vineyards which they could not otherwise afford. Where it feels able to redistribute land effectively it intervenes to block transfers.

Recent decades have seen a signal improvement in overall quality at every level in terms of consistency, typicity and reliability as well as of absolute quality. This is largely the result of a change in perception as producers came to appreciate the rewards of excellence. Most now appreciate, as an entrenched article of principle, that the devil is in the detail, that 'excellence is the accumulation of seemingly inconsequential minor and weightless details. Yet, if you gather them together lovingly and patiently … [and with intelligence] – it is possible to create weight and density. For a fleeting second, one may feel that one has touched excellence' (Raymond Blanc, *A Taste of My Life*, 2008).

In general, standards have risen throughout the region as has the number of sources producing wine at four- and five-star rating. Apart from the realisation that excellence pays, this is

attributable to three factors: an increase in technical competence, research-driven improvements in resources, and an increasingly sophisticated and exigent market willing to pay top dollar for serious wine.

Research and information now drive practice in vineyard and cellar through a knowledge base which is both wider and more secure. Although past generations strove for excellence, their knowledge was comparatively rudimentary. Viticulture was imprecise and vinification often 'seat of the pants' and especially vulnerable to adverse vintage conditions. Many had a strong instinct for quality but lacked the know-how to achieve it consistently. That so many great wines were produced is a tribute to the skill and instincts of those post-war *vignerons*.

The modern Domaine owner has a vast technical armoury at his behest. In the vineyard: expertise on canopy and soil management, sorting tables with ultra-violet lights to facilitate the removal of substandard fruit and a growing library of quality clones. In the cellar: a more detailed understanding of the fermentation sequence, temperature control of vats to a fraction of a degree, gentler, programmable presses, a far less opaque window onto the processes involved in malolactic fermentation and *élevage* and sophisticated analytical techniques to better inform racking, fining and filtration. In short, the *vigneron* intent on making the finest possible wine has resources undreamt of by his father or grandfather and thus limited excuse for underperforming.

Regular visitors to top Domaines have a palpable awareness of the ongoing quest for improvement. A passionate younger generation, freed from the isolationism of the immediate post-war decades, is open-minded, willing to share knowledge and ideas and to experiment in search of perfection. Looking again at traditional practices – horse ploughing, hand bottling, etc – has led to a re-evaluation of modern conventional wisdom and provided a further source of inspiration. Great wines were made before technology, so what were the great-great-grandparents doing right?

More consistency and better wine all round is good news. However, not all the mistakes of the past are easily corrected. Vineyards still have old 'volume' selections planted on overvigorous rootstocks in ground overfertilised with potassium in the 1950s and there are still patches of the poor quality upright-growing Pinot Droit. Time will eliminate these problems as the potassium degrades and as vineyards are replanted. Today's quality evolution is in the hands of a conscientious core of talented *vignerons*, passionate about their *métier* who well understand that improvements only come through attention to the minutest detail, whether from a millimetre increase in the width of the cork to ensure a tighter fit or lowering tractor tyre pressures to reduce soil compaction, rather than from grandiose eco-inspired gestures to flaunt on their websites.

Increased expertise not only delivers better overall quality but also serves to eliminate the extremes. This is not a matter of vintages coalescing and becoming standardised rather that truly execrable years (for instance, 1963, 1965) are almost unthinkable now. This is because techniques in promoting fruit ripeness and skill at vinifying dilute or marginally ripe grapes have enabled decent and correct wine to be made from what in recent history would have been considered indifferent raw material. For example, increasing concentration by bleeding vats of juice or removing water by reverse osmosis, and the now widespread use of cooling technology make for better balanced wines than would have otherwise been the case in problematic vintages.

Additions have been matched by excisions. Top-quality Domaines no longer use systemic herbicides and pesticides; spray regimes are more refined, avoiding the blanket preventive treatments of the past irrespective of need. In many areas sprays have either been eliminated altogether (for example, replacing pest control with natural predators or by disrupting reproductive cycles); soils are managed so as to avoid compaction from heavy machinery and thus loss of drainage permeability. Of particular note has been the development and evolution of organic and biodynamic viticulture on the Côte. In the cellar, handling fruit is altogether more sensitive; racking is performed on a cask-by-cask basis as needed rather than to a pre-determined regime etc. In short, viticulture and vinification are flexible and better adapted to the requirements of the individual vineyard or vintage. These production skills have trickled down from the glitziest Côte d'Or estates throughout Greater Burgundy. Small family Domaines in less grand villages on the Côte and beyond have improved immeasurably; wines are less simple and rustic throughout the range.

Apart from a few generic wines for the bulk export market, almost all Burgundy is now bottled at source. Duvault-Blochet had been bottling Domaine de la Romanée Conti wines at the estate since the 19th century, but the trend really evolved from the original trio (Gouges, Angerville and Grivot) in the 1930s who were openly dissatisfied with the way their wines were being handled by the négoce, and spread rapidly during the 1970s and 1980s. In 1970 a mere 5% of all wine produced was sold in bottle by the Domaine which produced it; the current figure probably exceeds 80% by volume. Estate bottling removes an important source of fraud and provides reassurance that only what the shipper produced, good, bad or ugly, ends up in the bottle.

The market for Burgundy is now international and sophisticated. The last twenty years of the 20th century saw the emergence, pari passu with the rise in wine quality, of specialist importers, retailers and commentators imbued with a mission to bring fine Burgundy to a wider, mainly Bordeaux-fixated, clientele. This reacts back on producers: those internationally minded and well travelled grasp the opportunity to broaden their sales base and thereby to generate the income needed to improve viticulture and to buy the latest presses, thermo-regulated vats and other high-tech desirables. A few were briefly thrown off the quality track by importers insisting on an excess of new wood and consultants who advocated high levels of sulphur during vinification, but these relatively short-lived phenomena were no more than a passing ripple on the general trend.

The sustained upturn in the overall quality and consistency of Burgundy has not entirely eliminated the shockers who exploit the market with substandard wine. At the quality end of the supply chain, a scarcity of wine from the finest Domaines has fed through to prices, although much of the upswing has been driven by importers and wholesalers rather than by the Domaines themselves. This seems likely to continue with the widening market interest in top-end Burgundy. Fortunately there is value to be found in lesser appellations and less sought-after vintages from an increasing band of reliable sources.

Burgundy has never produced so much consistently fine wine. It has looked tradition in the eye while absorbing the benefits of technology, to everyone's considerable advantage. A continuing sense of history pervades the place but producers now reckon with an increasingly sophisticated international market. This works two ways: greater demand improves profitability and develops a loyal customer base; increased vigilance keeps quality under pressure and the Domaines under constant surveillance. Supported by its wider markets, Burgundy is on an unstoppable path to excellence at every level. Consumers should be heartily grateful.

Debudding in Criots-Bâtard-Montrachet

CHAPTER 2
THE GENIE OF TERROIR IN THE CÔTE D'OR

Burgundy is justifiably regarded as the cradle of the modern notion of *terroir*. In this regard it continues to provide a model for the world. A place of complex and varied geology where a few metres often separate different rock and soil types, it is here, above all, that the ideas of vineyard-specific qualities and a hierarchy of quality across the vineyard ensemble have been nurtured, developed and protected. It must be nonetheless borne in mind that *terroir* is an entirely human construct – a convenient shorthand for describing viticultural arrangements. Land itself has no interest in *terroir* or in its expression. At the time Burgundy chose the concept of *terroir* as the yardstick for organising its appellations, other regions opted for different systems – Alsace: *cépage* (although delimitation of *Grands Crus* has now brought it into the *terroir* fold); Bordeaux: châteaux as brands; Champagne: marque, etc. Given its geological diversity and production history Burgundy's choice is entirely understandable. Although *terroir* is used somewhat indiscriminately in defining origins of production, it is the term *climat* – which designates a particular vineyard – that is perhaps more appropriate for Burgundy where it is the specificities of site which, above all, determine quality and personality. The concept is not confined to Burgundy – differences in soil, exposition, subsoil, local climate, etc exist everywhere; what is unique is that for around two thousand years those responsible for wine production here have expressly sought to link their wines to the characteristics of their origins. They have jealously preserved Pinot and Chardonnay as unique varietals in the translation of the differential qualities of place without which the notion of *climat* is meaningless.

The observation that some vineyards consistently produce better wine than others was well noted before the French authorities interested themselves in the matter – the monks were no fools when it came to supplying themselves with wine – but it took the arrival of an official classification to spark the debate in earnest. Although this has been an evolution spanning centuries it is in the decades since the Appellation Contrôlée (AC) system was codified in 1936/37 that the process has accelerated and attracted worldwide interest. This has lost none of its vigour in recent years either in Europe or the New World where regions wrestle with the problems of determining their own classification and indeed, whether to classify at all.

Although the importance of site to quality has long been understood, until the early part of the 20th century *terroir* did not have the significance it has today. Indeed, describing a wine as having a *goût de terroir* was mildly pejorative, denoting a certain coarseness and rusticity rather than anything more positive. Veneration for *terroir* came gradually, following the establishment of the AC system and its subsequent evolution across viticultural France and beyond. The modern concept crystallises the belief that important and systematic differences exist between the wines from one vineyard and another. The first-century agronomist Columella had already noted that vines planted on land on which corn was grown produced inferior wine and it is likely that more detailed observations were being made in Burgundy by the 10th century. Modern elaboration of the concept of *terroir* relies heavily on its burgundian ancestry and it is no accident that discussion of *terroir*, both inside and outside its European homeland, invariably returns to the Côte d'Or. The reason is simple: it is here that site-specificity is at its most striking and highly refined.

The concept of *terroir* bears a latitude of construction. It is most compelling in regions where wines are produced from a single grape variety – Burgundy, Piedmont, Rhine/Mosel, Alsace, northern Rhône, etc. At these marginal latitudes where ripening is not always guaranteed, it might be thought that blending different varieties would be one route to promoting balance and interest in wine. It is thoroughly counter-intuitive to find the reality is the opposite. In northerly regions, the greatest and most precise wines come from single varieties, and producers accept the consequences of marginality in the pursuit of quality. On the European cocktail circuit where multiple varieties are planted – southern Rhône, Bordeaux, Languedoc, Midi, Rioja, etc – the additional blending possibilities add a variable which muddies the concept of site specificity, compromising the purity both of varietal expression and vineyard identity. Moreover, where the blend is elective – for example in red Châteauneuf-du-Pape, where the permissible mix comprises up to thirteen grape varieties – the relative contributions of *terroir* and grape become impossible to disentangle. Where a single variety is planted, although the wine may comprise a blend of multiple different clones, the evidence is sharper. In Burgundy, prima facie support for the concept comes from two critical observations: first, that the quality supremacy of the greatest vineyards is maintained irrespective of seasonal conditions; second that identifiable vineyard characteristics reappear vintage after vintage.

Is *terroir* really the key to understanding Burgundy or is it some kind of factitious construct? The validity of the concept is not universally accepted. A high-profile non-believer is the

Aerial view of Vosne-Romanée

internationally respected viticulturalist Richard Smart. In his view, journalists are the main culprits in giving *terroir* its near-cult status and what significance it has is limited to a site's water-absorbing and retentive properties. Without doubt, *terroir* has been played up in the quest for distinction and market advantage and the drainage properties of soil arguably trump other variables. However, deciding what limits wine quality does not amount to accounting for it. Smart's variables, taking into consideration landscape parameters such as slope, exposure, altitude, microclimatic influences and human action, are certainly part of the enigma but fail to explain the total variance. In any case, research is beginning to tease out the microvariables in soil and indicates that other, subtler, factors are at work. Others express scepticism on the grounds that finished wine bears little or no relationship to what is evident in the fruit to start with; how therefore can *terroir* have any significant influence? This argument is specious: the constituents of grapes include certain compounds (flavour and aroma precursors) which only become discernable after fermentation, so differences are not invariably evident at an early stage. It is subtle reactions between chemical compounds accumulated in the grape throughout the growing

season which account for much of a wine's aroma and flavour. 'Must' (unfermented grape juice), as has been rightly said, is mute yet *terroir* is certainly able to contribute significantly after fruit has been picked.

Another powerful anti-*terroir* argument is that there is no overwhelming identity in a line-up of wines from different producers from the same burgundian *climat*. In other words, is the concept of *terroir* reinforced by the difference between say Roumier's Bonnes-Mares and his Amoureuses or negated by the difference between Mugnier's Bonnes-Mares and de Vogüé's? The fact that in any given cellar each *climat* produces consistently different qualities year after year makes a stronger case for site specificity than the cellar manipulation that some claim as the true basis for *terroir*. In my experience, differences between different Domaines' interpretation of the same site lie well within the bounds of variance to be expected in the overall envelope that is a vineyard's identity.

What *terroir* sceptics must ultimately confront is the overwhelming empirical evidence. In Burgundy, this is particularly strong, especially the long-standing observation that wine from adjacent vineyards with similar soils and vinified by the same winemaker show consistent differences vintage after vintage. Take Richebourg and Romanée-St-Vivant, *climats* separated by a narrow track where it would be untenable to posit significant differences in mesoclimate yet the wines differ: Richebourg fuller and more robust, Romanée-St-Vivant more delicate and elegant. It is difficult to see an explanation in terms of soil drainage, so how is this to be accounted for other than in terms of *terroir*? Burgundians themselves castigate the naysayers in uncompromising terms: 'Some in the modern world deny the existence of *terroir* or put it into question in the view that it is retrograde or too complex for the demands of modern consumerism. Some deny from ignorance, others from impatience or cupidity' (Etienne de Montille, quoted in *Le Terroir et Le Vigneron*, Jacky Rigaux, 2006). Others go even further in their advocacy, claiming the ability to identify a vineyard from tasting its grapes or even smelling its vine-flowers, pushing the idea of vineyard identity well back from finished wine. Until a more plausible case is made, *terroir* will remain the Côte's conceptual backbone.

Terroir does not exist *in vacuo* yet it is often portrayed as no more than a combination of specific physical, chemical and climatic factors. This is a profound mistake. In addition to its physical and situational components, *terroir* has an inalienable human dimension. Sit over a bottle or two of great Burgundy and discussion rapidly comes round to how far the hand of man, as much as that of plant, site and climate, is reflected in the wine. At one level, the human contribution should indeed be self-evident: owning a top of the range item – golf club, piano, video camera or vineyard – is no guarantee of an ability to extract the best from it. This requires time, experience and skill. It therefore makes sense for *terroir* to be regarded as representing potential rather than actuality – a promissory note rather than a receipt. The factor which realises the one from the other is man. Man has shaped, worked and perfected the Côte's vineyards over centuries and it is this transmitted history, culture, experience and accumulated wisdom that coaxes from them their quality and defining character. Tradition weighs heavily on the Burgundian *vigneron*, obliged by the Institut National des Appellations d'Origine (INAO) to work within a framework of *usages locaux, loyaux et constants*. For a few, such obligation

Winter Pruning in Bâtard-Montrachet

is a straitjacket; for most, this recognition of history represents an inspiration.

Man's contribution is diverse: he selects, prepares and often encloses the site – walls are built, stones and alien vegetation removed and drainage installed; he chooses plant material – scion and rootstock – and decides on soil preparation and planting configuration. Walls are particularly important as they trap soil and alter the air- and heat-flow over the vines. Seasonal work – training, pruning, debudding, leaf and crop thinning, etc – are at the call of the *vigneron* and to a large extent elective. Individual decisions are driven by the need to ensure that vines are maintained in the best possible relationship with their environment and the realisation that preserving the natural microbiology of the soil is essential to conserving a site's essential character. In short, man has a considerable influence on site, soil and how grapes are grown, and is thus an integral part of the *terroir* enigma; beyond doubt this influence is reciprocal. *Terroir* is thus not static but continually evolving.

Scepticism has been taken to the limit with the proposition that *terroir* is essentially a human construct. It is argued that nature per se is disinterested in the notion of *terroir* and that without human intervention there would be no *grands terroirs*. The idea of man as the active partner in revealing and preserving *terroir* is unanswerable, but the implication that this somehow makes it independent of nature is less secure. *Terroir* is certainly a human construct in the sense of being a useful explanatory concept for certain accumulated observations, but is no more man-made than is the atom or black holes.

If one accepts that *terroir* potential exists independent of human activity and that man is responsible for its realisation in wine, one must equally accept that it is in his gift to compromise or destroy it, typically by poor viticulture or inept winemaking. Sometimes the project is deliberate. This is obvious from overblown offerings from Bordeaux and elsewhere produced in pursuit of international acclaim. In minor appellations this is perhaps of less concern; in great *terroirs* it is positively criminal.

A variety of more or less exotic metaphors and similes has been wheeled out to give resonance to the idea of *terroir* beyond its purely observable manifestations. Among these one finds translation and language: *terroir* is translated through the language of the grape; likening *terroir* to an energy source – for example a unique radio frequency that has a more or less strong signal (Matt Kramer, *Making Sense of Burgundy*, 1990); *terroir* as a musical instrument which is of no use unless you

know how to play it; the simile of *terroir* as a 'rough diamond' in the soil waiting upon man to be discovered and fashioned into something beautiful. The more exotic efforts tend to be anthropomorphic: great *terroirs* have been described as sites uniquely capable of resolving natural deficiencies and imbalances more elegantly, as taste memories of their origins, and so on. All these make the point that in nature, expression is a joint venture between man and the raw material he works with; they affirm site specificity as an essential determinant of wine quality and reposition the once omnipotent winemaker as a midwife whose role is to facilitate the birth of a wine rather than as a chef who works his secret magic on whatever ingredients arrive on his chopping board.

Some have taken the energy analogy one stage further. For example, take Louis Jadot's supremely cerebral winemaker Jacques Lardière, whose philosophy is based on the need to understand 'the life and power' which come from a vineyard's substrata and the ability of the mother rock to 'demineralise, to liberate potential and life'. In this sense, *terroir* is a matter that is awakened, a force which is transmitted to wine, bringing with it complex vibratory fields which influence flavours and aromas. 'Dynamising' the ecosystem and releasing geochemical energy profitably is the province of delicate human viticultural activity. For Lardière, Burgundy's relatively warm and active *terroir* allows a better 'demineralisation' of these molecules which then delivers a finer, more subtle expression of perfume and odour. He envisages two separate stages to the process: the first is essentially constructive, creating an impression of fruit but less of place; the second, largely post-fermentation, is a destructive process which releases the stored energy into aroma and flavour development. It is in this latter phase that site specificity becomes evident. The rhythm of vinification – its temperature cycle, duration and general conduct – will determine whether this energy remains inert and thus the wine dull, or facilitates its liberation to produce wine with dimension and interest for the consumer. Those forms which are released and give great force to a wine are the best signature of place. This is not 'mumbo-jumbo' or new-age cant, but recognition that great wine has core energy and power which transcends its constituent components. The theme of dynamic force in nature is forcefully espoused by those who practise biodynamic viticulture (see Chapter 10 for more on this).

As well as reflecting the hand of man, *terroir* and *climat* encompass the influences of soil, topography and grape variety.

SOIL

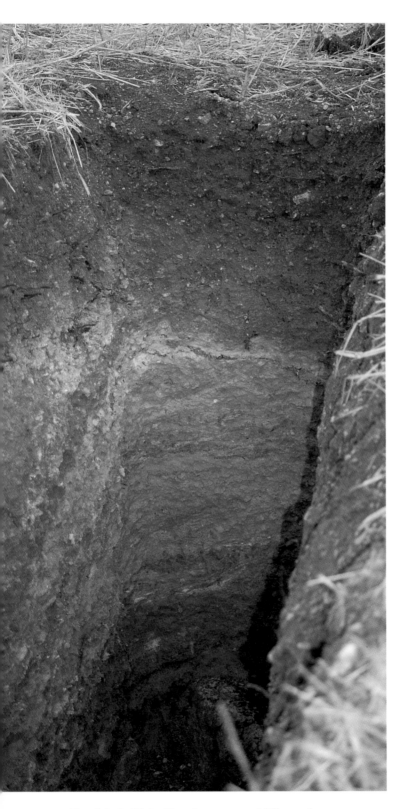

Trench in La Tâche. Note the pronounced difference between soil layers

The most frequent question asked is whether certain soil types correlate with certain wine flavours. For example, does the 'flintiness' in Chablis derive from a flinty soil or is the minerality of Puligny a reflection of minerals in its soil? The definitive answer is that there is no systematic correspondence between soil type and flavour: wine from ferruginous soils, for instance, does not invariably taste of iron and mineral presence does not necessarily produce specific mineral flavours or indeed minerality in general. A soil's trace elements act as catalysts to promote the growth and development of flavour compounds but are not direct contributors to flavour in any simple sense.

If one cannot correlate specific flavours with soil types, is it possible to relate quality level to soil character either in the sense of listing minimum criteria for top quality or, if not, a common factor shared by soils producing *Grand Vin*? One only has to consider the diversity of soil occupied by some Bordeaux First Growths to see the impossibility of such a project: Latour, Ausone, Pétrus and Cheval Blanc are grown on markedly different soil types: Latour on Médoc gravels; Ausone on alkaline limestone; Pétrus on blue clay and Cheval Blanc on a complex mixture of gravel, clay and sand. Or take the differences between *Grand Cru* Chablis and Puligny – wines from perfectly distinguishable soil-types showing consistently different typicities. The relationships between soil and overall quality and soil and specific taste qualities remain an enigma. In Burgundy, considerable effort has been expended to discover the essential elements which make for fine *terroir*. Holes have been drilled all over the place and erudite theses worked up but with little by way of conclusive analysis of the factors common to the *Grands Crus* or the minimum requirements for top-class *terroir*.

If it is impossible to state with any certainty which soil-types correlate with high quality Pinot Noir and Chardonnay, we can readily specify the characteristics which limit quality. Ground that is too hot, poorly drained or contains heavy clays will not produce fine wine. When it comes to chemical composition, nitrogen is a particular problem. Free (though not bound) soil nitrogen promotes natural vigour, which is the opposite of what is wanted for wine quality. At the opposite extreme, low nitrogen soils (for instance, those of volcanic origin or gravel beds) build up a potential for hydrogen sulphide (H_2S) in the vineyard. Vines use up nitrogen at they age, so old vines often suffer from problems related to nitrogen deficiency. In general, controlling nitrogen availability is often problematical: it may be present in the soil but not reaching the vines; also as nitrogen is water

Rock is not far from the surface in Vosne's Premier Cru Les Suchots

soluble it could be available in high concentrations at the start of the growing season but low later on after rain.

Soil comprises topsoil, subsoil and the mother rock upon which a vineyard lies. The diversity found along the Côte's 53 kilometres (33 miles) must be seen in the context of the wider canvas of its 9,000 hectares of vines, 33 *Grands Crus*, 800 individual *climats* in the Côte de Nuits, 400 in the Côte de Beaune. As anyone who has visited the region in any depth will know, a few metres or a narrow path may separate a *Grand Cru* from a *Premier Cru* or *Village* vineyard. The reason for this lies not on the surface, where there is often little visible sign of soil difference, but in the subsoil and bedrock below which exhibit a plethora of faults and strata variation (see Chapter 3). The fault-riven nature of the Côte's geology is well documented and it is this, rather than simply 'the soil' as most commonly understood, that determines how grapes grow on any particular site.

It is clear that broad measures of grape constituents are a poor guide as to how wine will turn out: two analytically identical bunches of grapes will not necessarily produce identical or even similar wine. The subtle variations in composition that differentiate one wine from another appear beyond measurement with the technology currently available which might otherwise provide some indications to correlate fruit composition and wine quality.

Soil has a multiplicity of factors that influence the plant's immediate environment. Its physical composition determines possibilities for root development, heat retention and reflection, and drainage, and its chemical composition determines the possibilities for interaction between nutrients and the vine via the root system. Many believe that soil drainage is a major determinant of site quality – very well drained soils are less able to provide water needs in years of great heat (water stress) unless the vine is old enough to have developed deep roots while highly water-retentive and humid soils are more conducive to the development and spread of rot and other airborne diseases than drier environments.

Then there is the all-important matter of clay. Clays are iron and aluminum silicates produced by microbial and vine-root interaction both with ancient rocks and with newer soil material. They are generally defined in terms of grain size together with plasticity and hardening characteristics; unfortunately, different disciplines use different measures which complicates the subject. A soil's granular composition affects behaviour during rain and drought, its reflectivity at the surface and also its compactability from vineyard operations such as tractor work. It also has an important influence on the general activity of soil fauna and microbes which interact with the vine. From their extensive research in Burgundy, agronomists Claude and Lydia Bourguignon conclude that the important variable is not the quantity of clay but its quality, in particular its internal surface area. They find that no two *climats* on the Côte have identical clay composition even if they have an equivalent overall percentage. The implication is that chemically identical soils do not guarantee identical mineral/ion exchange with vines planted on them and there is thus every prospect of subtle differences in grape composition. The striking difference is between red and white *Grands Crus*. Whereas in Puligny, the *Village* vineyards have clays with the greatest internal surface areas, the *Grands Crus* the least, for reds in both Côte de Nuits and Côte de Beaune the finding is the opposite: *Grands Crus* have the larger internal surface areas. This working hypothesis is reinforced by the finding that the flatter slopes have a mixture of clays of different origins giving *vins ordinaires* of no great quality or interest.

So what is soil's role in *terroir*? At present, the only secure conclusion is that soil is an important factor in wine quality but in an indirect rather than a direct manner. Its chemical and physical properties clearly matter but, as yet, beyond generalisations on drainage and water retention, the mechanisms involved remain imperfectly understood.

TOPOGRAPHY

Topography describes the situation of the land. Where a vineyard is sited – in particular its elevation, orientation and exposure – matter greatly to viticulture. More elevated sites tend to be cooler and thus later ripening but less frost prone as cold air spills downslope; orientation markedly affects how much sunlight and heat both soil and vines receive (as well as the time of day they receive them); some sectors of a given *climat* may be shaded in that they catch less warmth and sunlight. Exposure is certainly a key factor on the Côte; vineyards in evening shadow ripen later and sometimes less fully whereas those better sited enjoy more light and heat. As growers in Pernand-Vergelesses will tell you, an extra hour's evening sun can make a significant difference to ripening; they might wisely add that the south and westerly exposition of their vines is often what makes the quality of a fine Corton-Charlemagne. Depending on the prevailing wind direction, some sites are more exposed than others to desiccating or cold air and frost. There is also the relationship of a vineyard to nearby topographical features – for example, forests and hills can provide shelter, low-lying ground tends to be damper and rock outcrops are a source of reflected heat. Some vineyards have particular problems – proximity to one of the Côte's many streams which descend the *combes* from the escarpment may facilitate rot. This is all part of the *terroir* mosaic.

The *combes* or dry valleys (see page 31) which cut into its western hillsides are a striking and important feature of the Côte's topography. They are relatively young in geological time, created around 20,000 years ago as a result of glacial activity which also deposited scree material along the Côte's flanks. They are more pronounced and jagged in the Côte de Nuits, softer and less dramatic in the Côte de Beaune. *Combes* are also important as conduits for hail storms and for beneficial cooler air from the Hautes Côtes during warm summer months which allows grapes to ripen without burning.

Of all the Côte's major topographical features, slope is arguably the most important. Some vineyards slope gently, others more steeply. While the steepest sites are more prone to soil erosion, even mildly sloping sites (Clos de Vougeot or Montrachet, for instance) may also suffer because of local hard limestone bedrock with a thin soil cover resting on it. Slope and planting configuration determine how much sunlight and sunheat vines receive. East-facing vineyards enjoy morning and afternoon sun but there is often a significant difference in ripening between the north- and south-facing sides of each row which therefore require different handling.

The position of a vineyard is critical to wine quality and there are marked differences between top and bottom of the Côte's slopes. The upper sectors are zones of sediment transfer where progressive erosion has left a relatively thin covering of topsoil; lower sectors – especially those on flat ground near to the RN 74 – being net recipients of eroded and scree material, have deeper, clay-rich soils with more nitrogen (which promotes vigour and growth) and are less well drained. There are exceptions, as in the thick soils at the top of Monts-Luisants in Morey. As a general rule, the shallower the soil, especially if it gives directly on to the limestone beneath, the more elegant the wine (for instance, Chambolle-Musigny and Volnay) while deeper soils generally, but not invariably, promote more heavily structured wine (Pommard and sections of Clos de Vougeot). The finest wines come from sites where there is sufficient soil to provide body but not enough for leaden-footedness. This dream combination forces the vine to work for its nourishment by tapping into the underlying rock – an indispensable condition for the production of low yields and concentrated wine.

In this complex *terroir* mosaic the optimal conditions for the steady maturation of grapes are therefore a subtle amalgam of heat, light, exposition and water regime, many of which are within the scope of human influence (from canopy and soil management in particular). Nonetheless, some sites not only seem to have a knack of ripening fruit without undue assistance but also manage to avoid the problems associated with incomplete phenolic ripeness (where the non-sugar elements of the grape such as tannins and pigmentation remain unripe when sugar levels would suggest the time for picking had arrived or vice versa) and are less prone to disease and rot. *Grand Cru* sites almost define themselves as better places to grow Pinot Noir and Chardonnay – places whose situation delivers lower yields and better, more consistent ripeness year-on-year; in short, an ideal compromise in a region where fruit ripeness is not guaranteed.

What are the limiting factors? The short answer is that anything which alters *terroir* limits its expression. Over the years many of the Côte's *vignerons* overfertilised their land to promote growth (no longer, thankfully), compacted the soils as a consequence of using heavy tractors and overcropped their vines. Worst of all, the use of powerful herbicides, fungicides and insecticides severely compromised the microflora and fauna of the soil – yeast populations, earthworms and benign insects such as typhlodromes (a predatory mite which feeds particularly

Topographical features, like this striking combe behind Chambolle-Musigny, play an important role in fruit ripening on the Côte d'Or

on the pestilential red spider mite) which keep the soils clean and aerated – essential elements of *terroir*.

Claude Bourguignon has drawn attention to the importance of soil bacteria in *terroir* expression. It is these micro-organisms which facilitate the absorption of nutrients through the vine's roots. If soils are rendered biologically inert, poisoned with chemicals, their ability to transmit *terroir* identity is compromised. In his view, biologically dead soils produce indistinguishable wines. Nowadays there is much greater awareness of the importance of 'living' soil which organic and biodynamic viticulture have taken to a higher level. Burgundy's soils are once again fully alive and active to the benefit of the long-term health of the vines. That is perhaps a fundamental clue to understanding the mechanisms by which a *climat* expresses itself.

The micro-organisms affected by viticulture include yeasts. Harvested grapes come with a bloom of yeasts which mediate fermentation and which some believe are site-specific. While that question is, as yet, unresolved, burgundian *vignerons* are steadfast in the belief that yeasts are indissolubly linked to their originating *climat* and a critical partner in the expression of place. This is not to say that the yeast population from one *climat* remains immutable, rather that each year a *climat* builds its basket of yeasts – which may well differ in composition from season to season but will always differ from that of neighbouring *climats*.

Is the expression of *climat* truly compatible with technology? The answer is that technology can be put to its service or used to traduce it. Lighter tractors, gentler presses and dynamising machines for making biodynamic products help preserve *terroir* and typicity; artificially concentrating juice or wine and systemic sprays to combat vine disease mute them. What matters is that technology be employed at the service of tradition, not as its master. Producers, but probably not consumers, might worry that the advance of technological wizardry will be such that fine wine could be made almost anywhere, greatly diminishing the importance of *climat*. There are no obvious reasons why this is not a practical proposition; but while fine wine might become producible in hitherto unthought of locations, this is not equivalent to saying that great Burgundy or great anything else might be made anywhere, irrespective of prevailing conditions. There is thus no immediate fear of Mexican Musigny or Congolese Corton.

Is *terroir*'s existence, or at least its importance, confined to the Old World? Undoubtedly the weight of tradition and experience in the Old World gives *terroir* emphasis which is not necessarily shared by winemakers elsewhere for whom *terroir* is not yet a cultural and marketing driver, but otherwise the proposition is absurd. However, the fact that many high-profile new wine regions have markedly warmer climates than their Old World counterparts means that any *terroir* differences are likely to be less obvious. What is certain is that the New World's voyage of *terroir* discovery is in its infancy, which is both frustrating and exciting. It has been suggested that *terroir* trumps grape variety as the most important determinant of the taste of a wine. Whilst *terroir* imparts a certain character to a wine, it is not validly portrayed as one of many taste components competing for attention. This idea is implausible and has negligible momentum.

GRAPE VARIETY

Choosing which grape to plant is an indissoluble element in consideration of both the definition and individuality of *climat*. Indeed it is critical: what is planted on a site can either enhance or constrain its expression. It is tempting, but facile, to suppose that a great *climat* will show its class irrespective of what is planted upon it. To a certain extent this may be so, but in Burgundy above all, a significant factor in the development of quality has been the refinement of plant material and the preservation of genetic population from which it originated. The diversity of character this provides is considered an important component in the production of top-class wine. Here the grape is regarded as part of the region's heritage – *un patrimoine sans prix* – and the desire to retain as wide a range of *plants fins* as possible evidence of the way in which mass selection is seen as enriching *terroir* expression. This has led some forty Domaines to pool resources to preserve and nurture a selection of Pinot Fin, with the further aim of more rapid progress to refining a diversity of plant material for future use. As Pinot Noir is almost certainly of burgundian origin its inextricable link by association to the concept of *climat* is hardly surprising.

The distillation of all this is that while there is a powerful argument to be made for *terroir* in terms of specificity and typicity, we are far from understanding how it works. In this it shares much with homoeopathy and biodynamics. However, in both cases it is an abuse of logic to take the fact that no one has yet unpicked the mechanism as justification for denying the phenomenon itself: 'unexplained' does not mean 'inexplicable'. The fact that differences between wine from one site and another are subtle and fragile and not always pronounced is not to imply that they don't exist. Nor is there any cash-value for sceptics in the fact that much mediocre wine comes from great *climats*. *Terroir* and its expression in wine are an amalgam of many components, a synthesis of infinite subtle details, in which the contribution of geology has been overstated and that of man understated. The role of what intervenes to mediate *terroir* expression is barely understood. For example the notion that yeasts are site specific is entirely plausible but as yet unproven. What is certain is that great *terroir* does not guarantee great wine – it merely provides the potential and thus the raw material from which can then be fashioned something which is both special and reflective of its origins. Typicity is thus the product of the

Left: Harvested Pinot Noir

Grapes arriving - note the unripe, green fruit

behaviour of a given *cépage* on a given *terroir*. It follows that *terroir* is, as it were, an 'anti-standard' – its *raison d'être* being to express individuality, to privilege difference, whatever the taste characteristics of each particular plot.

What interest has the consumer in all this? Certainly, for the concepts of *terroir* and *climat* to make sense for him, the signature of the site must override that of the winemaker more often than not. The reality is that for most drinkers, beyond obvious broad regional differences, *terroir* is meaningless and its deeper manifestations complications they can certainly live without. The more sophisticated are probably aware of gross differences in soil types – the Médoc's gravels, Beaujolais' granite, Mosel's slate and Burgundy's limestone – and that these affect wine quality, but regard any greater intricacies as of marginal interest.

Although it may turn out that *terroir* is reducible to a specifiable amalgam of components, I somehow doubt it; analysis rarely inspires synthesis. At present and in the absence of any such formulae, the aim for the burgundian *vigneron* remains the maximum expression of *terroir*; this requires a relationship of a special kind: supportive yet respectful, sensitive yet guiding, vigilant but minimally interfering. What is certain is that *Grand Cru* is infinitely more subtle and interactive than *terroir* so often portrayed as a simple amalgam of pedology, topography, climate and so forth might suggest.

Chapter 3
The Origins of the Côte

The very mention of soil and geology makes even seasoned winelovers glaze over and turn the page to something more immediately appealing. With Burgundy this is a pity since the Côte's geological composition is a major key to understanding its wines and, far from being dull, the story is fascinating and indeed well worth telling. Unfortunately, much of what appears in wine books on this subject is sentimental imagining, misleading or plain wrong, often recycled wholesale from other sources. Although delving too deeply into geological complexities is fraught with danger – the more you look the less you tend to discover – this chapter aims to disentangle the subject in as uncomplicated and comprehensible a manner as possible. Considerable effort has gone into making what follows both accurate and intelligible; where unfamiliar terms are required, these are explained. Just as it is possible to appreciate beauty and structure in a building without architectural qualifications, so may the Côte's essential geological complexities be understood without expert training.

Geology influences the wine-related Côte in three principal ways: it determines its shape and relief (morphology), its underlying rock formations (geology) and its soils (pedology).

Spring flowers bordering Vosne-Romanée Premier Cru Les Chaumes

MORPHOLOGY

The Côte d'Or covers a strip of 53 kilometres (33 miles) from Chenôve to Cheilly-lès-Maranges just south of Santenay. It forms the western side of the Saône river from plain to plateau (above which it becomes the Hautes Côtes) and comprises two contiguous units: the northerly Côte de Nuits (CdN) from Dijon to Corgoloin and the southerly Côte de Beaune (CdB) from Ladoix to Santenay. Together these dominate the Bressan plain southwards from Dijon covering, from north to south, the eastern border of the Burgundy plateaux from the Ouche valley to the Dheune valley. In shape the Côte is roughly rectilinear; the CdN more so than the CdB. Whereas the former is oriented north–south with vineyards mainly exposed east and north-of-east, the CdB has a north/east-of-north to south-south-west orientation with vineyards exposed to the south east. Notable exceptions are the east and south-west facing portions of the hill of Corton and the south/south-east facing bowl of *Premiers Crus* north of Gevrey-Chambertin (Clos St Jacques, Lavaux St Jacques, Cazetiers, etc). It should be noted that these changes in exposure are strongly associated with the dry valleys (*combes*, see below) rather than thinking that the slope is not a straight line in these places.

The viticultural strip is narrow, varying in width from 200 metres at Comblanchien to 2 kilometres near Gevrey at an altitude of between 240 and 395 metres (in the Champs Perdrix vineyard just south of Marsannay). The slope angle varies from zero on the plain to 20% with an average of 5% for the *Grands Crus*. The best slopes are exposed to the morning sun and well sheltered from cold winds and spring frosts. Above the vineyards, at the westerly limit, are pine forests or scrub – all that will survive on the hard, unplantable limestone rock. This vegetation gives shade locally and provides limited protection from rain and wind. In earlier times the forests were exploited for wood, as was the case at Vosne-Romanée and Meursault, and what remains after deforestation is dry growing scrub known locally as *chaumes*, comprising juniper, box, grasses, and even wild orchids. In some places, forests planted at the end of the Second World War by youth teams (*chantiers de jeunesse*) now influence local climate; for example the Austrian pines above Gevrey's Belair and Clos de Bèze vineyards shade vines and may retard grape ripening.

A striking feature of the Côte's hillsides is that they are split transversely by a series of dry valleys (*combes*) which pierce the plateaus above. These are significant topographical features in that they act as conduits for cooler air from the Hautes Côtes – a mixed blessing which can amortise extreme heat but also delay ripening in nearby vineyards – and as an occasional funnel for hailstorms. The flanks of the *combes* below which vines are planted are steeper in the CdN, smoother, wider and less dramatic in the CdB. Because they do not cut into the same kinds of substrata, these *combes* are not of the same rock type in the CdN than the CdB – Nuit's *combes* are of Comblanchien limestone while Beaune's *combes* are nicked out of marl deposits (marl is defined as a mixture containing 35–65% clay and 65–35% limestone). Because of a higher shale content (shale is rock composed of layers of fine-grained clay and marl sediments) the *combes* of the CdB are gentler and vines can be grown on their slopes. They emerge in vivid relief in the Combe de Lavaux at Gevrey and the Combe d'Ambin at Chambolle-Musigny. Both have particular points of interest: the former for having Alpine vegetation on its north-facing flank and Mediterranean vegetation on its south-facing flank and a rock thickness of some 110 vertical metres which gives an idea of the depth of this limestone layer; the latter for the outcropping of four distinct and visible geological origins; from higher to lower these are: Comblanchien, Prémeaux, *calcaire argileux* and *calcaire à entroques* (see page 33). Each *combe* has an alluvial fan – a balloon-shaped area of scree material spreading outwards and downslope from the neck of the *combe* where material has eroded and been deposited as surface soil.

The shape of the Côte has been sculpted by millennia of erosion, with a mainly concave contour produced by rainwater and receding seas in distant geological time. These progressively deformed the rocks to create scree and some of this material further degraded into the finer soil in which today's vines are planted. Sustained water run-off also sculpted tiny hollows – a good example can be seen in the Vosne-Romanée les Suchots vineyard which adjoins *Grand Cru* Romanée-St-Vivant. In a few places erosion-resistant limestone has created convexity – as, for example, in much of Chambolle-Musigny Les Amoureuses.

GEOLOGY

In general, the geological history of an area determines and constrains the shape of the landscape – different geologies give different 'skeletons' upon which erosion and human activity superimpose flesh. Geologically, the Côte d'Or is a heterogeneous mixture of clay and limestone on a mother rock of limestone of varying periods. Given this diversity, the range and variegated nature of its wines should come as no surprise. The essential fact to absorb is that although its rocks and soils are of varying types and geological origins, the Côte is, with negligible exceptions, comprised entirely of Jurassic limestone and it is this that accounts for its shape, character and viticultural suitability. Within this overall framework, the present landscape must be understood in terms of three seminal events:

Some 165–141 million years ago, in the Middle and Upper Jurassic periods, when tropical conditions prevailed and shallow sea water covered the land, warm muddy lagoon-like conditions proved ideal for the accumulation of mud and other marine material which deposited then solidified into multiple layers of limestone and marl. As the prevailing conditions changed so did the form and properties of the rocks, hence the Côte's complex geological layering. On top of all this, around 100 million years ago, layers of chalk were deposited. This basic stratification remains unchanged although the younger layers disappeared through erosion between 65 and 35 million years ago when the sea was displaced by a tropical continental environment. Vestiges of this tropical climate are still found – for instance, near the Château de Pommard in the CdB – where nodules of iron represent remains of tropical soil alteration which have been eroded and transported by water run-off.

Thirty-five to twenty million years ago, during the Oligocene epoch, when sedimentation had stopped and the Alps appeared from massive upthrust of material from the earth's crust burying the outcropping Jurassic rocks in the Saône valley, significant rifting occurred which created the Côte's broad relief. This process consisted of stretching of two geological plates – rather like pulling apart a soft bread stick – which provoked a massive inward collapse producing two cliffs broadly oriented north–south: one stretching from Bourg-en-Bresse to Besançon, the other from Lyon to Dijon. These formed the Saône rift plane and the Alsace rift of which the Côtes of Burgundy, Alsace and the Beaujolais constitute the western border, with the Jura to the east and a wide rift valley in between. These escarpments provoked a myriad of smaller cliffs, sectioned at various levels by the accumulation of clays, marls and limestone.

Not a geological fault but the result of ancient quarrying in Bonnes-Mares – vines often encounter seemingly impenetrable rock

Finally, around 20,000 years ago, during the last glacial age, repeated seasonal freezing and thawing eroded the gross rock formations and sculpted the slopes and dry valleys (*combes*) as we now see them. During this period, faulting and collapsing of taller rocks produced the alluvial fans of debris at the outlets of the *combes* that fanned out rather like honey might spread from slope to plain. These fans are the result of *combes* burrowing or cutting and typically contain a mixture of pebbles and shales which have carpeted the lower slopes with well-drained clay and stone scree several metres thick, locally extending the vignoble down to meet the plains of the Saône. The debris can be found on or near the surface in many vineyards (a good example is next to the road to the Combe de Lavaux at the base of Lavaux St Jacques in Gevrey). Of different formation but similar dispersion are *cônes de déjection*, formed by the action of summer heat melting the top ice layers to form water which then penetrated the rock layers but, lacking sufficient force to erode them, merely rounded off small lens-shaped pieces in the more fragile, looser sectors near the surface; these were later deposited in the soil. Both alluvial fan deposits and *cônes de déjection* are to be found in the deeper soils – for example, at the base of Les Cazetiers in Gevrey by the road to Combe de Lavaux.

PEDOLOGY

The third process to influence the Côte is largely pedological. This saw the main development of soils in warmer conditions some 10,000 years ago. When the last glacial age petered out, the landscape changed from tundra to forest which allowed rich organic matter to develop and accumulate along the slopes both through progressive integration of organic matter from forests degraded by micro-organisms and through further rock erosion and scree deposition. This completed the formation of everything responsible for the modern viticultural environment.

To summarise the geological sequence of events: layers of different rock-types were laid down; rifting then sculpted the Côte's gross morphology and finally erosion and incorporation accumulated debris and organic matter along the slopes which we now refer to as soil. Today's mosaic of *terroirs* is the result of these events and the interactions between the various forces, including man, which have progressively shaped it. As for the geology, one can visualise the different strata being deposited one upon another, consolidating and then rifting, as a giant layer-cake which stretched apart and then collapsed inwards. Weather and water then caused further deformation transforming coarse material into smaller fragments and finer still into soils. In short, mud became rock which transformed into land which eroded into soil.

As stratification patterns are highly significant for viticulture on the Côte, it is worth describing the principal rock types. Geologists usually work from youngest to oldest but here for ease of comprehension this order has been reversed.

Sandy marls: These are the oldest, and thus deepest, rocks on the Côte, formed of a clay-limestone mixture. They outcrop between the villages of Couchey and Gevrey-Chambertin in particular, in *climats* such as En Champs (Gevrey), Les Herbues (Fixin) and En Sampagny (Marsannay). These marls constitute the main substratum for the Jura vineyards on the east side of the Saône rift valley.

Crinoidal limestone: Known as *calcaire à entroques*, this rock-type appears in many *Grand Cru* vineyards. It is the result of accumulation and subsequent decomposition of marine animals of the urchin family called sea-lilies or crinoids (meaning 'flowerlike'). What remains is skeletal material made up of calcite (crystallised calcium carbonate; the major constituent of limestone) most often ochre-coloured due to weathering but with a visible brilliant sparkling profile when cut, full of small shell fragments. It is particularly evident in the lower part of Bonnes-Mares, Clos de Bèze, Clos de Tart and Vosne's Les Suchots. A narrow *entroques* strip, 150–200 metres wide, traverses the lower slopes from Morey to Gevrey village straddling the Route des Grands Crus and re-emerges as a much wider band from north of Gevrey to Marsannay. The prominent rock of Solutré is made up of crinoidal limestone of similar age. Although hard, *entroques* is less resistant to weathering than Comblanchien and Prémeaux limestones, hence its widespread use for house and wall building in earlier times. Its presence is often marked by old quarry workings along the Côte's vineyards – very obviously, for example, in Clos de Bèze and Bonnes-Mares.

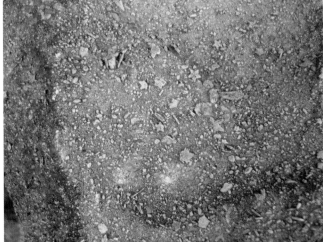

Crinoidal limestone

Various forms of Crinoid

Ostrea acuminata marls: These are formed of innumerable tiny intact oysters around one centimetre across that accumulated on muddy/marly marine beds. This decomposed fossil material is of marine origin; not oysters and crustaceans as in the *Grands Crus* of Chablis, rather the limestone residuum of marine lily-like creatures. Such marls are very tender and friable and erode easily, a factor which has contributed to the Côte's concave morphology. Erosion-resistant Prémeaux limestone generally overlays *Ostrea* with crinoidal limestone often found beneath. Notably, the mid-section of Bonnes-Mares, the top of Romanée-Conti, the Clos de Tart and lower part of La Tâche contain a significant proportion of *Ostrea acuminata* marls, as do Les Bievaux and Les Champs Carafes in the upper sectors of Santenay; it often occurs at the limit with the forest north of Gevrey and west of Marsannay (Les Vaudenelles, Les Echézots). None is observed in Meursault, Puligny or Volnay.

Shaly limestone: The transition between layers of *Ostrea* and younger, harder, lighter-coloured Prémeaux limestone is progressive and marked by shaly limestone – intermediate between marl and limestone. Along the hillsides between Vosne and Nuits this shaly limestone occupies the mid-section of the slope, as in Les Boudots.

Prémeaux limestone: This is widespread along the Côte and, like all Jurassic limestone, was formed in a lagoon environment under tropical conditions. When deposited it was limy mud with a high percentage of water; the weight of surrounding strata that deposited afterwards exerted pressure that squeezed out the water – a long, progressive, process (not an event) – and was highly conducive to cementation of the mud that transformed into hard, pure limestone. In appearance, Prémeaux stone is light coloured, white to light pink, with a white limestone interior without visible grains. Nodules of silica called *chailles* (*rognons silicieux* or cherts) are typical of this limestone level. Prémeaux is highly resistant to erosion and distinguishable in the Côte's landscape because of man-made *meurgers* (= stone accumulations) of which there are plenty (notably in Santenay) and a lightly convex form in the landscape. Good examples are *Grands Crus* Ruchottes (especially Rousseau's Clos des Ruchottes), the upper part of Clos de Bèze, the upper part of La Tâche and much of Vosne-Romanée les Brulées, which is particularly stony. There is an outcrop by the office of Domaine de la Romanée-Conti, another in Laurent Ponsot's cellar and yet another in Bernard Gros' cellar in Vosne-Romanée. Prémeaux is not evident in the Côte de Beaune although its equivalent

Ostrea Acuminata limestone

Shaly limestone

appears as Pierre de Chassagne limestone (visible as a prominent cut above Chassagne on the Puligny/St-Aubin side).

White oolite limestone: This derives from strong wave action – *action de la houle* – reworking the seabed and creating permanent movement. Limestone (chemically carbonates) precipitated in tropical conditions and these deposits collected round a seed (like a pearl) which then grew with constant wave movement to create oolites, as notably in the Great Bahama Bank and the Persian Gulf. The name oolite comes from its egg-like appearance as it resembles small fish eggs (in Greek oos = egg; litos = stone). The resulting limestone is bright white, relatively soft and friable made up of numerous millemetric to infra-millemetric oolites. On the Côte it is usually found interbedded between two hard, resistant limestones – Prémeaux below and Comblanchien above – and very often covered by Comblanchien debris/scree. Good examples are the Nuits les Damodes vineyard (upper part), Les Petits Monts in Vosne and the middle section of Monts Luisants. Both Prémeaux and oolite change in form to become Pierre de Chassagne in the CdB. It is worth pointing out that the deposition conditions were not identical for the CdN and CdB; in the former warm lagoon conditions were followed by wave action, in the latter wave action preceded the arrival of deeper waters.

Comblanchien limestone: This is notoriously hard rock, being 99 percent pure limestone (calcium carbonate) deposited in a lagoon environment as mud which consolidated over a long period as further layers were stacked above it. As with Prémeaux stone, water was progressively squeezed out by weight from above, producing a hard, light-coloured stone without any distinguishing organism debris or visible grains of sand. Comblanchien is often found at the upper vineyard limits in the CdN. It also forms the *combes* of the CdN, often appearing as dramatic outcrops. The northern flank of the Combe d'Ambin behind Chambolle-Musigny is an exception; here the upper part is Comblanchien, the middle outcrop Prémeaux and the lower part is transitional shaly limestone (see above). Due to its low clay content, Comblanchien is generally unsuitable for viticulture, except where it occurs in mid or lower slope where it is excellent – for example the upper part of Clos de Vougeot, all of Chambolle's Les Amoureuses and the lower section of Charmes- and Griotte-Chambertin, and Roumier's Morey Clos de la Bussière. In the CdB the Comblanchien layer is much thinner becoming 'dolomite' – crystallising calcium/magnesium carbonate – as opposed to limestone alone which is calcium

Prémeaux limestone

White oolite - minute eggs clearly visible

carbonate without the magnesium. This is not cultivated because the soils are too thin, rather used as building stones, evident from the many old quarry workings in non-cultivated patches of Meursault around Puligny's Le Dos d'Âne and Meursault's Chaumes de Narvaux. Comblanchien stone has been used in construction since the 19th century, in particular for the Château du Clos de Vougeot (hence Vougeot la Perrière). Quarried at Comblanchien in the CdN, its marble was used in the building of Paris' Charles de Gaulle airport and the Louvre pyramid.

Dijon–Corton limestone: This is found at Dijon and Corton, mainly at Corton, but is rare in vineyards. It is a hard, yellow and blue limestone containing shale debris, deposited as sand which further cemented. It is known as Dijon because of its use in house building there from quarries around the town. At Corton it appears in the lower-middle and lower sectors of the vineyard.

Ladoix limestone: This sits just above (therefore younger than) Dijon-Corton and results from sandy deposits in a tidal environment. It forms the upper section of Volnay Caillerets and at the point where Meursault, Monthélie and Volnay meet there are many Ladoix limestone quarries. Outcrops in the form of horizontal beds are visible in old quarry working in Volnay Caillerets and Monthélie Champs Fulliot. Their form – sigmoidal, or in the shape of a transverse letter S – is due to tidal deposits and their thickness to lunar action. Up to the start of the 20th century Ladoix limestone (*laves*) was used for roofing tiles (*tuile de lave*). *Lave* is a deformation of *lève* (*la pierre qu'on lève* – meaning the stone that is removed). In contrast, Dijon–Corton limestone is no good for roof slabs because it forms thicker beds but an excellent material for walls.

Oligocene: This is (geologically) more recent material of heterogeneous composition – old galets (round or oval stones formed as seas receded) mixed with eroded clays and marls of 150 million years old which form conglomerates and marl deposits with a typical salmon pink colour. Oligocene generally occurs in the lower part of vineyard slopes where sediments accumulated when the creation of the relief generated erosion around 30 million years ago. It is not conducive to top wine quality as evidenced from the lower third of Romanée-St-Vivant, whose fruit Romanée-Conti exclude from their St-Vivant *cuvée*, and the lower portion of Clos de Vougeot which is borderline *Grand Cru* quality. Excavating for houses and cellars in Vosne-Romanée, the first five metres of ground were found to be of Oligocene type.

It is important to visualise these layers as retaining the same relationship as they were deposited, lying flat one upon another as they outcrop, throughout the various upheavals with the different strata following the contour. Thus geologists surveying the Côte tend to find that rock type B is likely to have rock type A above it and type C below it wherever it appears. Because of the rifting 30 million years ago, wide stair steps have been created generating disturbances in the logical geological organisation, so that the stratification pattern does not invariably occur as expected; so, two formations with different ages can be found close to each other along the hillside as, for example, in the Clos St Jacques and Lavaux St Jacques at Gevrey which profiles as Prémeaux limestone in the forest, marls with *Ostrea acuminata* in the upper part of the vineyard, *calcaire à entroques* in the mid-section then, because of faulting, Prémeaux limestone next to the road. The adjoining vineyard, Les Cazetiers, has completely different stratification with *Ostrea acuminata* marls upslope and *calcaire à entroques* all along the slope. Gevrey's *Grands Crus* are different again: below the forestation one finds oolite, Prémeaux limestone in the middle of the hillside then (faulting again!) *calcaire à entroques.*

Comblanchien limestone

FAULTS

If the geological picture were simply a repeating pattern of identifiable layers of rock following the Côte's contours, understanding would be greatly simplified. Any such predictability is complicated by the fact that the Côte's hillsides are intensively cut by faults resulting from tensions pulling rock layers and forcing them to break apart. Stretching usually occurred on an east–west axis producing fault lines running on a north–south axis. The process created fissures or fault lines parallel to the relief in the form of narrow strips 200–1,000 metres long in an east-west direction which can run for up to 10 kilometres on a north-south axis. These punctuate the Côte irregularly: some communes are more faulted, for instance, Gevrey-Chambertin, others, like Vosne-Romanée, less so. A few faults are visible most invisible. A major fault line between the Côte's limestone plateau and the trough below explains the hillside relief and the geological diversity along it. It is this major fracture which has generated minor ones that more or less intensively affect the vineyards and account for the Côte's geological complexity. The outcrops due to these fault lines make it possible to appreciate the complexity of the *terroir* and to a certain degree understand the personality of each wine.

The presence of a fault is sometimes indicated by a slight deformation in the landscape and often coincides with a vineyard track or road. Not all undulations signify faults; many are hollows made by water run-off, the introduction of new soil or quarrying activity. Faults are more often visible when they feature two different rock types – for instance, *Ostrea acuminata* against Prémeaux limestone – less visible where two resistant limestones are involved. A prominent example of faulting is visible at the top of Le Montrachet in the form of a highly striated outcrop the lower part of which has slipped downwards towards Puligny.

While it is incorrect, as has been claimed, that on the Côte there is on average a geological fault of 100 metres every kilometre, one of 10 metres every 100 metres and one of 1 metre every 10 metres, this is not so much of a distortion as to be a wild exaggeration. Suffice to say that the Côte is a landscape feature that is highly faulted and that the relevance of all the displacement for viticulture is that from top to bottom of a given slope one is likely to be traversing several different geological compartments. This further emphasizes the complexity of the Côte's *terroir* but is neutral as to how this translates into wine difference.

Visible faulting at the top of Le Montrachet

THE TWO CÔTES

The Côte de Nuits and Côte de Beaune differ in geological age and consequently in predominant rock type. The CdN has older, limestone-dominated terrains (Middle Jurassic, 170–154 million years old – technically Liassic to Callovian series) whereas the CdB's lithology (Upper Jurassic, 154–141 million years old – technically Oxfordian to Kimmeridgian series) is marl-dominated. Travelling south from Gevrey-Chambertin, the Jurassic rock substratum exhibits layers of different ages with younger rocks toward the south. The CdB is somewhat different from the CdN. The white marls of the Upper Jurassic age outcrop from Aloxe-Corton to the north of Meursault, while Middle Jurassic strata outcrops of Dijon-Corton and Ladoix limestones dominate the vineyard between Volnay and Meursault. The Middle Jurassic strata which characterise the CdN plunge down at Ladoix, resurface at Meursault and run through to Santenay.

Soils are the key to understanding the qualities of Burgundy both in the sense of the qualitative hierarchy and, to a lesser degree, the individual aroma and flavour profiles of particular vineyards. In wine writing, 'soil' is often a loosely used term covering everything apart from rock in which vines grow, both what is seen on the surface and what is below (subsoil). Clearly, given the heterogeneous nature of its geology it is not surprising to find a range of soil-types and compositions throughout the Côte. While science has yet to provide detailed explanations for observed differences it is beyond doubt that soils are a major factor in the variety of wine produced at every level. The quality and classification of the Côte is closely related to its geology and geomorphology. These determine a vineyard's slope, exposition and soil composition – the proportion of rock fragments, clay fraction, calcium content, and so forth.

The Côte's soils reflect human activity as much as its geological history. It is important to appreciate, especially in today's *terroir*-fixated mindset, that soil is not a static, immutable element, a mere growing medium upon which man has no influence. Two thousand years of human activity and intensive cultivation since the Roman invasion have modified the landscape and made profound changes to its soils. In particular the construction of enclosures, tracks and roads has affected the downward displacement of both coarse and fine material. Stone walls block water run-off and often accumulate soils which would otherwise have been washed away. The

Parochial sculpture in Puligny-Montrachet

effects are particularly noticeable in the lower section of Clos de Vougeot and almost everywhere where roads are built among the vineyards. Early cultivation required earth to be imported from the plains of the Saône Valley to render land suitable for plant growth. Documents from the Middle Ages testify that soils were brought in for viticulture – including in Romanée-Conti!

Fertilisation, digging and routine mechanical operations have changed the land's structure and drainage properties and altered its health and microbial life. Ever since husbandry has involved mechanisation there has been much trouble with soil displacement. On the Côte, the mean rate of erosion is 1–2 millimetres per year on the steeper slopes, sufficient to present a serious long-term problem both with loss of soil and the accumulation of clay-rich material lower down. For example, the fact of a 3-metre difference in soil depth between the upper and lower part of Fixin's Les Hervelets due to a wall cannot be indifferent to its wine.

Understanding soil requires a broad awareness of what it contains and how it works. Soils influence the quality of grapes grown on them in two major ways: depth and physical structure determines in part how effectively (or badly) they drain away excessive water, their overall heat-retentive properties and how well they are aerated (essential for microbial and other life). Chemical and biological make-up – in particular the amount and type of mineral, organic and nutrient material soil contains – influences both vine growth and fruit composition. The same selection of Pinot Noir or Chardonnay grown on adjacent vineyards with different soil and rock types in the same season will produce more or less subtle differences in the final wine. That soil and situation affects quality should be obvious to anyone who grows vegetables. This proposition is the foundation of Burgundy's remarkable diversity.

As the geological events described above unfolded erosion further altered and complicated the Côte's landscape. Scree, pebbles and debris of various kinds were deposited in varying quantities and depths depending on the speed of water run-off. This essentially mechanical process fashioned and deposited the material which now covers the slopes.

Although this activity produced highly varied *terroir*, the Côte's soils are essentially similar, being formed from changes in sedimentary rock – well-drained Jurassic limestones, marls and shales. The Upper Jurassic rock produced more marls – ideal for white varieties; the Middle Jurassic more limestone – ideal for Pinot Noir. Soil compositions on the Côte range from

An old vine in leaf in Romanée Conti

the extremes of heavy clay to a strong predominance of active limestone (which affects uptake of soil nutrients and eventual grape composition) with limitless permutations in between. In general, the soils are pebbly with a shaly matrix and not conducive to vigorous growth. A relatively high percentage of active limestone and low proportion of clay make them ideal for Pinot Noir and Chardonnay which perform well on a limestone base but indifferently at high yields. This mix of constituents promotes a burgundian typicity characterised by a savoury element and notable minerality which overlay each grape's varietal personality.

In both CdN and CdB greyish-brown, humus-rich, gravelly and stony soils developing on scree predominate. These, known as rendosols, are particularly associated with the weathering of compact limestones containing active carbonates and brown soils. The scree is a mixture of gravel (broken up by frost) and red silt that has slipped downslope onto marly bases or limestones. The best are either brown limy or brown with active limestone, delivering wines of considerable finesse and complexity. On the brown limy soils the limestone is active and generally dominant which can cause yellowing of vine leaves (chlorosis) when the limestone stifles the vine root; the brown limestones have less active limestone offer the vine a better balance of carbonates. Certain poorly drained brown soils contain no limestone because it has either been completely washed out or else was never there in the first place; they are mainly made up of alluvial clay and found at the foothills to the east of the D 974 (the Route des Grands Crus) where the plains begin. Vines are only planted here because their roots can eventually reach limestone and

these areas are classified only as *Appellation Régionale*.

The depth of soil available to vines before they hit bedrock is a major determinant of finesse. Along the Côte, the upper slopes which, through erosion, have a paucity of topsoil – in Chevalier-Montrachet or parts of Musigny, for instance – tend to deliver wines of greater finesse and less substance, while those from deeper and richer soils produce the reverse. It is no coincidence that the finest wines come from vineyards in the mid-section of the slope where the soils combine sufficient depth to impart substance but not enough to destroy finesse.

Differences in soil and rock account for Pinot Noir's supremacy in the CdN. Theoretically, though of course not in practice, the CdN is better for white grapes than red with higher, cooler, east-facing slopes and the CdB better for reds being lower, hotter and south facing. It took the monks to work out that the reverse is true. The Middle Jurassic strata that characterise the CdN are ideal for Pinot Noir which is perfectly at home on well-drained limestone soil and moderate slopes. It is on such terrain that one finds Burgundy's great red *Grands Crus*. The composition of these wines, in particular their tannin/acid balance fuse into almost seamless harmony with their power and profundity; wines with subtlety and solidity, body and bouquet and with longevity built into their structures. The predominance of active limestone explains why there are very few whites in the CdN and indeed the rather *sui generis* and curious character of those there are. A handful of plots are good for whites and, once again, the monks found them!

At the same time as rifting collapsed the land by faulting, erosion continued and accumulations of conglomerates, often as large, salmon-pink marls, known as 'pudding stones' (also strikingly evident in some parts of the Hermitage hill in the northern Rhône) occurred in the lower part of the rift valley. These make for well-drained soils combined with potentially good water storage properties. Residual scree from this process composed of material of various ages but mainly Jurassic limestone debris and marls, appears along the Côte as Oligocene deposits – notably in the village and lower vineyards of Vosne-Romanée (Clos des Réas and the lower sections of Romanée-St-Vivant and Clos de Vougeot). In such situations the vine's expressiveness is compromised.

The hill of Corton forms the transition between CdN and CdB with both red and white *Grands Crus*. Its upper section, being marlier in composition, is planted with Chardonnay (Corton-Charlemagne), whereas to the east and in the lower

Autumn vineyard on limestone soil above Chambolle-Musigny

climats the Upper Jurassic-derived soils are planted with Pinot Noir (Corton). Wine from Chardonnay planted on red Corton territory may not be designated Corton-Charlemagne but only Corton Blanc; there is very little of it and it is rather unusual.

In the Côte de Beaune, the dominance of marls over limestone is ideally suited to Chardonnay and centuries of experience confirm that these soils produce the finest results. From Ladoix to Meursault the bedrock is Upper Jurassic (Oxfordian and Kimmeridgian) with strata that contribute to bases that vary according to their proportion of limestone or clay; from Meursault southwards it is of Middle Jurassic origin. Here, and notably in the CdN at Morey-St-Denis, one finds the white marls on which Chardonnay thrives. From halfway southwards in Chassagne (roughly from Morgeot on) through to Santenay and Maranges the proportion of marls to limestone diminishes strongly. Pinot Noir does well here, giving supple, fruity wines, although less tannic and structured than those of the CdN. Soils of the CdB tend to be markedly less pebbly than those of the CdN, although pebbly alluvial fans, often several metres thick, are found below the *combes* marking the foot of the slope and the start of the plain.

In general Chardonnay dislikes pure limestone, which tends to increase yields, preferring marly terrain with moderate clay: the Kimmeridgian marls of Chablis, the Oxfordian deposits of Corton-Charlemagne or the southern part of the Côte de Beaune. Here Upper Jurassic marls and limestone dominate (more marls than limestone) with Oxfordian marly limestone and marls with iron-bearing oolite and hard Middle Jurassic Dijon-Corton limestone forming the substrate of vineyard soils. These are residues of the deeper seas in this area which deposited the layers found on the tops of the hills above the vineyards to the east. Thirty million years ago water deposited scree containing enough clay to thicken the soils.

One final factor to be mentioned in discussing the CdB is the water table. At Puligny this is near the surface hence the absence of the underground cellars found in next-door Meursault. Subterranean water carries nutrients and other elements to vines and its depth and constancy is clearly relevant to how much they receive. It is tempting to speculate that differences in water table account in part for differences in vineyard classification. This is unproven beyond the known dislike of many plants, vines included, of having their roots waterlogged.

One can know a great deal about the Côte's wines without knowing anything of its origins. Knowing something of its morphology, geology and soils provides the basis for a more profound understanding of the differences between vineyards and communes and thus adds another dimension to the appreciation of its wines.

PART 2

THE CONCEPT OF GRAND CRU

CHAPTER 4
THE UNIVERSALS OF QUALITY

The working idea of *Grand Cru* is both thoroughly burgundian and thoroughly pragmatic. It reflects the fact that over the centuries the quality of wines from certain plots has consistently out-performed that of their neighbours, irrespective of the grape variety planted on them. Despite being trafficked around the world as a superior designation for wine, of whatever origin, with or without legal sanction, it is in the notion of vineyard ranking rather than wine classification that the concept of *Grand Cru* finds classic expression. In this system it is the quality potential of a specific site that is classified and only by derivation the wine produced from it. In Burgundy, the designations of *Grand* and *Premier Cru* are indissolubly tied to place: not *Grand Cru* wine, rather wine from a *Grand Cru* vineyard. It is entirely consonant with these arrangements that part of a garden, a courtyard and a vegetable plot retain *Grand Cru* status (Clos de Tart) and land containing little beyond a few trees and a religious statue (Côte Rôtie, Morey) remains a *Premier Cru* despite having not a single vine planted upon them.

There is a seminal distinction often confused – or at least confounded – in discussions of *Cru*, between the quality level of a wine and its individual qualities. The former determines a vineyard's hierarchical status, the absolute level of quality of which it is deemed capable and reflects what might be termed 'universals' of quality. The latter denotes the particular taste qualities of an individual *climat*. In Burgundy, hierarchy is represented by the ascending scale from *Régionale* (Bourgogne Rouge or Blanc) through *Village* and *Premier Cru* to *Grand Cru*. This is a matter upon which neither winemaking skill nor viticultural expertise has any bearing but crystallises the observation that the produce of one vineyard surpasses that of another in terms of consistency and class irrespective of vintage conditions. These rankings are robust, having withstood the test of time and recurrent mutterings about the need for revision. As any intellectually honest producer will aver, a *Village* vineyard cannot be cajoled into producing the depth, richness, balance and complexity of *Grand Cru* however determined the effort or skilled the craftsman. This is entirely as it should be and as credible a vindication of the hierarchical system as one can expect.

The other aspect of quality refers to the particular taste qualities from any given vineyard site. In this sense, parity of ranking does not amount to parity of taste. Musigny tastes different from Chambertin, and both from Bonnes-Mares or Corton. Even within a given village one *Premier Cru* or *Grand Cru* will exhibit a different spectrum of aromas and flavours from another. Superimposed on these complexities are overall differences in character between one village and another. So it is that Puligny Premier Cru Les Pucelles differs from Puligny Premier Cru Les Folatières and Gevrey Village from Chambolle Village. In contrast, Gevrey *Premier Cru* differs from Musigny both in absolute quality and in individual qualities. These distinctions are essential to understanding Burgundy.

Site specificity relies in part on the conventional wisdom that the higher a vineyard's classification the more defined and resilient its taste characteristics. This makes it possible to talk of typicity at least at *Premier* and *Grand Cru* level. To add further interest, Musigny or Bonnes-Mares from one source will taste subtly different from their counterparts from another. It is such nuances which help make Burgundy so intriguing.

How are such differences to be explained? While there can be little doubt that soil composition and siting of vineyards are major determinants of what ends up in one's glass, some have sought to depict these arrangements as a French ploy designed to maintain hegemony over the rest of the wine-producing world. It is beyond doubt, and entirely understandable, that the Old World has wheeled out *terroir* as an unique selling point, but this does not *ipso facto* invalidate the concept or justify extending the argument to the proposition that only the Old World has five-star vineyard sites. No-one who has deep experience of Burgundy would for a moment entertain the proposition that *terroir* is merely an ingenious marketing tool. Indeed, those who argue in this way ignore the obvious fact that a system which has proved notoriously difficult to understand hinders rather than facilitates marketing.

Nor are the existence of execrable bottles of *Grand Cru* (there are unfortunately plenty) or the fact that *Village*-designated wines in expert hands may eclipse *Premiers Crus* from the less competent (which they often do), or that in exceptional vintages *Régionales* are as good as normal *Villages*, *Villages* as *Premiers Crus* and *Premiers Crus* approach *Grand Cru* quality, credible arguments against the classificatory hierarchy. On the contrary, such apparent anomalies are entirely consistent with it. Recent progress, particularly in viticultural know-how, has, if anything, emphasised differences in both quality ranking and taste qualities between *Crus* as top Domaines strive for minimum interference in the grapegrowing and winemaking

Towards Le Montrachet

process, allowing the vineyards to express themselves in as pure and untrammeled a manner as possible.

Thus it is that the 33 vineyards of the Côte d'Or designated *Grand Cru*, a mere 1% of Greater Burgundy's production, represent the summit potential of which Pinot Noir and Chardonnay are capable. They are scattered throughout the Côte – some villages have several, others none. Their status is signified by having only the vineyard name on labels. Thus Montrachet and Chambertin are *Grands Crus* whereas Puligny-Montrachet and Gevrey-Chambertin are the corresponding villages. In fact the villages themselves were Puligny and Gevrey, until status-conscious late 19th-century municipalities decided to tack on the name of their most illustrious *Cru* to enhance their village's reputation. This was largely a Côte de Nuits phenomenon; many in the Côte de Beaune did not follow suit: Beaune itself, Chorey, Volnay, Pommard, Meursault, St-Aubin, Monthélie and Santenay chose to remain, as it were, 'single'. Conventional wisdom has it that this was a deliberate decision to protect the brands of the then all-powerful négoce; superficially plausible perhaps but hard to square with the reality of little in any of these villages which might even be candidates for *Grand Cru* status.

As it stands now, the classification is not entirely uncontroversial. In the original determination of which vineyards merited *Grand Cru* status, politics as well as wine quality contrived to cloud the picture. For example, Gevrey-Chambertin's Premier Cru Aux Combottes was not so classified and, given its situation bordered to the north, south and west by *Grands Crus* one has to wonder why. Its wine is certainly often as good, if not better than neighbouring Mazoyères/Charmes-Chambertin. Part of the answer may be because the committee in Gevrey charged with the determination in 1936 discovered the vineyard's proprietorship was mainly vested in citizens of Morey and not a single Aux Combottes vine belonged to a *vigneron* in Gevrey. The Clos St Jacques in Gevrey also suffered because the then owner was unpopular for his reluctance to participate in the life of the commune; so the vineyard was classified *Premier* rather than *Grand Cru* – political vengefulness if you will. There were other instances: many considered that Les Saint-Georges merited *Grand Cru* but the burghers of Nuits, led by Henri Gouges, felt that their village was of sufficient renown without one. Other proprietors saw no advantage in the superior designation at a time of widespread economic difficulty and were content

to remain at *Premier Cru* level; Domaine Lamarche for example, whose La Grande Rue in Vosne was only upgraded to *Grand Cru* in 1992. One hears such stories up and down the Côte and while it is tempting to question the sanity of those early recusants it is worth recalling that in the 1930s the markets lacked today's international dimension, with often marginal difference between the price of *Premier* and *Grand Cru* for the majority of wines on offer. In current circumstances, were the classification to be revisited without prejudice there would undoubtedly be revisions, especially among the *Premiers* and larger *Grands Crus*.

The list of *Grands Crus* is not immutable but given the requirement for an act of the French parliament, not to mention the legions of experts, bureaucrats and committees, and the quantity of dossiers and circumlocution required elevating or demoting a vineyard at *Grand Cru* level, evolution is understandably sluggish. Some revisions are now widely recognised as desirable: sections of some larger *Grands Crus* are generally considered unworthy of their status – including parts of Les Echézeaux, Clos de Vougeot and Corton – while some *Premier Cru* vineyards deserve promotion. At the top of the list are Chambolle's Amoureuses, Gevrey's Clos St Jacques and Puligny's Pucelles and Caillerets.

Why is Burgundy so diverse? Part of the answer is historical and part geological. Centuries of monastic ownership followed by the destruction of monopoly ownership at the French Revolution has evolved into today's fragmented mosaic. However, it is the region's unusually complex geology which really underpins modern Burgundy's system of classification. This has been imaginatively described as a geological keyboard – each key separated from the next by a crevasse. Faults, largely invisible on the surface, occur all over the place. They mark changes in subsoil structure, determine water run-off or bring the terrain of one level down to the next (see Chapter 3).

What, geologically, differentiates *Grand Cru* land from *Premier Cru* or *Village* and indeed, one *Grand Cru* from another? While rock and soil diversity undoubtedly play important roles in determining the quality potential of a vineyard and the individual taste qualities of grapes grown on it, the relationships are complex and far from being understood, even by experts. If to geological variation one factors in drainage, surface soil type, exposition, slope, microclimate and, most importantly, the experience accumulated and transmitted by generations who have worked this land, it is not difficult to understand why the classification has evolved as it has.

What is beyond dispute is that there are demonstrable geological differences between vineyards and that these matter. Both the physical structure and chemical make-up of soil influence the growth and composition of grapes grown on it. In turn the characteristics of the grape – skin thickness, concentration of sugars and minute differences in flavour compounds, etc – determine the taste qualities of the resulting wine. The studies – and there have been many – are inconclusive, indicating no obvious correlation between soil composition and either quality level or individual flavours. Recent work by Claude and Lydia Bourguignon on clay profiling has started to throw light on this enigma (see page 25). At a phenomenological level, *vignerons* have never doubted the active ingredients of their unique *terroirs*: 'It is the nature of the soil and subsoil which, given favourable exposition for maturation of fruit, imprints its profound personality on each *Cru*, its aromatic specificity in particular, but the style of its body and flavour also. We believe that calcium and active limestone are essential factors. We propose that the "fat" and roundness of wine [are] dependent on limestone, that clay favours the extraordinary and paradoxical alliance between tightness (*fermeté*) and softness (*moëlleux*), that silica brings power and finesse, that iron develops colour intensity. We know that deep-coloured soils favour red wine production, while white soils (*marnes blanches* in particular) favour white wine production; this is very obvious from the Montagne de Corton' (Henri Jayer, quoted in *Ode aux Grands Vins de Bourgogne*, Jacky Rigaux, 1997).

Classifying the vineyard rather than the wine it produces compounds the difficulties for the consumer. Finding the best in a region in which vineyards are generally owned by multiple proprietors all making their own wine comes on top of mastering the differences between one *climat* and another. Even at *Grand Cru* level there is much indifferent wine so the consumer's wisest recourse is to rely on the quality and integrity of the grower. With, to use the oft-quoted illustration, over fifty Clos de Vougeots produced in any given vintage it is hardly surprising that many do not merit *Grand Cru* status (or the price asked). Unfortunately, too many producers still underperform: many cut corners in pursuit of maximising income; some simply lack competence, while others have a poor appreciation of what constitutes *Grand Cru* quality. While it should not be beyond the wit of any producer not making the grade to seek help from a colleague making a better fist of it, this rarely happens, so many continue turning out wine which damages the collective image of what Côte d'Or *Grand Cru* should be.

One of the most difficult messages to communicate to those seeking to understand Burgundy is why one vineyard is classed *Grand Cru* while its neighbour across a narrow track is mere *Premier Cru* or even *Village*. This reflects the fact – which many, particularly from regions with vast tracts of geologically uniform vineyard have difficulty accepting – that even within the compass of a few metres geology can vary significantly. It is clear that there are a myriad of variables, many poorly understood, but it is probably no coincidence that the majority of *Grands Crus* and finest *Premiers Crus* are found mid-slope on well-exposed, moderately sloping ground, on soils combining optimal proportions of clay and limestone with pebble size which promotes heat retention and good drainage. Most of these vineyards are sited outside the extended influence of the *combes* which funnel colder and often humid or rain-bearing air from west to east.

It is sometimes suggested that Burgundy's fine divisions are distinctions without differences. This is far from the case; these distinctions deliver real differences and the characteristics of each vineyard emerge in the wine vintage after vintage. Ask any *vigneron*: Bruno Clair will tell you that working with neighbouring *Premier Cru* vineyards in Gevrey over many vintages – Clos St Jacques and Les Cazetiers – same scions on same rootstock, ripening and picked and vinified at the same time, the differences between these *Crus* are systematic and consistent. Anyone having difficulty accepting this has only to make some comparisons for themselves.

For the *vigneron*, the signal mark of a *Grand Cru* is its ability to produce fine wine year after year, ripening fruit fully whilst retaining acidity. These exceptional sites enjoy relative immunity to seasonal conditions not shared by lesser vineyards which suffer more obviously from vintage differences. They are favoured by their position and soil composition to produce ripe fruit incorporating subtle elements of aroma and flavour which allow sympathetic and skilled hands to transform a humble bunch of grapes into a wine of magic and distinction. These privileged plots are the *Grands Crus* of the Côte d'Or.

CHAPTER 5
THE GRANDS CRUS & FINEST
PREMIERS CRUS OF THE CÔTE D'OR

The following pages describe each *Grand Cru* vineyard with a listing of its major owners and identify the best sources for its wine. The topographical and geological descriptions use the rock and soil terminology outlined in Chapter 3. The *Premiers Crus* which come closest to *Grand Cru* status are also included. The selection of these latter is a matter of personal judgement and reflects my view of those vineyards with that extra indefinable 'something' which puts them above their peers. This is not a matter solely of wine quality – there are many excellent wines from vineyards which do not justify a rating above their current classification – but of vineyard potential and, above all, consistency. The fact that fine wines are currently made from one vineyard and not from another does not *ipso facto* make the first better than the second. Fine wine is a necessary, but not alone sufficient, condition for *Grand Cru* status. There will inevitably be disagreement on the choice, particularly the inclusion of Nuits' Les Saint-Georges and the exclusion of Vosne's Cros Parantoux. This will hopefully enliven the wider debate about quality in Burgundy.

Cros Parantoux well illustrates the problem: owned by two talented Domaines (Méo-Camuzet and Emmanuel Rouget), the international cult status it currently enjoys is due to the exaggerated reputation of the wine produced by the late, legendary, Henri Jayer who cleared and replanted it after the Second World War (the fact that it was abandoned then says much). If it were not for him, this would just be one *Premier Cru* among the pack. Today's Cros Parantoux bottlings are fine wine indeed, sometimes at *Grand Cru* level, but not of the quality or consistency to elevate it above other fine Vosne *Premiers Crus* such as Malconsorts or Suchots. What is also clear is that the geology of this vineyard puts it outside the band of Vosne *Grands Crus* so on this criterion alone an application for upgrading would almost certainly fail. Supporting historical reference comes from Lavalle (op. cit.) who ranked Cros Parantoux in the fourth division in his 1855 ranking. The 1936 classification of Vosne's vineyards was well done and has stood the test of time; its validity is not automatically repudiated by the fact of mediocre wines from great sites or great wines from lesser sites. It bears repeating that the basis of Burgundy's classification is the potential of its land, of which wine quality is one, but not the sole criterion. There is no compelling reason to depart from this general principle.

The choice of *Premiers Crus* as *primus inter pares* is complicated by the fact that in some communes the general standard of winemaking is notably high and consequently many candidates would vie for promotion. In Volnay, for example, one finds Clos des Ducs, Taillepieds, Mitans, Caillerets and Bousse d'Or all capable of excellence. I include Caillerets in *Grand Cru*

Maturing wine

Tending Pinot Noir vines on the Hill of Corton above Pernand Vergelesses

aspirants as it seems to me to produce the most consistently fine wine, almost irrespective of vintage – a signal criterion of top quality. This assessment is shared by several of Volnay's top *vignerons*.

Nuits' Les Saint-Georges is generally considered as its finest *Premier Cru* but its suitability for elevation to *Grand Cru* is controversial. Are the wines really fine enough to justify promotion? Is the vineyard capable of producing at the topmost level? Is the finest Saint-Georges really a notch above other *Premiers Crus* – for example, Grivot's Vosne Boudots, Roumier's Morey Clos de la Bussière, Frédy Mugnier's Chambolle les Fuées, d'Angerville's Volnay Clos des Ducs, Lafarge's Clos du Château des Ducs or de Montille's Taillepieds or Mitans? Probably not, but when consistency is factored in, the conclusion has greater force. A similar difficulty arises in Puligny where Pucelles and Caillerets are knocking on the door of their adjacent *Grands Crus* – Montrachet and Bâtard-Montrachet. I have included both as they seem to me to meet the eligibility criteria of quality and consistency and share the same geology as their neighbours.

As I believe descriptors are of limited value in transmitting the idea of quality, I have largely avoided these in characterising the wine from each vineyard. In truth, the impact of great wine is as much emotional as sensorial and, in any case, at the topmost

level one rapidly runs out of distinctive superlatives. What I have, however, tried to achieve is a description of broader structural qualities as it seems to me that these do provide elements of constancy which transcend variation in vintages and growers' styles. In general, Richebourg is denser and more muscular than its neighbour Romanée-St-Vivant but that is not to say that a St-Vivant from a dense, hot vintage will necessarily feel lighter than a Richebourg from a more elegant year. Such anomalies and inconsistencies are part of the Burgundy's enduring fascination.

I have deliberately avoided the thorny debate as to whether parts or all of some *Grands Crus* should be downgraded. There are clearly instances where known differences in soil-type would suggest that the classification is inappropriate and others where, for reasons of incorporation, parts of an appellation are questionable. My view is that, although there are a few cases where revision is probably justified, this kind of argument is distinctly shaky as it is difficult to disentangle indifferent quality due to producer ineptitude from that ascribable to deficiencies in the vineyard itself.

In the end, readers must make up their own minds. Collectors will doubtless enjoy sharpening their vinous wits comparing bottles from these vineyards with others to prove me wrong. No-one has a monopoly of wisdom on this topic which is still hotly debated by the *vignerons* themselves and which, given the tortuous ramifications of French bureaucracy, is likely to remain academic for the foreseeable future.

A NOTE ON PRESENTATION

Area: 1. The area attributable to the principal owners of each vineyard is listed alongside their entry (**best sources in bold**). Where an individual connected to a Domaine owns vines worked by that Domaine, these are listed as if owned by the Domaine itself which, as far as the consumer is concerned, they are. 2. The area given for each vineyard is the full extent granted the AC; the area actually in production may differ slightly.

Vine Age: This information follows the ownership entry and comes in several forms: planting dates, e.g. (1959, 1964, 1973); planting period, e.g. (1962–1984); average age (50); age span (40–80). Some Domaines chose not to supply vine age details so none is given.

Average Annual Production: Figures are obviously approximate and subject to annual variation. Those given average the years 2003–2007. (For yield conversion factors see Measures in the Appendices, page 232. NB 1 ha = 2.471 acres.)

Further information: for details of a Domaine's vineyard holdings see *The Great Domaines of Burgundy*.

Combe aux Moines

Clos St-Jacques

BROCHON/
FIXIN

Gevrey-
Chambertin

Ruchottes-
Chambertin

Mazis-Chambertin

Combe de Lavaux

Route des Grands Crus

Chambertin
Clos de Bèze

Chapelle-
Chambertin

Griotte-
Chambertin

280

D 122

Charmes-Chambertin

Chambertin

Charmes-
Chambertin

N

0   400 m

Latricières-
Chambertin

Mazoyères-
Chambertin

Combe Grisard

Monts-Luisants

Aux Combottes

MOREY-ST-DENIS

50   GRAND CRU

CHAMBERTIN

Gevrey has the greatest number (nine) and the second largest area (87.06 ha) of *Grands Crus* on the Côte, although well behind Aloxe-Corton which has 232.07 ha. The picture is needlessly complicated by administrative idiosyncrasy which permits Mazoyères-Chambertin to be labelled Charmes-Chambertin, and Clos de Bèze as Chambertin, but not vice versa in either case.

Gevrey's *Grands Crus* occupy two strips to the south of the village separated by the Route des Grands Crus (the D 974). Within this short compass – some 1,200 metres long and 250 metres wide – soils and slope vary significantly and there is a definite gradation of quality potential and taste qualities between the different vineyards. The *Grand Cru* strip extends from below the forest to the west to the easterly plain on a gentle slope. Beneath the woods, the bedrock is hard Prémeaux limestone extending to an invisible fault line which cuts north–south some 100–200 metres above the road; a narrow band of *entroques*, maximum width of 150 metres, occupies the next portion either side of the road, then, after another fault line, a wider band of hard Comblanchien limestone emerges to the east. Further downslope, on flatter land, the clay content is unsuitable for quality viticulture. It is the differences between these three soil-types which characterise and define Gevrey's *Grands Crus*.

Chambertin and Clos de Bèze are rightly regarded as *primus inter pares*, showing more depth and complexity than other Gevrey *Grands Crus*. This is not to say that these latter are in any way shabby – far from it – just a shade less exciting.

STATISTICS: *Area*: 12.9 ha. *Owners*: 25. *Average Annual Production*: 5,250 cases.

PRINCIPAL OWNERS: **Armand Rousseau**: 2.15 ha (1930–1997); **Jean-Louis Trapet**: 1.90 ha (1919 & on); Camus: 1.69 ha; **Rossignol-Trapet**: 1.60 ha (1919–1972); **Jacques Prieur**: 0.84 ha; Louis Latour: 0.81 ha; **Leroy**: 0.50 ha; Pierre Damoy: 0.49 ha (1974); Rebourseau: 0.46 ha; Belland: 0.41 ha; Louis Remy: 0.32 ha (30–40); Tortochot: 0.31 ha; **Dujac**: 0.29 ha (40); Philippe Charlopin: 0.21 ha (1950); **Ponsot**: 0.20 ha (15 & 49); Bouchard Père et Fils: 0.15 ha (30–40); **Denis Mortet**: 0.15 ha (c. 1960); Bertagna: 0.20 ha (1965); Bichot/Clos Frantin: 0.17 ha; **Dugat-Py**: 0.05 ha (1920).

ORIGINS: Received wisdom is that 'Chambertin' is a contraction of 'Champs Bertin' (Bertin's field) after one Bertin who, owning land adjoining the Clos de Bèze belonging to the Abbaye de Bèze and seeing the quality of wine the monks made there, decided to plant Pinot grapes. By the late 13th century Chambertin was well-established as a premium wine-producing site. Chambertin and Clos de Bèze were sold to the Chapitre de Langres in 1219 and remained in religious ownership from then until the French Revolution at the end of the 18th century.

TOPOGRAPHY/GEOLOGY: The vineyard, a broadly rectangular strip, is bordered by Clos de Bèze to the north, Latricières to the south and Charmes to the east. In the main it is flat, although the upper sections towards the forest are on a shallow slope – enough for soil to be washed down to the road during heavy rain. It lies in the influence of the Combe Grisard, just to the south, at an elevation of 270–300 metres. In the southerly part of the vineyard and in the lower sections, the white soils – due to the alteration in form of the Prémeaux limestone – are more evident. Here, as in Clos de Bèze, the soils are rather thin, 20–50 centimetres, with light-coloured stones dominating. The geology offers two distinct units: the upper two-thirds are Prémeaux limestone while the lower third has a subsoil of *calcaire à entroques*.

WINE: Chambertin's robe has been compared to 'seeing the best of Titian' (*Burgundy,* Stephen Gwynn, 1934). In general, it produces a dense, muscular wine with plenty of natural stuffing. Unfortunately, a number of owners of this great vineyard are underperformers, so careful selection is necessary. With less obvious finesse and noticeably firm tannins at the outset, the best examples need several years to integrate and unpack their considerable aromatic and flavour complexity. Chambertin does not have the sheer sophistication of say Musigny or the top Vosne *Grands Crus*, but is invariably well concentrated with an appealing breadth and density. The most common epithets are 'masculine', 'austere', 'fleshy' with a character which emphasises the darker elements of flavour: black fruits, dark cherry, coffee, chocolate, liquorice and so on. The *terroir* is strong, giving powerful, rich, wine which has no difficulty absorbing 100% new oak in good vintages. If you want the best from Chambertin, leave it until at least its eighth birthday. The finest examples will evolve gracefully for several decades. A mature Rousseau Chambertin is one of Burgundy's greatest and most memorable wines. As Hilaire Belloc famously remarked: 'I forget the name of the place, I forget the name of the girl, but the wine was … Chambertin'!

CHAMBERTIN-CLOS DE BÈZE

Chambertin Clos de Bèze with the forest beyond

In 1860 the Comité de Beaune classified the *Grands Crus* of the Côte. It adjudged Chambertin and Clos de Bèze first class and the other *Grands Crus* second class. Though no such official designation exists today – *Grand Cru* is *Grand Cru* without sub-classification – Chambertin and Clos de Bèze are considered qualitatively superior to the other Gevrey *Grands Crus* and command higher prices on the secondary market. Clos de Bèze is 2.5 ha larger than Chambertin which it adjoins on its southern boundary with Mazis to its immediate north.

STATISTICS: *Area*: 15.38.87 ha. *Owners*: 18. *Average Annual Production*: 5,104 cases.

PRINCIPAL OWNERS: Pierre Damoy: 5.36 ha (1920–2000); **Armand Rousseau**: 1.42 ha (1935–2000); Drouhin-Laroze: 1.39 ha; **Faiveley**: 1.29 ha (1949, 1955, 1966 & 1983); Prieuré-Roch 1.01 (1929); **Bruno Clair**: (0.98 ha); Pierre Gelin: 0.60 ha (1979); **Louis Jadot**: 0.42 ha; **Robert Groffier**: 0.47 ha (1953); Bart: 0.41

ha; Rebourseau: 0.33 ha; Alain Burguet 0.27 (1955); **Prieur**: 0.14 ha; **Joseph Drouhin**: 0.12 ha (1999).

ORIGINS: Having been donated land by Duc Amalgaire in the seventh century, the monks of the Abbey of Bèze cleared and planted it. Thus the birth of Clos de Bèze, which has not altered in dimension since its creation in 630 AD.

TOPOGRAPHY/GEOLOGY: Clos de Bèze is marginally steeper than Chambertin, especially in the upper sections under the forest. This steepness also makes it sunnier – particularly in the early part of the day. The Combe de Lavaux immediately to the north brings down cooler air which retards maturity, especially in the sector near the woods, so Clos de Bèze is often harvested late. The soils here are shallow which, as so often in the Côte, tends to impart more perfume and less substance. The geology broadly continues that of Chambertin, with one notable difference: although both lie on prevailing Prémeaux limestone, Clos de Bèze has far more light-coloured soil which is whiter and more luminous than that at Chambertin. The top two-thirds of the vineyard are on Prémeaux limestone, the lower third is on *calcaire à entroques*. The forest above plays an important qualitative role in both Chambertin and Clos de Bèze. The microclimate it provides protects the vineyards from the north wind and from hail, though not from the cooling influence of the Combe de Lavaux. It is noteworthy that elsewhere in Gevrey (and throughout the Côte) where the forest-line is broken by *combes* or deforestation, hail damage is more likely. The Combe Grisard above Latricières and Chambertin is a good example.

WINE: There is a subtle difference between Chambertin and Clos de Bèze. While the former can be described as having greater muscle and flesh, the latter often shows more fragrance and aromatic openness at the outset with particular notes of spice. Side by side, Chambertin is generally more austere in character, firmly tannic and virile and a shade less dense in colour than Clos de Bèze which, as one chronicler of Burgundy's history, Gaston Roupnel, put it with rare Gallic restraint, 'combines grace and vigour, austerity and power with finesse and delicacy. All these contrary qualities compose an admirable synthesis with a unique generosity and … complete perfection'. Eric Rousseau suggests Clos de Bèze receives a little more light, which gives it a touch more ripeness and sweetness than Chambertin. Fortunately the majority of owners are of high quality, so disappointments with Clos de Bèze are statistically less likely than with Chambertin.

CHAPELLE-CHAMBERTIN

Chapelle-Chambertin lies below and to the east of Clos de Bèze, across the Route des Grands Crus and is bordered by En Griotte (Grand Cru Griotte-Chambertin q.v.) to the south and the little-seen Premier Cru Les Gerbaudes to the north. It comprises two principal sections: En la Chapelle (3.69.24 ha) and a parcel of Les Gémeaux (1.79.29 ha) which ajoins it to the north. This latter was incorporated at the delimitation of AOC in 1936.

STATISTICS: *Area*: 5.48.53 ha. *Owners*: 9. *Average Annual Production*: 1820 cases.

PRINCIPAL OWNERS: Pierre Damoy: 2.22 ha (1947–1990); **Ponsot**: 0.70 ha (5 & 14); **Jean-Louis Trapet**: 0.60 ha (1945 onwards); Rossignol-Trapet: 0.55 ha (1929–2001); Drouhin-Laroze: 0.51 ha; **Louis Jadot**: 0.39 ha; **Claude Dugat**: 0.10 ha (1902)

ORIGINS: As with many burgundian vineyards, Chapelle has religious origins. A small chapel – Notre Dame de Bèze – stood on the site until it was deliberately burnt down in the 1830s to add two *ouvrées* to the plantable area.

TOPOGRAPHY/GEOLOGY: The vineyard faces east on a well-drained, mild slope, with shallow, stony, surface soils (around 30 centimetres) giving on to compacted rock. In parts of the vineyard rocky outcrops are evident. The soils are marginally deeper than at Clos de Bèze, particularly in the lower sectors. The plots nearest the RN 74 (about one-sixth of the area) are largely on Comblanchien limestone; the remaining area closer to the Route des Grands Crus, the D 974, share the band of *calcaire à entroques* which straddles this road.

WINE: The quartet of *Grands Crus* below the Route des Grands Crus tend to be more feminine and elegant than the quintet above it. Chapelle is no exception, though it tends to greater masculinity than either Charmes or Mazis. In some versions it is more overtly fruity than the rest in this group, in others it show a more robust character. In reality, any such nuances are masked by differences in origin, vinification and *élevage*, particularly those related to vine age, extraction and oak treatment. The ground does not give wine which is powerful enough to tolerate heavy new oaking and the best sources use less new wood with this *cuvée* to preserve the wine's natural delicacy. Although a large *Grand Cru* – over twice the size of Griotte – the wine does not often appear on the consumer radar possibly because 40% of the vineyard is in the hands of one owner, Damoy, whose bottles may be unevenly distributed. However, from one of the top sources, it can be excellent.

Chapelle-Chambertin. Note the stony top-soil

CHARMES-CHAMBERTIN & MAZOYÈRES-CHAMBERTIN

For over a century and a half growers in Mazoyères-Chambertin have been allowed to label their wine as Charmes-Chambertin (but not vice versa). Today the distinction has almost gone to the extent that there are very few Mazoyères to be found. It therefore makes sense to consider the vineyards as one – although this might seem to purists as heretical as the vineyards and their wines do indeed differ.

STATISTICS: *Area*: 30.83.24 ha (Charmes 12.24 ha; Mazoyères 18.59 ha) *Owners*: 67. *Average Annual Production*: 12,230 cases

PRINCIPAL OWNERS: Camus: 5.90 ha Charmes + 1.90 ha Mazoyères; **Perrot-Minot**: 1 ha Charmes (55) + 1 ha Mazoyères (55); Taupenot-Merme: 1.42 ha; **Armand Rousseau**: 1.37 ha (1938–1990); Rebourseau: 1.31 ha; **Arlaud**: 1.14 ha (1957, 1973, 1989); Raphet: 1.0 ha; Dupont-Tisserandot: 0.80 ha; Domaine de la Vougeraie: 0.75 ha; **Dujac**: 0.70 ha (30); Pierre Bourrée: 0.65 ha; Tortochot: 0.57 ha; **Dugat-Py**: 0.47 ha (1965); Castagnier: 0.40 ha; Charlopin-Parizot: 0.40 ha (1950s); **Geantet-Pansiot**: 0.45 ha (1954); **Denis Bachelet**: 0.43 ha; Confuron-Cotetidot: 0.39 ha (65); **Christian Serafin**: 0.31 ha (1946); **Ponsot**: 0.30 ha (40); **Claude Dugat**: 0.30 ha (1976); René Bouvier: 0.30 ha (60); **Michel Magnien**: 0.28 ha; **Christophe Roumier**: 0.27 ha (1972); Pierre Amiot: 0.20 ha; **Bernard Maume**: 0.18 ha (c.1956); **Joseph Roty**: 0.16 ha; **Hubert Lignier**: 0.11 ha

ORIGINS: The wine of 'Charmes' is routinely described as 'charming' – which it frequently is. However, the origin of the name is more prosaic, being a corruption of the old French word *chaumer/chaumée* which means to clear a field of stubble and denotes an abandoned piece of land which is subsequently replanted. This in turn probably derives from the pre-Latin word calma which evolved into the parallel forms 'chaume' (thatch), 'charme' (hornbeam) and 'chaux' (quicklime). It is difficult to say whether the name of this *Grand Cru* comes from the tree or the dry calcareous grasslands. The term recurs many times in Burgundy – Vosne-Romanée les Chaumes, Meursault Charmes, etc. The origin of Mazoyères is obscure – possibly related to Mazis which in turn may be a corruption of 'maisons' reflecting the fact that small dwellings occupied the site several centuries ago. There are possible associations with the ancient Provençal words 'Mas' and 'Meix' which also denote dwellings.

TOPOGRAPHY/GEOLOGY: At nearly 31 ha this sizeable vineyard accounts for over one-third of Gevrey's *Grands Crus*. Charmes lies east of the Route des Grands Crus, below Chambertin and Mazoyères which adjoin it to the south, below Latricières and Premier Cru Aux Combottes. Both vineyards appear relatively flat although, as with much of the Gevrey vignoble, they actually slope from west to east (forest to the RN 74). Charmes lies at an altitude of between 262 and 284 metres (average 271 metres) on a gentle slope exposed due east. The underlying rock is *calcaire à entroques* in the upper, western part, faulting to Comblanchien towards the easterly plain. A north–south fault to the east of the road and a small 'croupe' to the west mark the limits of *entroques*. There is significant iron in these gravelly soils. In the southern section, alluvial fan deposits of shale and gravel cover the limestone. In Charmes proper, the soils are of an arable character some 30–35 centimetres deep, which would support the 'straw' theory of its etymology.

WINE: As Mazoyères is sold as Charmes, it is only of intellectual interest to discuss the differences. In general, Mazoyères is tighter and more austere than Charmes, itself somewhat plumper and more rustic. Within Charmes, the upper sections above the vineyard track which bisects this *climat* (Charmes du Haut) tend to greater finesse than muscle. Charmes is the most accessible and earliest maturing of the Gevrey *Grands Crus*; nonetheless, the best – good producer, good vintage – are capable of lasting many years. Roty's Charmes Très Vieilles Vignes from vines planted in 1881 is the greatest example from this *climat* – a magisterial wine, firm, densely packed and vigorous, combining density, power and finesse. Knowing the character of the late Jo Roty, it is hard to imagine him producing a delicate, feminine wine, certainly not from Gevrey! Care must be taken not to overpower the wine's fragrance and finesse with oak. One of the finest producers, Rousseau, gives his Charmes none. Overwooding in the belief that all *Grands Crus*, irrespective of vintage and vineyard, merit 100% new oak spoils many *cuvées*. Some feel that parts of the Charmes du Bas which adjoin the Route des Grands Crus do not merit *Grand Cru* status – or at least if they do then adjoining *Premier Cru*, Aux Combottes, should be promoted *Grand Cru*. All in all, by virtue of its size and diversity, Charmes is Gevrey's least interesting *Grand Cru*.

Working in Mazoyères-Chambertin

GRIOTTE-CHAMBERTIN

Griotte-Chambertin, the smallest of the Gevrey *Grands Crus*, is the filling in the sandwich whose outer teguments are Chapelle-Chambertin to the north and Charmes-Chambertin to the south. Its size and consequent small production means that it is rarely encountered, but it is nonetheless a vineyard well meriting its *Grand Cru* status.

STATISTICS: *Area:* 2.69.18 ha. *Owners:* 9. *Average Annual Production:* 1,012 cases

PRINCIPAL OWNERS: **Ponsot/Chezeaux:** 0.89 ha (19); **Joseph Drouhin:** 0.53 ha (1982); **Jean-Marie Fourrier:** 0.26 ha (1928); **Claude Dugat:** 0.16 ha (1957); **Joseph Roty:** 0.08 ha. There is also an excellent *cuvée* from Louis Jadot.

ORIGINS: There are two popular accounts for the naming of this vineyard, both almost certainly wrong. One has it that the summer heat captured by the concave shape of the *climat* which, amplified by the rock outcrops, makes it resemble a little grill or *grillotte*. The second ascribes the name to the whiff of griotte cherry that many detect in the wine. The more plausible etymologies are, first that it derives from the old French word *ruotte* which means *ruisseau* (= little stream), probable reference to a subterranean rivulet which flows between Chambertin and Clos de Bèze into Griotte and emerges as a couple of water sources at the top and in the middle of the vineyard. Excavations by the Ponsots while replanting a plot acquired *en fermage* in 1982 – the previous owner had apparently left it in a lamentable state with trees growing everywhere – unearthed a sort of man-made grotto to catch the water run-off from Chambertin thought to have been constructed in the 17th century. It was repaired and functions to this day. The most credible etymological candidate has it that Griotte derives from the predominantly chalky limestone soil type which the French call *criotte* or *crai*. Older vignerons in Gevrey still talk of Gruotte instead of Griotte.

TOPOGRAPHY/GEOLOGY: As with Chapelle, the topsoil is mainly the result of human activity, as Griotte is on the site of an old quarry. This topographic hollow was definitely not produced by meteorite impact, as has often been written, but is the result of stone excavation for wall and house building. Infill probably accounts for the pocket of soil four metres deep in the lower part of the vineyard. Because some of its soil may have eroded from Chambertin, it is sometimes said in jest that the best Chambertin

Marker stones are common on the Côte

comes from Griotte. Nonetheless, the soil is deeper in the lower sections of the vineyard and contains significant amounts of fragmented chalk. The bedrock in the upper section is *calcaire à entroques* of which there was a large quarry on what is now the Griotte vineyard; lower down there is Comblanchien limestone. The water table is high and a number of small springs punctuate the vineyard. Were it not for a capacious drainage pipe which carries water run-off via Aux Etelois, standing water would be a problem during heavy rain.

WINE: Griotte-Chambertin has more in common with Charmes than with Chambertin in the sense that elegance dominates muscle. It is well-structured, finely textured and complex in character and, yes, even the whiff of griotte cherry is there if you look hard enough, although the fruit is generally more redcurrant than cherry, certainly in the Ponsot version. However, there is far more to a great Griotte than that. In riper vintages it tends to show more dark fruits, coffee bean and liquorice, sometimes with a beguiling floral aromatic component. As it ages, in common with many great Pinots the *primeur* aromas vanish to be replaced by secondary and tertiary aromas of *sous-bois*, mushroom and spice; intriguing and complex, but different. Griotte is in the top league of Gevrey's *Grands Crus*; the real problem is finding it to taste in the first place.

LATRICIÈRES-CHAMBERTIN

Latricières-Chambertin is a medium-sized vineyard in tightly held ownership. Sightings are rare as only eight of the ten owners have significant holdings. Good bottles are findable – with seven producers being in the top division. It is generally – and rightly – regarded as a second-division *Grand Cru*.

STATISTICS: *Area:* 7.35.44 ha *Owners:* 10. *Average Annual Production:* 3,388 cases

PRINCIPAL OWNERS: Camus: 1.51 ha; **Faiveley**: 1.21 ha (1958, 1984, 1989); **Rossignol-Trapet**: 0.76 ha; **Jean & Jean-Louis Trapet**: 0.73 ha (1933–1969); Drouhin-Laroze: 0.67 ha; **Louis Remy**: 0.57 ha (30–40); **Leroy**: 0.57 ha; **Robert Arnoux**: 0.50 ha (1957); Simon Bize: 0.30 ha (1961, 1971, 1981)

ORIGINS: Latricières derives either from the Latin – de Triciae – or from old French word '*tricière*'. Both mean 'poor', or in this case 'infertile', in reference to the site's unpropitious growing conditions: thin, low-nutrient soils on hard rock.

TOPOGRAPHY/GEOLOGY: Latricières pegs the line of *Grands Crus* from Mazis, Clos de Bèze and Chambertin. Immediately to its south is the Premier Cru Aux Combottes whose southerly limit marks Gevrey's boundary with Morey-St-Denis. In shape it is rectangular, almost square, in inclination flat apart from a gentle slope in the upper sector towards its conjunction with the forest. Deprived of the protection of trees at its southerly extremity, where the Combe Grisard bisects the Côte, its situation increases the likelihood of hail and wind damage. Latricières' soil differs from that of Chambertin because of significant alluvial run-off (technically *cône de déjection* or alluvial fans) from the Combe Grisard which separates Morey from Gevrey. The evidence for this is the presence of round, calcareous pebbles in the vineyard. Beneath these alluvial fan deposits, deeper subsoils are the same Prémeaux limestone found in Chambertin.

WINE: Despite its proximity to Chambertin, Latricières possesses none of the presence or nobility of its illustrious neighbour. In the best hands it is quite robust, full, sturdy wine, but lacks the complexity and finesse which characterise both Chambertin and Clos de Bèze.

Gently sloping ground in Latricières-Chambertin

MAZIS-CHAMBERTIN

Mazis-Chambertin is the first *Grand Cru* one encounters on the Route des Grands Crus from Gevrey to Morey. It is surrounded by *Premiers Crus* to the east and north and by *Grands Crus* (Clos de Bèze and Ruchottes-Chambertin) to the south and west respectively. On the right-hand side of the road leaving Gevrey, Mazis is notionally divided into two sections – Mazis Haut (upslope) and Mazis Bas. The upper section is considered as the finer of the pair, but as the origin of the grapes is never stated on the label, for the consumer the distinction is academic. Various alternative spellings are tolerated – Mazy, Mazis, Mazi.

STATISTICS: *Area:* 9.10.34 ha. *Owners:* 28. *Average Annual Production:* 3,542 cases

PRINCIPAL OWNERS: Hospices de Beaune, Cuvée Madeleine Collignon (1.75 ha); **Joseph Faiveley**: 1.21 ha (1937,1959, 1974); Rebourseau: 0.96 ha; **Harmand-Geoffroy**: 0.73 ha (c. 1960); **Bernard Maume**: 0.67 ha (1932); **Armand Rousseau**: 0.53 ha (1945, 1978); Philippe Naddef: 0.42 ha; Tortochot: 0.42 ha; Camus: 0.37 ha; Dupont-Tisserandot: 0.35 ha; **Leroy/d'Auvenay**: 0.26 ha; **Dugat-Py**: 0.22 ha (1940); Frédéric Esmonin: 0.14 ha (1949–1959); **Joseph Roty**: (0.12 ha); Confuron-Cotetidot: 0.09 ha (65); Philippe Charlopin-Parisot: 0.08 ha (1946)

ORIGINS: Mazis has three putative derivations: from the old French *mazures*, which means 'ruin'; 'small house' in dialect; Mazis also denotes a hamlet or settlement, one of which was known to exist on this site. The name of the *lieu-dit* has the same origin as Mazoyères, with ancient houses probably built here.

TOPOGRAPHY/GEOLOGY: Mazis is largely flat with a gentle slope in the upper sections. Its soils are broadly similar to those of Clos de Bèze with which it is contiguous: brown limestone with the occasional rocky outcrop. The underlying rock is Prémeaux limestone in the upper sector (Mazis Haut) having abundant light-coloured stones in the soil, and mainly *entroques* in Mazis Bas with some Prémeaux limestone. The ground is cold – *terre froide* – made so by cool air funnelling down from the Combe Grizard Despite requiring a relatively long ripening period, its fruit is generally riper than Chambertin.

WINE: Mazis is masculine in character, coming close to the distinction and nobility of Clos de Bèze with all the usual attributes – deepish colour, firm, refined tannins, good acidity, plenty of fruit – emphasising black rather than red fruit, although both are found. The best are quite plush and develop attractively with bottle age showing good palate and aroma complexity and marked finesse.

Mazis-Chambertin with Ruchottes beyond

RUCHOTTES-CHAMBERTIN

The most northerly of the Gevrey *Grands Crus*, Ruchottes-Chambertin is a smallish vineyard somewhat overshadowed in reputation by its more illustrious peers. Tucked in a corner on the village outskirts, it is notionally divided into two: the lower section, Ruchottes du Bas, adjoins the north-west part of the Mazis vineyard; the upper section, Ruchottes du Dessus, has the Premier Cru Fontenys and the *Premier Cru* section of Bel Air as northerly and southerly neighbours respectively. The Clos des Ruchottes owned by Domaine Armand Rousseau is at the top of the slope above Les Mazis and Les Ruchottes proper, marked by a prominent stone portal.

STATISTICS: *Area:* 3.30.37 ha. *Owners:* 7. *Average Annual Production:* 1,122 cases

PRINCIPAL OWNERS: **Armand Rousseau** (Clos des Ruchottes): 1.06 ha (1950–2003); **Georges Mugneret-Gibourg**: 0.64 ha (1950); Frédéric Esmonin: 0.52 ha (1945–1959); **Christophe Roumier**: 0.54 ha (1967); Frédéric Magnien: 0.16 ha; Marchand-Grillot: 0.08 ha

ORIGINS: Disputed. The most plausible etymology for Ruchottes is that it derives from *rochers* which means 'rocks'; '-ottes' is a diminutive suffix, the burgundian equivalent of '-ettes'. This fits in with the vineyard's pronounced rockiness. Others believe the origin lies in *ruche* which means beehive. It is certain that the early monks kept bees and Les Ruchottes may denote the position of the monastic apiary.

TOPOGRAPHY/GEOLOGY: Ruchottes is the steepest of the Gevrey *Grands Crus* (at least in Ruchottes du Dessus). The soils here are thin – barely 20 centimetres onto hard Prémeaux rock – stony and nutritively poor, which promotes finesse in the wine and allows minerality and structure to show through. This impenetrable Prémeaux rock is clearly visible at the entrance to Rousseau's Clos des Ruchottes where it outcrops onto the vineyard track. Soils in the lower sector – Ruchottes du Bas – are marginally deeper and similar to those of Clos de Bèze which adjoins it to the south. The various walls and terraces visible in the southerly part of Ruchottes are the work of man and not geological faulting as has been suggested.

Immediately adjoining Ruchottes to the south is the Bel Air vineyard – part *Premier Cru* and part *Village*. The owners

(Domaine de la Vougeraie) have noted significant problems with shading from the nearby forest and have been seeking permission to fell trees; however this remains a controversial matter as it would remove important protection from the *Grand Cru* vineyards immediately below.

WINE: The situation of the vineyard and its poor soils make for wine which is generally rather austere in its youth with tight-grained tannins and a marked mineral undertone. Thin, limestone-based soils give good acidities – which in well-made Pinot translates as palate freshness. In youth a Ruchottes offers flavours more of red fruits than black and even a softness overlaying its hallmark minerality often quite spicy in character. In thin-skinned vintages (e.g. 2007) careful use of oak tannins may help support a natural structural deficiency without overwhelming the fruit. With such structural components, it is not surprising that a good Ruchottes ages well, fleshing out and developing fine aromatics. Not perhaps the grandeur of Chambertin, but from good sources, abundantly satisfying and well worth buying and keeping. The offerings from Roumier, Georges Mugneret-Gibourg and Rousseau are unquestionably the pick of this select, classy, bunch.

Entrance to Domaine Rouseau's Clos des Ruchottes

GEVREY-CHAMBERTIN PREMIER CRU AUX COMBOTTES

Aux Combottes is surrounded by *Grands Crus* and situated on the soil band which stretches from Morey-St-Denis village to Gevrey-Chambertin. A small vertical strip which belongs to Camus is actually classified as Grand Cru Latricières-Chambertin. Historically, it appears that the owner at the time of delimitation was not from Gevrey, which possibly led the local committee deliberating the classification to declare it *Premier Cru*. The view is also heard that the vineyard's situation puts it in the draught zone of the Combe Grisard which is a conduit for colder air that results in less even ripening and thus compromises quality. This argument would carry more weight were it not for the fact that the adjacent Gevrey *Grands Crus* are in a similar situation.

STATISTICS: *Area:* 4.58 ha *Owners:* 6 +. *Average Annual Production:* 2,015 cases

Small flower has implanted itself in an old vine root

PRINCIPAL OWNERS: **Dujac**: 1.15 ha (30); Pierre Amiot: 0.61 ha (45); **Leroy**: 0.46 ha; **Arlaud Père et Fils**: 0.45 ha (1925–1964); Georges Lignier: 0.42 ha; **Rossignol-Trapet**: 0.14 ha (2001); **Hubert Lignier**: 0.14 ha (49); Marchand Frères (in Gevrey): n/a (45); also *cuvées* from Odoul-Coquard and Gérard Raphet (both based in Morey) and David Duband (Chevannes), and Thierry Beaumont (Gevrey)

ORIGINS: 'Combottes' derives from old French in which '-ottes' or '-ettes' signifies a diminutive. So the name means 'little Combe'.

TOPOGRAPHY/GEOLOGY: Such is the geological complexity of the Côte d'Or that it is not necessarily reasonable to assume that because a vineyard is surrounded by others of one degree it automatically merits their classification. The Combottes vineyard faces east on a gentle slope below the Monts Luisants section of Clos de la Roche with Mazoyères/Charmes to the immediate east and Latricières-Chambertin to the north. The majority of its extent sits on the narrow band of *calcaire à entroques* which stretches from Morey to the southern edge of Gevrey. A fault separates this from Prémeaux limestone underlying the remaining area to the west. The easterly limit of this band is identifiable from a small stone cabin (*cabotte*) next to the Route des Grands Crus which marks the site of a disused *entroques* quarry which provided stone for wall and house building. As its underlying rock strata demonstrates, the same lithological succession encountered along the slope as Clos de Bèze and Chambertin – *entroques* then Prémeaux – there is no credible geological argument why Aux Combottes should not be *Grand Cru*.

WINE: The wine is generally expressive and quite open aromatically, with floral components and fresh mineral flavours; elegant, somewhat feminine in character and more redolent of Chambolle than either Gevrey or Morey in structure – red fruits rather than black. Compared with its southerly neighbour Clos de la Roche, Combottes rarely shows its amplitude and plushness, being rather more restrained and brighter in feel and perhaps a shade less full. It ages well; the best examples need 5–10 years to show at their best.

Gevrey's fine Premier Cru Aux Combottes with Morey's Monts Luisants in the mist beyond

GEVREY-CHAMBERTIN PREMIER CRU CLOS ST-JACQUES

The splendid swathe of *Premiers Crus* which form a semi-circle to the north of the road leading through the Combe de Lavaux to Chambœuf produces some of Gevrey's finest and most interesting wine outside the *Grands Crus*. Surprisingly, none was considered for *Grand Cru* status at the time of original delimitation. While Les Cazetiers, Lavaux-St-Jacques, Les Goulots and Estournelles-St-Jacques are well capable of excellence, the undisputed jewel in this vinous coronet is the superbly sited 6.7 ha walled vineyard of Clos St-Jacques. Lavalle's 1855 ranking puts it in Gevrey's second division, below Chambertin and Clos de Bèze, along with the best parts of Mazis, Ruchottes, Chapelle and Charmes. Its ownership is confidential, concentrated in the hands of five highly competent producers, so good bottles are findable and, compared with the grandest *Grands Crus*, relatively affordable. It is considered and treated by these producers as of *Grand Cru* quality and priced as a junior *Grand Cru*. Clos St-Jacques well merits space in any serious cellar.

STATISTICS: *Area:* 6.70.49 ha. *Owners:* 5. *Average Annual Production*: 2,950 cases

PRINCIPAL OWNERS: **Armand Rousseau**: 2.22 ha (1935–1993); **Michel & Sylvie Esmonin**: 1.60 ha (1961–1970); **Bruno Clair**: 1.0 ha (1957 & 1972); **Louis Jadot**: 1.0 ha: **Jean-Marie Fourrier**: 0.89 ha (1910)

ORIGINS: It is said that there used to be a small chapel in this area and that the names of several vineyards here have 'St-Jacques' as part of their name.

TOPOGRAPHY/GEOLOGY: The vineyard occupies a steepish vertical strip extending from top to bottom of the slope, exposed south of east on the northern flank of the Combe de Lavaux and at a similar elevation to the upper sections of Chambertin and Clos de Bèze. Its five owners all have parcels which cover the vineyard's entire vertical extent. The geology of Gevrey's northern sector, of which the Clos St-Jacques is part, differs significantly from that of the southern sector. It is thought, though not yet definitively established, that Clos St-Jacques is highly faulted, with some five separate faults running transversely across the vineyard from north-west to south-east. The base rock differs

from the band stretching from Clos de Bèze to Clos de la Roche in that it contains significant proportions of *Ostrea acuminata* marls and *calcaire à entroques* in the upper sector with probable Prémeaux limestone downslope but no Comblanchien. This is complex geology beyond simply well-drained mixed soils. In the upper part of the vineyard, the *entroques* outcrop makes for very thin, stony soils; lower down, where run-off accumulates more readily, soils are finer-grained and less stony. Soil erosion is a problem here as is the wind which funnels down the Combe retarding ripeness. This causes the vineyard to be cool in comparison with those outside the influence of the Combe – the largest in the Côtes de Nuits – especially on summer evenings. It may be that the Clos' southerly wall provides an element of protection from winds sliding down from plateaux along the Combe de Lavaux, protection not enjoyed by its immediate neighbours Lavaut and Estournelles St-Jacques.

WINE: A good Clos St-Jacques can easily be mistaken for a Chambertin. Domaine Rousseau has always considered that it outclasses their Ruchottes, Mazis and Clos de la Roche, fine as these are, and this potential is reflected in its having more new wood. The wine has fine poise and balance and is rich, full and tightly structured, often with a strong mineral undertone. It carries the class and complexity of a *Grand Cru* with perhaps a shade less finesse and opulence – but that is a minor matter for what is unquestionably Gevrey's finest *Premier Cru* and one of indisputable *Grand Cru* potential.

Newly harvested fruit from Rousseau's Clos St Jacques

The walled vineyard of Clos St Jacques with Lavaux and Estournelles beyond

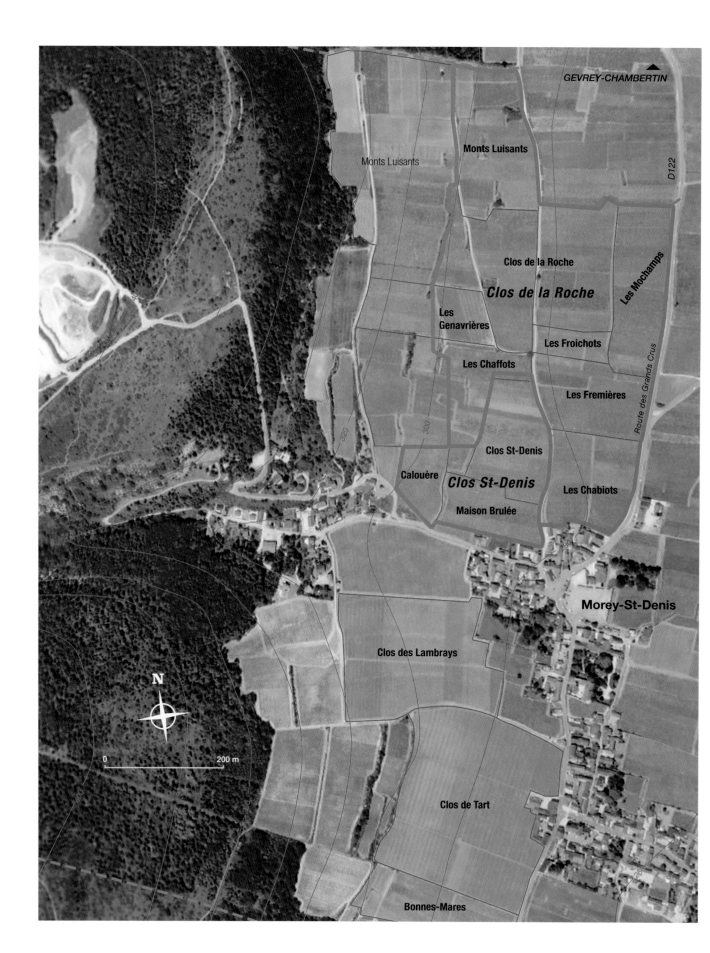

GEVREY-CHAMBERTIN

Monts Luisants

Monts Luisants

D122

Clos de la Roche

Clos de la Roche

Les Mochamps

Les
Genavrières

Les Froichots

Les Chaffots

Les Fremières

Route des Grands Crus

Clos St-Denis

Calouère

Clos St-Denis

Les Chabiots

Maison Brulée

Morey-St-Denis

Clos des Lambrays

N

0   200 m

Clos de Tart

Bonnes-Mares

CLOS DE LA ROCHE

eing by a good margin the largest of the Morey *Grands Crus*, Clos de la Roche is certainly the best known. It happens also, in the most competent hands, to produce some of Morey's greatest wines. As with Clos St-Denis, it has expanded considerably, in the latter half of the 19th century, from its original size of 4.57 ha, to its present size of 16.9 ha by absorbing the lower section of Monts Luisants (3.74 ha), Mochamps (2.57 ha), Fremières (2.28 ha), Chabiots (2.15 ha), Genavrières (part, 0.88 ha), Chaffots (0.70 ha) and Froichots (0.64 ha) into the original 4.57 ha Clos de la Roche *climat*. The qualitative heart of the *Cru* is the flatter section of Clos de la Roche itself.

The Clos has a wider significance for Pinot Noir as the plant material selection made by Laurent Ponsot's grandfather in 1954 is the source of many of Burgundy's finest clones – 113/114/115/667/777/778 and others. These remain highly regarded and indeed are planted worldwide. Many post-war selections were made to maximise quantity; these were selected for quality.

STATISTICS: *Area:* 16.90.27 ha. *Owners:* 40. *Average Annual Production:* 6,120 cases

PRINCIPAL OWNERS: **Ponsot**: 3.40 ha (62); **Dujac**: 1.95 ha (30); **Armand Rousseau**: 1.48 ha (1961–2008); Pierre Amiot: 1.20 ha (35); Georges Lignier: 1.05 ha; **Hubert Lignier**: 1.01 ha; Philippe et Vincent Lecheneaut: 0.82 ha (1959); **Leroy**: 0.67 ha; **Louis Remy**: 0.65 ha (30–40); Guy Castagnier: 0.57 ha; **Arlaud**: 0.44 ha (1979, 1990); Hospices de Beaune: 0.44 ha; also a worthy *cuvée* from Louis Jadot.

ORIGINS: The name is curious – meaning Clos of the Rock rather than several rocks – which suggests that there was one prominent rock from which the vineyard took its name. Henri Cannard in *Balades en Bourgogne* surmises that the historical evidence, such as it is, points to the existence of a large rock outcrop between Latricières-Chambertin and Clos St-Denis. In pre-Roman times, there were gibbets in the Chaffots vineyard and a site named Pierre Virante (roughly translated as 'sweeping' or 'revolving' stone) which was linked to a Celtic or Druidic cult. A prominent, visible, rock outcrop, believed to have been a sacrificial stone, still adorns the Pierre Virante vineyard.

TOPOGRAPHY/GEOLOGY: The Clos shares broadly similar soils with its neighbours: Clos St-Denis on the Morey side and Premier Cru Aux Combottes and Grand Cru Mazoyères on the Gevrey side. The Clos has relatively rich brown limestone soils admixed with abundant limestone scree material which imparts breadth, flesh and ultimately finesse to the wine. The soils are deep, especially in the upper sectors of the vineyard where the ground is stonier, with more than 80 centimetres of soil before the bedrock is reached. Its situation, under the lee of Monts Luisants, provides a particularly sheltered microclimate which favours fruit ripening. The vineyard is gently sloping, more steeply in the upper section through the topmost boundary of which the 300 metre contour line passes. The precision of delimitation is exemplified by the fact that the top section of Monts Luisants, beneath the Ponsot's small villa, is classified *Village* (there are some ancient Aligoté vines here), the mid-section is Grand Cru Clos de la Roche and the lower, flatter sector is *Premier Cru* Monts Luisants.

WINE: Clos de la Roche is an ample, rich wine with a touch of Morey earthiness and distinct class. In character, it resembles a somewhat muscular Latricières, perhaps because of the high proportion of *marne*. Here is not to be found the sheer muscularity of Bonnes-Mares, the lacy distinction of Musigny, or the tight early austerity of Chambertin – rather something that seems to combine in its character elements of each. It has a slightly 'wild' side to it, often distinguished by a hint of truffle on the nose. The class of Chambertin is there, as is something of the richness of Bonnes-Mares and the promise of the aromatic panoply of Musigny but none so obvious. If anything its character leans toward Gevrey in general and Chambertin in particular, with which it is easily confused in blind tasting. In youth it can appear rather straightforward and uncomplicated but is transformed by age into something magnificent and even rather surprising.

CLOS DES LAMBRAYS

This is essentially a *Monopole* – a vineyard in single ownership. To be precise, it is not strictly so as there are three other owners. In two cases it is their gardens which are classified *Grand Cru* but not planted; in the third, 420 square metres are owned by Domaine Taupenot-Merme. The Taupenots do not produce an individual bottling from their holding, so for the consumer there is effectively only one Clos des Lambrays.

The vineyard was known and documented (in the archives of Cîteaux) as the Cloux des Lambray as early as 1365, a date engraved into a plaque in its northern wall. After the Revolution, the vineyard was sold parcel-by-parcel into the hands of no fewer than 74 separate owners. In 1938, having been painstakingly reassembled, as it were, the Clos was acquired by the Cosson family during the earliest years of whose ownership were produced some of its greatest wines.

The vineyard was passed over for *Grand Cru* when the original classifications were determined. The Algerian brothers, Lucien and Fabien Saier, who bought the vineyard in 1979, petitioned for an upgrade to *Grand Cru* which was granted in 1981. In 1996 the Domaine was acquired by M. and Mme Gunther Freund.

STATISTICS: *Area:* 8.83.94 ha *Owners:* 4. *Average Annual Production:* 2772 cases

PRINCIPAL OWNERS: **Domaine des Lambrays**: 8.66 ha (1902–1988)

ORIGINS: Nothing documented

TOPOGRAPHY/GEOLOGY: The Clos adjoins the Clos de Tart on its south side and the Clos St-Denis to the north. The site is oriented broadly south of east at an elevation of 250–350 metres, crossed in its mid-section by the 300 metre contour. The slope is not even – if you view the Clos from Domaine Ponsot's parking area it is clear that, far from being flat, the plane is undulating. In fact, the north-west corner, in the *climat* Les Bouchots, is a microclimate – with a distinct depression which attracts cold air from the *combe* above and cools this part of the

Clos; this, coincidentally, is the 2.45 ha which were replanted in the 1980s.

The Clos shares the same basic geology with the Clos de Tart. Soils are dominated by white limestone admixed with clay which varies in proportion from the top (less) to the bottom (more) of the vineyard. The soil structure is relatively sandy, which makes for less stability and greater likelihood of rain-induced erosion although, unlike the Clos de Tart, only some of the vine rows are oriented north–south. The layer of marlstone which runs through Bonnes-Mares and the Clos de Tart peters out in the upper section of the Clos des Lambrays where the subsoil is made up of shaly limestone. An ancient quarry runs between the Clos des Lambrays and the Clos de Tart.

As elsewhere on the Côte, the topography is such that soils in the lower sectors are thicker and richer in clay, giving greater water retention. In rainy summers (e.g. 2007) this allows the vines at the bottom of the Clos to pump water and the fruit to become more dilute. Conversely, in hot, dry vintages (e.g. 2003) the top sectors of the Clos suffer more and the wine loses finesse. Its location, adjacent to the combe to the north, may well account for differences in fruit composition and ripening from its neighbours.

WINE: The wines of the Cosson era provide ample testament, if any were needed, to the quality potential of this vineyard. If one dined in the Castel de Très Girard in Morey in the 1960s or 1970s the wine list offered an extraordinary array of mature Mme Cosson's Clos des Lambrays dating back to the great vintages of the 1940s – in particular, the especially fine trio of 1945, 1947 and 1949 which appeared sporadically on the UK market during this period. These were remarkable for their intensity, depth and beauty. Not silken Musignys or aristocratic Vosnes but finely wrought nonetheless; vigorous characters with developed old Pinot aromas and flavours and plenty of stuffing; deeply satisfying wines whose intensity and complexity brought one back to the glass again and again. Recent owners have poured money into the estate and with the meticulous, intelligent management of Thierry Brouin there is every sign that the Clos des Lambrays is returning to its former glory.

Clos des Lambrays looking towards Morey St. Denis. Clos de Tart vines and cuverie to the right

CLOS DE TART

The Clos de Tart is an ancient *vignoble* even by burgundian standards. Then known as the Clos de la Forge, its documented history dates from 1141 when it was sold, along with a press and vineyards at Brochon, ajoining Gevrey-Chambertin, to the sisters of the important Abbey of Tart-le-Haut, in Genlis, a small town between Dijon and Dôle, which was attached to the Cistercian foundation at Cîteaux. By judicious dealing, through donations and purchases, they augmented the Clos from around 5 ha to its present size. Its current name dates from 1184 when the sisters were granted the rights to harvest 'before, during or after the *ban*' (*de vendanges*). In the following 860+ years there have been only three owners: first, Monsieur Charles Dumagner of Nuits who acquired it from the French State after sequestration during the Revolution in 1791; shortly thereafter it passed to the Marey family (of Marey-Monge lineage – the family who owned a large slice of Romanée-St-Vivant since the late 18th century before selling it to the Domaine de la Romanée-Conti). The present owners, the Mommessin family, took over in 1932. The reconstitution of the estate was due to the inspiration and energy of Ferdinand Marey-Monge, direct descendant of the original purchaser Claude Marey. By 1855, it was considered as a *tête de cuvée* by Dr Lavalle in his treatise *Histoire et Statistique de la Vigne et des Grands Vins de la Côte d'Or*. In 1956 two small parcels of adjoining Bonnes-Mares totalling 32 ares were officially incorporated into the Clos. Clos de Tart used to be distributed by the negociants Mommessin but this firm now belongs to Jean-Claude Boisset and is no longer involved with the Clos or its wine. The wine is now made, matured, bottled and marketed at the fine old buildings in Morey-St-Denis, presided over by its affable *gérant* Sylvain Pitiot.

STATISTICS: *Area:* 7.53.28 ha (average vine age: 60) *Principal Owners:* 1 – *Monopole* of the **Mommessin family**. *Average Annual Production*: 2,299 cases

ORIGINS: The name dates from its 12th-century ownership by the sisters of Tart-le-Haut.

TOPOGRAPHY/GEOLOGY: The vineyard, enclosed by a dry stone wall which defines it as a *clos*, is a mixture of stones and clay lying on three distinct geological units: *calcaire à entroques* outcrops downslope and also in the Domaine's cellar. This is overlaid in the upper part of the vineyard by light-coloured,

greenish to yellowish, *Ostrea acuminata* marls; these progressively change to shaly limestone. As with most *Grands Crus*, the soils are a heterogeneous compound of components. Here, the broad soil type is *marne* (marlstone), defined as a mixture of clay and limestone with 33–66% of limestone, a layer of which traverses the Clos and the Morey section of Bonnes-Mares. These *marnes* are relatively impermeable and vine roots often spread at the upper limit of the marl where water and organic matter remain available for the plant, although they can manage to penetrate through fissures in the rock. The soil profile is the result of eroded rock material mixed with limestone pebbles sliding down from the hillside above. A recent study by the agronomist Claude Bourguignon (op. cit.) identified two main soil types: i) decarbonised limestones, concentrated in the lower sectors of the vineyard, low in active lime – mainly *entroques*; ii) more active limestone-rich soil which covers the upper sector of the vineyard.

Soil erosion is a perennial problem here due to the marly nature of the subsoil. The Domaine's solution is to orient the vines north–south rather than the more conventional east–west. This helps soil retention but means that drainage is less efficient as the vines block the natural flow of water. The priority of maintaining a high vine age is achieved by replacing individual vines rather than by mass replanting.

WINE: Things have improved considerably from the 1980s and 1990s when quality was distinctly patchy. In particular, the introduction of a second wine, La Forge de Tart, has greatly strengthened the credibility of the *Grand Vin*. Recent years have seen more precision viticulture, thoughtful vinification and rigorous selection for what appears under the Clos de Tart label. Nowadays, the fruit from the different subsoils in the Clos is vinified separately before selection and *assemblage* for the final *cuvée*. In general, there appears to have been a shift towards a plusher, more modern style with a touch more obvious oakiness than hitherto. The wine is none the worse for that. The keys to the Clos' quality are a rich mid-palate, plenty of ripe fruit and excellent length. There seems to me a touch of the Morey earthiness in the wine which sets it apart from the *Grands Crus* of both Chambolle and Gevrey. The best vintages start out full and masculine with plenty of firm tannin, developing typical Pinot secondary *sous-bois* and considerable finesse. Great wine indeed.

Opposite: discussing vintages?

CLOS ST-DENIS

The Clos St-Denis is the smallest of the four *Grands Crus* wholly situated in Morey. It has fluctuated in extent over the centuries – expanding from a relatively small 2.15 ha in the 19th century to its present size by absorbing the lower (eastern) section of the Les Chaffots (1.33.92 ha), Maison Brulée (1.82.94 ha) and most of La Calouère (1.30.85 ha). It is separated from the Route des Grands Crus by Les Chabiots which is part of neighbouring Clos de la Roche (q.v.). The heart of the appellation is the Clos St-Denis *finage* (2.14.89 ha). Lavelle places it in the third division – the first, *tête de cuvée*, being Clos de Tart solo, the second comprising Bonnes-Mares, Les Lambrays (*sic*) and Clos de Laroche (*sic*). It may seem surprising that the burghers of Morey chose Clos St-Denis as their preferred suffix when Morey became Morey-St-Denis on 19 January 1927; they probably had little choice: the Clos de Tart was excluded, as being in single ownership, the Clos de la Roche would sound awkward and the Clos des Lambrays was, of course, not then a *Grand Cru*.

STATISTICS: *Area:* 6.62.60 ha *Owners:* 20. *Average Annual Production:* 2,255 cases

Above: Clos St-Denis
Opposite: Spring ploughing in Clos St-Denis

PRINCIPAL OWNERS: Georges Lignier: 1.49 ha; **Dujac:** 1.29 ha (35); **Ponsot/de Chezeaux:** 0.70 ha (104); **Bertagna:** 0.53 ha; Castagnier: 0.35 ha; (1980); Charlopin-Parizot: 0.20 ha (c. 1950); **Arlaud:** 0.18 ha (1970); **Jadot:** 0.17 ha; Pierre Amiot: 0.17 ha; Michel Magnien: 0.12 ha

ORIGINS: The original Clos belonged to the Canons of the Chapter of St-Denis de Vergy. Planted by monks in the 13th century, it then passed into the hands of the Marey-Monge family and thereafter was sold and became fragmented.

TOPOGRAPHY/GEOLOGY: The major macro-influence on Clos St-Denis is the Combe de Morey which channels east to west above Morey. This means that fruit on the south-facing exposure ripens faster and better than that on the north-facing side. It is possible that this more favourable exposure promotes malic acid production over that of tartaric acid which means reduced acidities in the finished wine. The vineyard slopes relatively evenly from Calouère to Chaffots – steeper and stonier in the former, flattening out in Les Chaffots. The soils continue the hard (mainly Prémeaux) limestone, a band which stretches south from Gevrey, with a good larding of rock fragments evident, strewn with flat, angular stones – most probably limestone – and overlain by thick gravelly scree. As is to be expected where the gradient is marked, soil tends to collect in the lower sections of the vineyard. Here the soils are deep, up to 80 centimetres without reaching bedrock, marginally heavier, containing fine-grained gravels. The wine of Calouère is a touch less rich than that from the other *climats*.

WINE: Clos St-Denis consistently produces the most elegant wines of all the Morey *Grands Crus* – finesse, subtlety and delicacy are its hallmarks. Though not showing the aromatic intensity of Musigny, Clos St-Denis is certainly the most Chambolle-ish of Morey's *Grands Crus* with fruit style redolent more of red than black fruit. This character is not achieved at the expense of concentration, far from it; Clos St-Denis fuses depth and richness with its fragrance, albeit with a shade less structure to it than Clos de la Roche, even more pronounced in comparison with Bonnes-Mares. Here the emphasis is on nuance whereas with Bonnes-Mares it is on substance. As one expects from any *Grand Cru*, finesse is balanced by concentration and power – that elusive energy which great vineyards bring to their wine.

MOREY-ST-DENIS

La Bussière

Bonnes-Mares

Combe d'Ambin

Route des Grands Crus

La Combe

300

260

Chambolle-Musigny

280

300

Les Amoureuses

320

N

340

0   300 m

Le Musigny

Combe d'Orveaux

Les Petits Musigny

Château du Clos de Vougeot

VOUGEOT

BONNES-MARES

Chambolle-Musigny fields a pair of fine *Grands Crus*: Bonnes-Mares and Musigny. There could not be a greater contrast between them. Bonnes-Mares, which extends north of the village up to, and indeed in to, Morey-St-Denis which has a 1.52 ha slab within its curtilage, produces wine best described as substantial and heavy-framed; Musigny, at the southern end of the parish is elegance and restrained aristocracy personified. While both are fine, Musigny indubitably has the quality edge for its remarkable suavity and finesse.

STATISTICS: *Area:* 15.05.72 ha (1.51.55 of which is in Morey St-Denis) *Owners:* 35. *Average Annual Production:* 5,115 cases

PRINCIPAL OWNERS: **de Vogüé**: 2.66 ha (1945–1995); Drouhin-Laroze: 1.49 ha; **Fougeray de Beauclair**: 1.20 ha; Bart: 1.03 ha; **Robert Groffier**: 1.00 ha (1960–1970); **Domaine de la Vougeraie**: 0.70 ha; **Dujac**: 0.58 ha (30); **Bruno Clair**: 0.41 ha (1941, 1978); **Roumier**: 0.39 ha (1967); **Jacques-Frédéric Mugnier**: 0.36 ha (1961,1980, 1988); Castagnier: 0.33 ha; **Louis Jadot**: 0.27 ha; **Leroy/d'Auvenay**: 0.26 ha; **Bouchard Père et Fils**: 0.24 ha (30–40); **Joseph Drouhin**: 0.23 ha (1967); **Arlaud**: 0.21 ha (1979); Pousse d'Or: 0.17 ha; Charlopin-Parizot: 0.12 ha (1980); Patrice Rion: 0.06 ha (1979)

ORIGINS: The etymology is unclear despite three plausible theories. The most prevalent is that Bonnes-Mares is a corruption of Bonnes-Mères – a reference to early owners, the Nuns of the Abbey of Tart-le-Haut. A second notion is that 'Mares' derives from *marer* meaning to cultivate (hence *maréchage*). Since much of the Côte was under monastic control from the early Middle Ages, possibly even earlier, it is more plausible to think that a good vineyard would take its attribution from a religious source rather than a secular source. The third idea is that Bonnes-Mares refers to the 'Mères', the deities who protected and blessed the harvest. *Au choix!*

TOPOGRAPHY/GEOLOGY: Bonnes-Mares follows the line of fine *Premiers Crus* Cras and Fuées at broadly similar altitude, exposed east and south-of-east on a moderate but irregular slope. The vineyard has two distinct subsoil types that match those in its northern neighbour, Clos de Tart.

There is a well-defined soil gradation between the northerly section into Morey and the southerly section adjoining Les Fuées. The line of separation is more or less co-terminus with a track which runs from the vineyard's north-east corner to the point where it meets Les Fuées. The upper section is characterised by the presence of *Ostrea acuminata* marls, rich in active lime, in the lower part the base rock is *entroques*; here red soils dominate imparting lower acidity to the wine. While these latter are shallow, in the upper sector subsoils are much deeper. Pick up a handful on either side of the path and the difference is clearly visible. The upper part is rich in small crenellated *Ostrea* fossils of a clay-like consistency, the lower part is more friable and darker; it also contains (*entroques*) fossils but of a different character. Two other important factors are first, that the majority of the overall vineyard area is *terre rouge* (lower sector) and second, that the nearer to Chambolle the more the soil resembles the upper sector. The upper sector's light-coloured marls are finer-grained and less permeable imparting finesse and minerality to the wine. The reddish-brown soils that develop above the *entroques* are thin (40–50 centimetres) with lowish acidity which gives the wine a sappy, more obviously fruity quality. So different are these soil types that were the classification to be reviewed it is probable that Bonnes-Mares would have two appellations rather than one. Note that the prominent rock profiles next to the Route des Grands Crus in Bonnes-Mares and Clos de Bèze are not geological faults but remains of ancient stone quarries; *entroque* limestone was widely used for walls and shelters.

WINE: Generalisations about a *Cru* as extended and with such soil variation as Bonnes-Mares are of limited value. One producer may have vines in both main sectors from which to compound his *cuvée* (Christophe Roumier does) while another may have only one (de Vogüé does – lower sector). Tasting a single vintage from the two sectors in one cellar well illustrates the contribution of soils. *Terre rouge* gives round, fleshy, broad-shouldered and muscular wine, redolent of red fruits and relatively approachable; light-coloured marls (*terre blanche*) impart florality, minerality and spiciness with firmer tannins – altogether more elegant and direct. This is not to say that one sector produces better wine than another, just to mark the difference. The ideal is a blend from both sectors. Where the character of Bonnes-Mares becomes most obvious is in its contrast with Musigny, and here there can be no doubt the role soil plays in wine character. Taste these side by side from the same source – de Vogüé, Roumier and Mugnier have both – and the differences shine out: the broad, muscular Bonnes-Mares alongside the balletic poise and silky elegance of Musigny. This is not to disparage Bonnes-Mares, rather to highlight its distinctiveness.

MUSIGNY

Musigny is not only one of the greatest wines of Burgundy it is also one of the greatest wines on earth. It also enjoys the distinction of being the only Côte de Nuits *Grand Cru* to produce both red and white wine. Poets – usually French, be it said – have stretched the bounds of credibility, even by their own fantastical standards, in evocation of this wine, whose poise and nobility have long been known and admired. Some descriptions border on the erotic while the more restrained invite one to imagine 'little Jesus slipping down the throat in velvet trousers' or 'a wine of silk and lace, supremely delicate, with no hint of violence, yet great hidden strength… savour it deliberately…. Smell the scents of a damp garden, the perfume of a rose, a violet bathed in morning dew' – this, from Gaston Roupnel who is responsible for much vinous literary euphoria. One might think that the prospect of swallowing anything, however small, in velvet trousers might be something of a deterrent, not to mention a hazardous biomechanical challenge, but obviously not to the French. Taken as pure marketing copy, such purple prose does rather well.

Shorn of its velveteens, the vineyard itself is tripartite – the lower and smaller section of Le Combe d'Orveaux (0.61.28 ha) bordering Les Echézeaux, which was reclassified from *Premier Cru* to *Grand Cru* in the 1960s; Les Petits Musigny (4.19.35 ha) which extends to the wall of Clos de Vougeot at the level of the Château, and Les Musigny itself (5.89.60 ha). After the Revolution the vineyard was sold piecemeal and thus became heavily fragmented in ownership. Today, 90% is in the hands of four principal owners.

STATISTICS: *Area:* 10.70.23 ha. *Owners:* 17. *Average Annual Production:* 2,904 cases (red), 242 cases (white)

PRINCIPAL OWNERS: **de Vogüé:** 6.46 ha Pinot (1953–2007), 0.65 ha Chardonnay (1986–1997); **Jacques-Frédéric Mugnier:** 1.14 ha (1947, 1962, 1997); **Prieur:** 0.76 ha; **Joseph Drouhin:** 0.68 ha (1980); **Leroy:** 0.27 ha; Domaine de la Vougeraie: 0.21 ha; **Louis Jadot:** 0.17 ha; Drouhin-Laroze: 0.12 ha; **Domaine Roumier:** 0.10 ha (1930); **Joseph Faiveley:** 0.03 ha (1945)

ORIGINS: It is said that Musigny came into existence in the 11th century when Pierre Gros donated his 'Champ de Musigné' to the monks at Cîteaux. The name is well-documented in local archives from the 1500s. Otherwise, the etymology is obscure.

TOPOGRAPHY/GEOLOGY: The soils of Musigny vary with location. In the upper (and qualitatively superior) sectors near the village of Chambolle, the soils are relatively deep and composed of *marnes calcaire*, a friable, oolitic limestone and degraded fossil material. It is this soil-type which imparts Musigny's hallmark finesse. The underlying rock in this sector is *Ostrea acuminata* marl. Lower down in the Musigny Bas and indeed in Les Amoureuses, the rock is largely hard, white compact Comblanchien limestone. These lower sectors have more clay and less active limestone and are shallower (around 30 centimetres deep).

The vineyard lies on several north–south faults which separate different geologies; these occur in places where the ground starts to slope. There is a fault line at the limit between Musigny and the brush, with Comblanchien limestone above the vineyard. Around one-third of the way up from the road, near the inflexion point of the slope where it changes from weakly to more strongly inclined, there is another fault; this separates the marls to the east from Comblanchien limestone to the west. In the upper sectors the substratum is more friable and marly; downslope the rock is hard and compact Comblanchien limestone. All round, Musigny is well drained.

The altitude ranges from 262–283 metres for Petits Musigny and 270–305 metres for Musigny. The slope is around 12% in the upper part of both vineyards, lower in the bottom sectors, locally higher (15%) in Musigny. These inclines are enough to produce soil erosion during rainy periods. In that event, the soil washed down is meticulously collected and returned. In general, Musigny's soils have a significant proportion of stones (20% plus) and contain red clays, particular to this vineyard. The prominent drop from Musigny onto Les Petits Vougeots is not in fact a geological fault but the scar of disused quarry workings; this is reinforced by the vineyard below which is basically quarry debris on Comblanchien and white oolite. An administrative curiosity is a small, flat bench of vines below the road which are in fact classified Musigny rather than Petits Vougeots.

WINE: Let's deal first with Musigny Blanc which comes exclusively from de Vogüé's 0.65 ha of Chardonnay planted in the upper, marlier sectors of Petits Musigny and Les Musigny. This is highly individual, *sui generis*, full and robust and noticeably phenolic in character; white wine grown on red wine soils – definitely not to be compared to the *Grands Crus* of Puligny or Corton-Charlemagne. The parcel was entirely replanted in the mid-1990s and thenceforth the production has been sold under the Domaine label as Bourgogne Blanc although the intention is to revert to Musigny Blanc when the wine is deemed worthy of *Grand Cru* status. (Even 15 years is still *jeunes vignes* here!) The wine is good and without doubt interesting but, in my experience of it, lacking the finesse and complexity for greatness.

There is, however, no doubt as to the greatness of Musigny. It sits at the summit of the Côte's output, Burgundy's Everest. Statuesque in structure, patriarchal in presence, Musigny derives its authority from its extraordinary purity, energy and outstanding class. The hallmarks of this remarkable *terroir* are delicacy, finesse and subtlety, 'velvet' and 'silk' being the most common descriptors. The difficulty is that words border on the pretentious when attempting to describe wine at this level of quality. The magic lies in the sensation, not in any descriptive deconstruction. Fortunately, this great vineyard is entrusted to a short dozen of hugely skilled and passionate *vignerons* so indifferent quality is mercifully a rarity. It has been suggested that Musigny fuses the characteristics of Les Amoureuses and Bonnes-Mares in that the one contributes finesse, the other body. This is one way of looking at it but not, I believe, particularly helpful in understanding the wine.

Musigny's largest owner, de Vogüé, finds no marked difference between the various parts of the vineyard and suggests that whatever differences there are may be the product of differing speeds of fermentation which might be traced back to fruit components and thence to location in the vineyard. Musigny starts life unforthcoming, sometimes austere to the point that one might even be forgiven for thinking it mediocre, but with none of the brutality of Bonnes-Mares. Harder work is required to get a line onto young Musigny than Bonnes-Mares. The seeds of future greatness lie in bright, refreshing acidity, silken tannins, magnificent presence and length and a purity which is almost essential in character. In young Musigny look for *petits fruits rouges* (redcurrant, *fraises des bois*, raspberry) and even white chocolate, rather than cassis, blackcurrant and the darker fruits found elsewhere on the Côte. But there is much more to come, given a decade or so in bottle. The rewards are an explosion of aromas – game, *sous-bois*, wild tea-rose and violets – almost exotic in their complexity and overwhelming in their intensity. Musigny is a wine of supreme breed and poise, the sublime sensuousness and graceful seductiveness of a perfect figure. It has an almost numinous quality, conveying an impression of effortless intensity without the slightest suggestion of solidity. This is no ossified aristocracy, rather the lithe, agile poise of self-assurance, suave and charming. Great Musigny has a class which leaves one marvelling in disbelief that this is the product of freshly squeezed grapes. Pretentious words: very possibly; great wine – most definitely.

Musigny with the wall of Château du Clos de Vougeot beyond

CHAMBOLLE-MUSIGNY PREMIER CRU
LES AMOUREUSES

In the pantheon of Chambolle's *Premiers Crus* Les Amoureuses stands supreme. Known until relatively recently as 'Musigny Amoureuses', Lavalle puts it on a par with Bonnes-Mares and the *Premiers Crus* Cras, Fuées and Varoilles. Among producers there is widespread agreement as to its primacy and eligibility for *Grand Cru* status and this superior status has long since been reflected in its price. Indeed, one producer regularly charges more for his Amoureuses than for his (excellent) Bonnes-Mares even though he has more of this. The vineyard, as well as its wine, is striking. Apart from a prominent wall-sign proclaiming its largest owner – Robert Groffier et Fils – it is noteworthy for its terraced configuration which takes the vineyard from the heights of Chambolle almost down to the level of the Clos de Vougeot. Visitors leaving Chambolle by the southerly by-road to turn onto the direct road to Vougeot pass between Les Amoureuses on the left and Musigny on the right. The prospect from Amoureuses towards the Clos de Vougeot with Les Echézeaux and Vosne-Romanée in the distance is an evocative sight for any Burgundy aficionado.

STATISTICS: *Area:* 5.40.13 ha *Owners:* 17 *Average Annual Production*: 2,300 cases

PRINCIPAL OWNERS: **Robert Groffier**: 1.00 ha (1968); **Joseph Drouhin**: 0.60 ha (1971); **de Vogüé**: 0.56 ha; **Jacques-Frédéric Mugnier**: 0.53 ha (1954, 1956, 1966); Amiot Servelle: 0.45 ha (1944–1999); **Christophe Roumier**: 0.40 ha (1947); Bernard Serveau: 0.35 ha; **Moine-Hudelot**: 0.20 ha; Pousse d'Or: 0.20 Patrice Rion: 0.18 ha (1979); **Louis Jadot**: 0.12 ha

ORIGINS: Whether Les Amoureuses (= the (feminine) lovers) merely suggests something of passion and delicacy or has a deeper significance in Chambolle's history is not known. Whatever its etymology the name seems somehow entirely appropriate.

TOPOGRAPHY/GEOLOGY: The vineyard follows the hillside from the source of the Vouge up to a plateau on which the major part is located. Amoureuses is distinctive in that, whereas the Côte is for the most part concave, here it is convex. This is evident from the croupe in Frédy Mugnier's Amoureuses vines which are sandwiched between Les Chabiots and Musigny on the upper side of the spur road from Chambolle to Vosne. This convexity and the vineyard's largely southerly orientation

means that it is in sunlight all day compared with Musigny on which the sun sets earlier. Thus, despite being exposed to wind which helps limit airborne disease and would normally delay the vegetative process, this orientation paradoxically makes for early budding and ripening. The lower, easterly, sector is steeply sloping and its location and proximity to the Vouge imparts greater coolness and humidity than on the plateau.

In general, Amoureuses shares much the same soil-types as Musigny although as with the lower sectors of that vineyard, the rocks are more friable. The ground here is very shallow – 20–60 centimetres only with a bedrock of compact Comblanchien limestone which is very mineral in character and contains a high proportion of pebbles at all soil levels. The top section is effectively a continuation of Musigny across a narrow road. The southerly sector of the vineyard lies beneath a disused quarry whose stone was undoubtedly used to build the Château du Clos de Vougeot with high stone walls which reflect heat back onto the vines. The topography is characterised by several faults which bring the terrain down towards Vougeot by a series of steps, softened in appearance by erosion. The predominance of active limestone here accounts for the wine's abundant finesse and silkiness. It has been incorrectly written that Les Amoureuses is on oolitic bedrock; in fact, it lies on Comblanchien limestone as can be clearly seen from the quarry profile which shows a deep layer of Comblanchien with oolite below. Here the soils are yellow and brown with a stony surface and highish clay content in the subsoil.

WINE: The intrinsic character of Amoureuses is difficult to capture, let alone express in words. No-one doubts its ability to produce heart-stopping quality but it is a nymph and hard to pin down. François Millet, winemaker at de Vogüé, talks of the 'wife of Musigny' – the first lady of Chambolle and a very elegant one at that. Christophe Roumier depicts its constant qualities as 'silky tannins, delicate texture, an ethereal character which has no need of mass to be intense … a wine of natural gracefulness'. Frédy Mugnier also refers to this taste impression of intensity without mass. It might be taken as damning with feint praise to regard Les Amoureuses as a junior Musigny but that would be a mistake. Amoureuses does not pretend to the sublime heights of top Musigny, but its wine often reaches *Grand Cru* quality. The best examples – especially from the likes of Groffier, de Vogüé, Roumier or Mugnier – are strongly redolent of Musigny with perhaps a shade less glamour and intensity, giving an

Varied topography. Vougeot from Les Amoureuses. Note the steep incline towards the east and the undulation towards the Château

impression of ethereal luminosity not found in Musigny. One grower, who has both, characterised the difference between Musigny and Amoureuses thus: 'Musigny is grander, deeper and richer; Amoureuses has vibrancy and charm which Musigny lacks.' It is often contrasted, as is Musigny, with Bonnes-Mares. Amoureuses is more restrained, less open and frank than Bonnes-Mares, which tends to wear its heart on its sleeve. Perhaps the more instructive contrast for Les Amoureuses is with Premier Cru Les Fuées. Although from the Bonnes-Mares end of the village, this wine (and there are only a few producers of whom the finest are Frédy Mugnier and Ghislaine Barthod) more resembles Amoureuses in tone and structure.

Aromatically youthful Amoureuses is redolent of spring – hawthorn, may, cowslip and the like – with notes of raspberry, grenadine and blackberry overlaid with a peppery spiciness, rose and violet. The best have a seductive, enticingly silky, florality to their fragrance. It is easy to be deceived by a relatively 'light', finely poised, taste profile into thinking that Amoureuses lacks the constituents for longevity. On the contrary, from a decent vintage and producer it ages beautifully; indeed, it is sacrilege to broach such a wine before its fifth birthday and even that is likely to be premature. What might put the elevation of Les Amoureuses to *Grand Cru* in doubt is a tendency to inconsistency. When it delivers at the highest level it does so spectacularly, but it does not invariably deliver. The character of the vintage marks Amoureuses more than either Bonnes-Mares or Musigny which makes its *terroir* expression less sure-footed.

CLOS DE VOUGEOT

If Musigny rarely disappoints, Clos de Vougeot rarely enthrals. This massive *Grand Cru* – over 50 hectares – crystallises years of land transactions by the Abbey at Cîteaux, mainly in the early 12th century. The Abbots knew exactly what they wanted and when parcels were not donated they bought them. According to the historian Camille Rodier, the last piece of the jigsaw was put in place in 1336. However, the date of the final establishment of the Clos' limits as we now know them is disputed: some put it between the 12th and 15th centuries, others as late as the 17th century. In any event, the monks of Cîteaux remained sole owners for almost seven centuries. After the Revolution, the Clos remained in state ownership, a *bien national*, until 1818, as unusually, the Revolutionaires decided to sell it as a single lot rather than subdividing. It was then bought by Jules Ouvrard who owned vineyard land throughout the Côte, in particular Romanée-Conti. On his death it was managed by his three immediate heirs who sold it on in 1889 to six local wine merchants. Subsequent subdivision has resulted in its present highly fragmented proprietorship.

The Clos de Vougeot, along with Corton and Echézeaux, are the most extended and least tractable of Burgundy's *Grands Crus*. Size apart, the mix of variables is daunting: differences in soil type, particularly between the upper and lower sections of the vineyard (see following); highly fragmented ownership – not only 80+ different owners but many with strips scattered here and there; and differences in vine age and in viticultural and winemaking competence from owner to owner. These factors make for considerable variability in both quality level and individual taste qualities. Getting to grips with the Clos' vinous identity is akin to giving eighty chefs everything from a free-range Bresse chicken to a battery-farmed bird, good stock to stock cubes and home grown to hydroponic vegetables and then trying to discern any homogeneity in the resulting Coqs au Vin.

STATISTICS: *Area:* 50.95.76 ha. *Owners:* 82 *Average Annual Production:* 17,523 cases

PRINCIPAL OWNERS: Château de la Tour: 5.48 ha; **Méo-Camuzet**: 3.0 ha (1920s, 1960s, 1979); Rebourseau: 2.21 ha; **Louis Jadot**: 2.15 ha; **Leroy**: 1.91 ha; **Grivot**: 1.86 ha (1964); **Gros Frère et Soeur**: 1.56 ha (1986–1989); Raphet: 1.47 ha; Domaine de la Vougeraie: 1.41 ha; **Eugénie**: 1.36 ha

(1949); **Lamarche**: 1.35 ha (1979); **Faiveley**: 1.29 ha (1940, 1974–1976, 1980–81); Prieur: 1.28 ha; Drouhin-Laroze: 1.03 ha; Thibault Liger-Belair: 0.75 (1938); **Hudelot-Noëllat**: 0.69 ha (1950); **Anne Gros**: 0.93 ha (1905); **Joseph Drouhin**: 0.91 ha (1977); Daniel Rion: 0.73 ha (1958–1973); **Louis Jadot**: 0.64 ha; Bichot/Clos Frantin: 0.63 ha; Mongeard-Mugneret: 0.63 ha (1954, 1964); Prieuré-Roch: 0.62 ha (1932, 1958, 1962, 1975); Jean-Jacques Confuron: 0.50 ha (1962); **Bouchard Père et Fils**: 0.45 ha (30–40); **Robert Arnoux**: 0.45 ha (1955); Charlopin-Parizot: 0.42 ha (1950, 1986); **Ponsot**: 0.40 ha (54); **Georges Mugneret-Gibourg**: 0.34 ha (1955); Henri Boillot: 0.34 ha (1985); **Chauvenet-Chopin**: 0.35 ha (40); **Denis Mortet**: 0.31 ha (c. 1950); **Bertagna**: 0.31 ha (1964); **Régis Forey**: 0.30 ha (1972–1986); **de Montille**: 0.29 ha; Confuron-Cotétidot: 0.25 ha (65); Jean Tardy: 0.26 ha (1954); **Michel Gros**: 0.20 ha (1987, 1988); Ambroise: 0.17 ha (40)

ORIGINS: Perhaps, in view of its monastic parentage, it should have been called the Clos de Cîteaux, but it wasn't. As other Clos de Cîteaux appear along the Côte, notably in Pommard and Meursault, this neatly avoids any possible confusion.

TOPOGRAPHY/GEOLOGY: Although from the road it appears flat, the Clos is in fact on a gentle 3–4 degree slope, with a vertical displacement of some three metres from top to bottom. Given its situation, bordered by Musigny and Grands Echézeaux, its complex geology and soil come as no surprise. A variation in quality potential from different sectors of this large vineyard has long been recognised. In his early 19th-century work *Topography of all the known vineyards*, André Jullien wrote of Clos de Vougeot: 'the products of different portions of this Clos vary in quality: the vines sites on the highest parts give a fine and delicate wine; the lower parts, above all those that border the Grande-Route give a much inferior wine.' This description oversimplifies what is a highly complex pattern of soils and local variation.

The Clos is underpinned by three separate geologies with soils that vary in depth and drainage; these broadly correlate with separate levels of quality. The upper section, where the vineyard joins Grands-Echézeaux to the south and Musigny to the north, is dominated by Comblanchien limestone with noticeably stonier and better-drained soils with less clay than lower down. These produce the finest, most distinguished and complex wines. Two particular *lieux-dits* are (unofficially) recognised here –

Le Grand Maupertuis and Musgni (*sic*) – producing notably fine *cuvées* from Anne Gros and Gros Frère et Soeur respectively. The Clos' mid-section is mainly clay-limestone with significant clay content and soils of 40–50 centimetres depth but is also stony and thus generally well-drained. Quality can be fine here but is more mixed. The lower, least propitious *quartier* is formed of deeper layers of mixed (Oligocene) eroded material which has accumulated since the current relief initiated some 30 million years ago; these are overlain with thick shaly deposits that stacked over time. Vines in this deep, clay-rich soil tend to give rather coarse, leaden-footed wine, considerable skill being required to counterbalance size with finesse.

In addition to soil variation, the Clos is a multiplicity of small inclines and depressions which affect exposition and ripening; for example, between the Chioure *climat* just below the Château and the Grand Maupertuis *climat* there is a small hillock which perforce affects the exposure and drainage of its vines. Elsewhere one finds measurable differences in humidity and temperature which also play a role in ripening. In other parts of the vineyard soils are relatively thin and stony (for example in parts of the Quatorze Journaux *climat*). Walls and deep soils increase humidity, which is not always the negative influence it is considered to be. For example, in the exceptionally hot 2003 vintage greater humidity helped sustain the vines which otherwise might have shut down altogether.

The Clos' quality spectrum is not exclusively due to natural variation; man has also played a part. When the RN 74, which abuts the eastern border of the vineyard, was raised in the early 1900s by France's Department of Water and Forests to counter flooding, the result was an excess of rainwater standing in the lower sections of the Clos already close to the water-table. This increased the flood risk and limited drainage. Of more beneficial human influence is the stone wall limiting the Clos to the west which efficiently prevents the cool air driven by the Combe d'Orveaux retarding fruit ripening.

None of this is to say that the obstacles to producing *Grand Cru* quality are insurmountable for today's viticulturally and technologically trained producers, rather to emphasise that there are identifiable differences which matter to the final product.

WINE: These complexities make describing the wine of Clos de Vougeot hazardous. There are some fine *cuvées*, especially those from parcels with older vines planted on the more propitious sectors. In its least appetising manifestations Clos de Vougeot is burly and truly rustic stuff, lacking in definition, coarse and thoroughly dull. Indifferent offerings often emanate from the second-division négoce and proprietors who either overwood, overcrop to stretch their production from a small plot, or simply overwork the fruit in the mistaken belief that this is the route to quality. The best bottlings come with the broad shoulders the Clos seems to deliver as a hallmark, but layered with elegance and dimension – a Vosne-ish succulence overlaying a firm frame. A worthy Clos de Vougeot has aromatic as well as palate complexity and tends to show the darker-fruited, spicier face of Pinot Noir.

The Clos has perhaps suffered unduly from a reputation for producing poor wine. Shop selectively and there are excellent bottles to be found. As with all larger *Grands Crus* there are less favoured plots but much of the quality variation is more reflective of vigneron ineptitude than inferior *terroir*. One grower summed it up succinctly: 'Clos de Vougeot is sometimes like a rough diamond who is trying to acquire some manners!'

Clos de Vougeot in winter

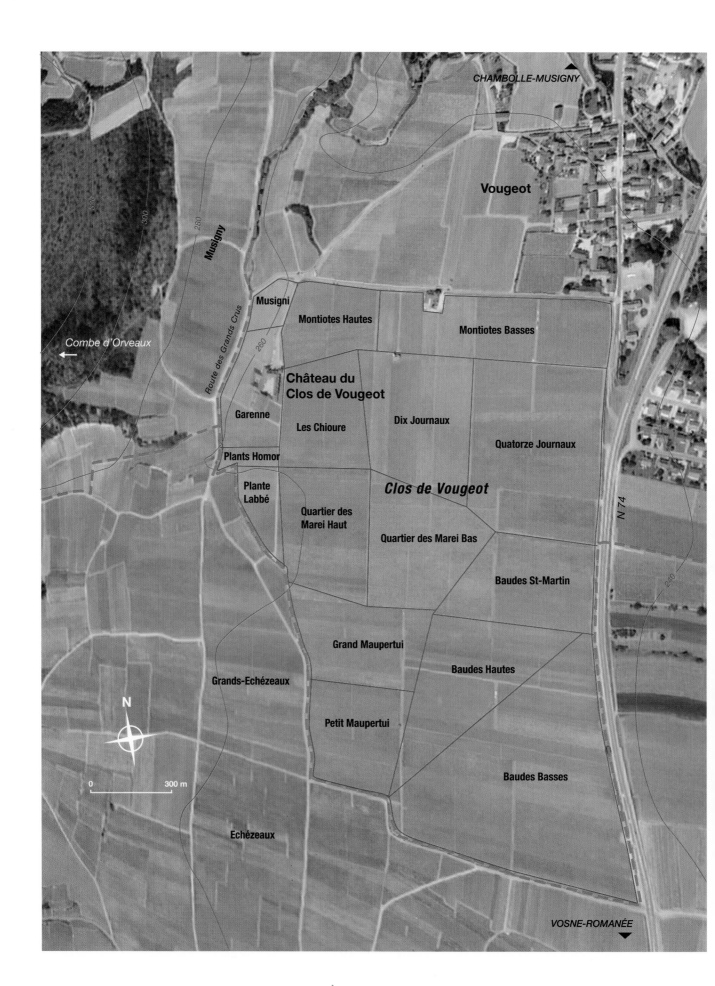

CHAMBOLLE-MUSIGNY

Vougeot

Musigny

Musigni

Montiotes Hautes

Montiotes Basses

Combe d'Orveaux

Route des Grands Crus

Château du
Clos de Vougeot

Garenne

Les Chioure

Dix Journaux

Quatorze Journaux

Plants Homor

Plante
Labbé

Clos de Vougeot

Quartier des
Marei Haut

Quartier des Marei Bas

N 74

Baudes St-Martin

Grand Maupertui

N

Baudes Hautes

Grands-Echézeaux

Petit Maupertui

Baudes Basses

0   300 m

Echézeaux

VOSNE-ROMANÉE

Map of Clos de Vougeot vineyard ownership
as at February 2010

ECHÉZEAUX

chézeaux is another of the Côte's large *Grands Crus*. A 'broad church' welcoming the fine and the less fine, it is among the most variable in quality and difficult to pin down in terms of typicity. There is no 'house style' here and the quality varies widely between growers, often dependent on the location of their vines. At its northern extremities Echézeaux touches both the south-west corner of the Clos de Vougeot and the Combe d'Orveaux *Premier Cru* of Chambolle-Musigny with Les Grands Echézeaux between it and the westerly wall of the Clos de Vougeot. At its southern end it is surrounded by the Vosne Premiers Crus Les Suchots and the lower section of Les Beaumonts.

While Grands Echézeaux reflects well-attested historical boundaries, there is a strong whiff of political expansion about the enlargement of Echézeaux to its present extent. Les Echézeaux is an amalgamation of no fewer than eleven distinct *lieux-dits*: bordering Suchots to the north are the Clos St-Denis

(nothing to do with the eponymous vineyard in Morey) and Les Cruots (aka Vignes Blanches); to the north of Suchots and the south of Grands Echézeaux is Les Treux which is bordered to the west by Les Loachausses and to the east by Les Quartiers de Nuits (part Grand Cru Echézeaux and part Vosne Premier Cru); west of Grands Echézeaux are the Echézeaux du Dessus and Les Poulaillères which in turn is bordered by En Orveaux to the north and west, Les Champs Traversins to the west. Echézeaux du Dessus is bounded to the west by Les Rouges du Bas. These subdivisions are not irrelevant; knowing the location of a producer's vines is a fair guide to the quality of his wine.

STATISTICS: *Area:* 37.69.22 ha. *Owners:* 84. *Average Annual Production:* 12,661 cases

PRINCIPAL OWNERS: **Domaine de la Romanée-Conti**: 4.67 ha (40–50); Mongeard-Mugneret: 2.50 ha (1969); Emmanuel

View over one of Echezeaux's eleven climats - Les Rouges

Rouget: 1.43 ha; **Lamarche**: 1.34 ha (1979); **Georges Mugneret-Gibourg**: 1.24 ha (1940, 1981); Perdrix: 1.14 ha (1922, 1947); Clerget: 1.09 ha; Jacques Cacheux: 1.07 ha; Bichot/Clos Frantin: 1.00 ha; **Gros Frère et Soeur**: 0.93 ha (1976–1995); **Faiveley**: 0.83 ha (1941, 1955–1958); **Jean Grivot**: 0.84 ha (1954); **Robert Arnoux**: 0.80 ha (1968); **Anne Gros**: 0.76 ha (1990); **Dujac**: 0.69 ha (25); Nudant: 0.66 ha (50+); **Liger-Belair**: 0.62 ha (65); **Eugénie**: 0.55 ha (1929); **Jayer-Gilles**: 0.54 ha (60); **Louis Jadot**: 0.52 ha (30–40); Confuron-Cotétidot: 0.46 ha (65); **Joseph Drouhin**: 0.46 ha (1977); **Méo-Camuzet**: 0.44 ha (1940s onwards); **Bouchard Père et Fils**: 0.39 ha (30–40); Jacques Prieur: 0.35 ha; Daniel Rion: 0.35 ha; Jean Tardy: 0.34 ha; Philippe Charlopin: 0.33 ha (1923); Capitain-Gagnerot: 0.31 ha; **Régis Forey**: 0.30 ha (1949–2004); **A F Gros/François Parent**: 0.28 ha (1940); François Gerbet: 0.19 ha; Robert Sirugue: 0.12 ha

ORIGINS: It is thought, but by no means certain, that Echézeaux is of Latin derivation which corrupted into Aux Cheusots or Les Cheseaux and referred to buildings. In support of this contention Marie-Hélène Landrieu-Lussigny, in her excellent book, *Les Lieux-Dits dans le Vignoble Bourguignon* (1983), cites the plots known as Aux Cheusots at Fixin, Aux Chezeaux at Morey St-Denis and Aux Echézeaux at Gevrey and Chambolle where remains of habitation have been discovered. It is likely that Echézeaux was home to dwellings and this derivation reflects that history.

TOPOGRAPHY/GEOLOGY: As an assemblage of eleven *climats* spread over nearly 38 hectares, Echézeaux has no identifiable geological identity. Topography and geology vary markedly: slopes in the upper sectors of Champs Traversins and Rouge du Bas reach 13–14%, while those of the lower portions are virtually flat. The top of the vineyard is on the 310-metre contour, the bottom some 70–90 vertical metres lower. These differences contribute significantly to ripening – both ripening date and ripeness level – and thereby to wine quality. There is also the matter of position relative to the sun. The *combe* above the northern end of Vosne/Flagey allows evening sunshine from the west through, so the northerly end of Les Echézeaux gets comparatively more sunlight than elsewhere. The upper *climats* – for example, Champs Traversin and Rouge du Bas – are still in sun when the adjoining *Premiers Crus* are in shade. The particular effect of these differences in micro-exposure is on acidity altering the all-important balance between malic and tartaric acid in the grapes. The cold air circulating downwards from the Combe d'Orveaux also influences grape ripening.

Even for the Côte this is particularly complex geology, with significant soil variation to be found within a few metres. In general, the lower the slope the deeper is the soil while the upper sectors are thinner and stonier. The totality is well drained; it is said that even after heavy rain one can walk here in carpet slippers a couple of hours later, whereas in Grands Echézeaux one must wait two or three days before venturing into the vineyard. Certain *climats*, notably Les Treux and Loachausses, are on brown clay-limestone soils while the Echézeaux du Dessus has clay-rich soils. One of the better *climats*, Rouge du Bas, has soils which are even richer in brown clays, quite deep in places: this is shared by Echézeaux du Dessus. In Les Cruots soils are dominated by limestone pebbles which drain well; one grower avers that his Cruots vines gave a good ripe harvest every year – even in a poor vintage such as 1984 when all the rest of his vines were damaged, the Echézeaux came up trumps.

Finding deep soils at altitude is a relative rarity on the Côte, where increasing elevation usually means poorer, thinner soils. This does not chime with the conventional wisdom which has it that rich deep clays usually give less refined wine. As Rolande Gadille points out in her 1967 treatise *Le Vignoble de la Côte Bourguignonne*, 'the concurrence of frost-riven stones, red lime, and Bajocien marls [actually *Ostrea acuminata*, RN] in one place with these exceptional, deep soils at such altitude permits the extension of the vineyard to higher levels at the expense of the forest on which vines were planted in the 19th century'. Mid-slope is essentially a continuation of the *Grand Cru* band of Musigny to the north and Romanée-St-Vivant to the south. For example, the Combe d'Orveaux *climat* has soils which more closely mirror those of Musigny which it nearly joins. The Echézeaux vineyard is thus varied and complex. If any generalisation holds good it is that the best wines come from the middle sections of the slope.

WINE: Echézeaux is Vosne-Romanée in all but name and it is with the finest Vosnes that its wines are generally compared.

Of the modern configuration, Lavalle put En Orveaux, Les Pouaillères, Echézeaux du Dessus, Cruots, Champs Traversins and Rouges du Bas in the second rank, with Grands Echézeaux alone in the first and the remaining, lower-situated *climats* in third rank. Not surprisingly a line-up of Echézeaux from any given vintage will show considerable variation, both in overall quality and individual taste qualities. Those from the upper sections of the vineyard are likely to be more classically structured while those from the lower vineyards less refined, more rustic and less complex. As usual, a producer's competence will influence the end result along with where his vines are

Winter pruning in Les Echézeaux

situated. Wine from Domaine de la Romanée-Conti, whose Echézeaux vines are in Les Poulaillères, is more likely to be fine than a wine from a Domaine whose vines are in Les Treux. Many *cuvées* benefit from having contributions from several different *climats* in much the same way as Chave's Hermitage Rouge from multiple sites has greater complexity than others from just one. In specific character, Echézeaux tends to have elegant fruit-based aromas – '*compôte*' according to Henri Jayer who made one of the finest – with a predominance of both red and black berry fruits. With age, these are transformed into aromas which reveal more *sous-bois*, musk, fresh leather.

On the palate the wine is usually rich and mouthfilling.

Attempting to describe a 'typical Echézeaux' is fruitless – no such wine exists. Inconsistency is built in. Although it is rightly regarded as a second-division *Grand Cru*, what can usefully be said is that the finest examples come close to the best of Clos de Vougeot, albeit with a shade more Vosne-ish finesse. One grower noted that while his (excellent) Clos de Vougeot invariably gets his dinner guests' conversation going, often to the point of heated dispute – the arrival of his Echézeaux (also excellent) invariably produces respectful silence! Material for many an interesting experiment!

GRANDS ECHÉZEAUX

Covering a shade over nine hectares, Grands Echézeaux was thought to have been created in the 12th century by Cistercian monks. At one quarter the size and with a quarter the number of owners it is a much more tractable *climat* than Echézeaux *tout court*. Its wines are much more homogeneous – if it ever makes sense to say this of fragmented Burgundy – and one can sense a typicity which defies most of the larger *Grands Crus*. Technically in the commune of Flagey-Echézeaux, it is situated in the easternmost extremity of Vosne-Romanée, its eastern flank being separated from Clos de Vougeot only by a stone wall; otherwise, it is surrounded by five of Echézeaux's eleven *climats*.

STATISTICS: *Area:* 9.13.45 ha *Owners:* 21. *Average Annual Production:* 3,058 cases

PRINCIPAL OWNERS: **Domaine de la Romanée-Conti**: 3.53 ha (40–50); Mongeard-Mugneret: 1.32 ha (1954, 1969); **Eugénie**: 0.50 ha (1984); Henri de Villamont: 0.50 ha; **Joseph Drouhin**: 0.48 ha (1986); **Gros Frère et Soeur**: 0.37 ha (1976, 1979); **Lamarche**: 0.30 ha (1979); Bichot/Clos Frantin: (0.25 ha); **Robert Sirugue**: (0.13 ha)

ORIGINS: One finds the term 'Grand' attached to many notable burgundian vineyards – Les Grands Epenots (Pommard), La Grande Rue (Vosne), Les Grands Charrons (Meursault), Les Grands Champs (Gevrey, Puligny). The word has two meanings – 'great' and 'large'. It is generally thought (for example, Landrieu-Lussigny, op. cit.) that its use as a prefix to a *climat* denotes the stature of the vineyard rather than its size. Indeed, this makes good sense with Grands Echézeaux which is a quarter the size of Echézeaux itself. However, for La Grande Rue which translates as 'main street', the adjective indicates size rather than quality. 'Chezeaux' is thought to signify a hamlet or small group of houses (from the Latin 'casa').

TOPOGRAPHY/GEOLOGY: It is worth asking what distinguishes Grands Echézeaux from Echézeaux, as it is generally felt to be a step up in quality. This is largely attributable to soil where there is a marked difference between the two *climats*. Indeed, there is more difference between them than there is between Romanée-Conti and Chambertin. While Echézeaux's soils are broadly shallow, giving onto rock, Grands Echézeaux is on deeper ground. In Echézeaux (and neighbouring Les Suchots) when the earth is tilled solid rock is often brought up on the plough. The fact of difference is highlighted by the road which divides the two – built on another of the Côte's many small convex reliefs.

At an altitude of around 260 metres, Grands Echézeaux is more or less flat in its lower section with a 3–4% slope in the upper part. Its deep brown, stony soils are mainly of a clay-limestone mix which gives onto hard Comblanchien limestone.

WINE: Despite its proximity to the upper (and finer) section of Clos de Vougeot, Grands Echézeaux has little of the character of that Cru. The differences in the two wines from the same source tend to be in definition and precision rather than in dimensions related to weight or intensity. In general Grands Echézeaux starts out quite tight, unforthcoming even ungenerous, often with little of the youthful perfume expected from the best Vosne-Romanées although with a characteristic note of *sous-bois*. You need to search diligently beneath the shell of an infant Grands Echézeaux to work out what it might bring forth as age transforms these wines and they slowly unpack. The best are altogether more subtle, aromatically expressive, and finely structured than their Echézeaux counterparts, showing both black and red fruits – dark cherry, blackcurrant, strawberry, raspberry – and plenty of ripe gaminess and *sous-bois* with subtle floral overtones. Expect greater consistency here than is found with either Echézeaux or Clos de Vougeot; the end results are well worth waiting for.

Harvesting in Grands Echézeaux

Another stone marker

LA GRANDE RUE

Until it was promoted to *Grand Cru*, La Grande Rue was one of those rare burgundian anomalies – a *Premier Cru* sandwiched between *Grands Crus*. In this case, its neighbours are among the most prized *Grands Crus* of the entire Côte – La Tâche and Romanée-Conti/La Romanée. This situation arose because Henri Lamarche, the father of the present owner, to whom it was given as a wedding present in 1933, did not consider that there was anything to be gained – except increased taxes – by applying for *Grand Cru* status so La Grande Rue was duly classified *Premier Cru*. In the context of an age in which *vignerons* were not as prosperous as today this was not the perverse decision one might be inclined to think. In 1984 his son, François Lamarche submitted an application for reclassification which was approved on 8 July 1992. On that day, he and his sister Geneviève became the sole proprietors of the 33rd *Grand Cru* of the Côte d'Or.

STATISTICS: *Area: 1.65.25 ha. Owners: 1 – Monopole* of **Domaine François Lamarche**, Vosne-Romanée. *Average Vine Age: 30 years. Average Annual Production*: 600 cases

ORIGINS: The name is descriptive. In France 'Grande Rue' designates the main street of many small towns and villages and this land lies parallel with the main road from Vosne to Chaux in the Hautes Côtes.

TOPOGRAPHY/GEOLOGY: La Grande Rue occupies a broad west-east oriented vertical strip separated from Romanée-Conti and La Romanée by a narrow road and shares in large measure both the geology and aspect of its illustrious neighbours, though not their soils. Twenty ares of Grande Rue are in fact Les Gaudichots (most of which is now La Tâche). Its elevation (250–300 metres) and slope run with La Tâche almost to its full extent, steeper at the top, flatter nearer to the village. As usual in these sloping vineyards, the negative compensating factor for better insolation is soil erosion. Over the centuries the eroded soils have accumulated lower down making these areas relatively richer, deeper and more water-retentive than the upper sections where the decomposed limestone and stony ground is better drained. However, unlike for example Clos de Vougeot, these differences are minor and not a significant problem for the ensemble of the vineyard.

The vineyard's geology is divisible into four separate sections: the uppermost part has 60 centimetres of brown limey soils before the Prémeaux bedrock is reached, the top 10 centimetres featuring a high proportion of stones which have eroded over the centuries from higher up; the middle section has a deep layer of brown soil giving onto impermeable rock; next a false plateau where the soil is thin – just 40 centimetres before rock is reached; the lower section consists of 40 centimetres of brown topsoil then a deep layer of light-coloured limestone-derived soils. A recent soil-profile photograph from the deepest section of the vineyard showed clearly distinct layers – the greater the depth the fewer the larger stony elements, except at around 130 centimetres where more sizeable limestone *limons* (silt agglomerations) are to be found.

WINE: Lamarche's Grande Rues of the 1970s, 1980s and early to mid-1990s, while often attractive, fell well short of top quality. This attracted criticism – some justified, much speculative and ill-informed – sloppy vinification, high yields, poor viticulture were all cited. It was during this period that the geological and other studies were undertaken which ended in reclassification. While promotion to *Grand Cru* might seem bizarre for a vineyard whose wine was often well below *Grand Cru* quality, it must be remembered that, in Burgundy, it is the land and its potential, not the wine, which is classified, although the process takes account of both actual wine quality and historical reputation.

Since then there have been welcome changes with recent vintages showing a marked upturn. The Lamarches have made considerable efforts to improve quality, in particular reducing yields across the Domaine. When it is on form, La Grande Rue has more in common with La Tâche, where the subsoils are similar in nature and distribution across the hillside, and with Richebourg than with Romanée-Conti. On top form, the wine is plush and poised, showing youthful aromas of *petits fruits rouges*, redcurrant and raspberry, with hints of blackcurrant and sometimes violets. These positive, complex aromas overlay a wine of substance with all the energy and finesse which typifies a Vosne *Grand Cru*. Nonetheless, there is still a worrying lack of the consistency one expects from any *Grand Cru* let alone from one of the situation and potential of La Grande Rue.

La Grande Rue with La Tache beyond

LA ROMANÉE

At less than one hectare, La Romanée is not only the smallest *Grand Cru* in France but also the smallest Appellation Contrôlée. It is generally believed that pre-1760 it formed part of the larger Romanée vineyard with the same name and conjoined to what is now Romanée-Conti. This history, though oft-repeated, is contested. The Domaine de la Romanée-Conti believes that only Romanée-Conti had the Romanée designation and that both La Romanée and Romanée-St-Vivant acquired the Romanée suffix later merely because of their proximity to Romanée-Conti. Rodier (op. cit.) cites a contemporary description of the verbal hearing from the Côte d'Or archives which avers La Romanée to be five *journaux* – the size of today's Romanée-Conti but surrounded on three sides by a stone wall, much of which remains and includes both vineyards. The Liger-Belairs, proprietors of La Romanée, on the other hand, claim that both vineyards were united until around the 14th century, most likely under an entirely different name, before part (which then became Romanée-Conti) was sold to the Prince de Conti. Whatever one's take on the history, what is certain is that La Romanée has never been part of Romanée-Conti. In any event, General Liger-Belair bought the six individual plots which constitute the present vineyard progressively from 1815 to 1826. It was declared a *Monopole* on 1 July 1927.

From 1947–2001, the vineyard was managed by Vosne *viticulteur* Régis Forey who also made the wine although because of part family ownership, half the crop was matured and marketed by Bouchard Père et Fils in Beaune. From the 2006 vintage, the Liger-Belairs, having bought out the other family interests, took over both vineyard and winemaking; the arrangements with Bouchard ended after the 2005 vintage.

STATISTICS: *Area*: 0.84.52 ha. *Owners*: 1 – *Monopole* of the **Comte Liger-Belair**, Château de Vosne-Romanée. *Average Annual Production*: 341 cases

ORIGINS: Discussed above

TOPOGRAPHY/GEOLOGY: La Romanée is situated in mid-slope directly above Romanée-Conti from which it is separated by a low wall possibly built on the line of a natural rock fissure. The vineyard slopes upwards at around nine degrees towards the Premier Cru Aux Reignots and is unusual in that it is planted to follow the contour. This probably reflects the desire for viticultural convenience, given that the vineyard is longer on its north–south than on its east–west axis. Such a planting configuration both limits soil erosion and helps fruit ripening. Excavations in the mid-2000s showed 50 centimetres of clay-limestone topsoil under limestone scree giving onto Prémeaux limestone. This base presents an irregular limit with the soil, probably reflecting the erosion surface pre-dating modern soil development. The obvious question is: are there any *terroir* or topographical differences between La Romanée and Romanée-Conti which would make a significant difference to wine quality? Apart from the slight increase in slope at the top of the La Romanée vineyard and an outcrop of Prémeaux limestone, clearly visible by the stone cross at the point where the vineyard meets Aux Reignots (this band of rock follows the contour marked by the stone wall above La Tâche), there are no significant differences.

WINE: Given its situation and pedigree, there is no reason why La Romanée should not equal Romanée-Conti in quality. However, for many years it did not do so. There are signs from the limited evidence available since the family took back responsibility for the operation that quality has improved considerably. In character it is relatively firm and masculine with plenty of flesh, developing complexity and interest as its layers unpack and its tannins resolve. The wine is clearly returning to where it belongs – as first-division *Grand Cru*.

La Romanée in the mist

LA TÂCHE

La Tâche is one of a handful of the world's truly great vineyards. Classed by Lavalle as *tête de cuvée*, together with Romanée-Conti, Richebourg and La Romanée, its wine represents the summit of which Vosne-Romanée, and indeed Burgundy are capable; the apotheosis of Pinot Noir.

The vineyard lies to the immediate south of La Grande Rue, which separates it from Romanée-Conti and La Romanée to the north. To its south is the fine Premier Cru Aux Malconsorts, which Lavalle ranked equal as *première cuvée* with Romanée St-Vivant, Grande Rue, Brulées, Varoilles and Beaux-Monts. It combines two individual parcels – the lower, southerly corner, La Tâche proper, 1.43.45 ha; adjoining it to the north and west Les Gaudichots (4.62.75 ha). Throughout the 19th century the Gaudichots parcel was also known as La Tâche according to Richard Olney (Romanée-Conti, 1995) having been bought by M. Duvault-Blochet, then owner of Romanée-Conti, in two transactions from its two owners, M. Morellet in 1862 and M. Lausseure in 1866. (Interestingly, in the mid-19th century Lausseure made sparkling red wine from his La Tâche grapes.) La Tâche proper joined it following its acquisition from the Comte Liger-Belair in August 1933. The Domaine's current co-owners, the de Villaines, are Duvault-Blochet's successors.

Another cadastral curiosity: some 0.50 ha of the adjacent Malconsorts Premier Cru vineyard is enclosed on three sides by La Tâche; it was acquired from the sale of the Thomas Moillard vines in 2005 by Domaines Dujac and de Montille; the latter bottle their share as Malconsorts Cuvée Christiane in memory of Etienne de Montille's mother who died in 2008.

STATISTICS: *Area:* 6.06.20 *Owners:* 1 – *Monopole* of the **Domaine de la Romanée-Conti**. *Average Annual Production:* 1,661 cases

ORIGINS: There are two contenders for the origin of this name. '*Tâche*' means 'task' in French, and many vineyards were worked *à la tâche*, which meant that those looking after a vineyard were paid for the task based on an agreed amount of time worked. However, it is difficult to explain why this particular plot rather than another should be so named. The alternative derives from another translation of *tâche* = spot. Once again, the explanation lacks credibility – both La Romanée and Romanée-Conti are considerably smaller than La Tâche and more merit that name. Marie-Hélène Landrieu-Lussigny (op. cit.) supports the former interpretation which has the greater plausibility of the pair.

TOPOGRAPHY/GEOLOGY: La Tâche occupies a vertical strip of nearly 200 metres at an elevation of 250–310 metres whose lower extent almost reaches the village. The slope is markedly steeper at the top, flattening as it approaches the village. The vineyard is crossed by three different rock strata: Prémeaux limestone at the top, shaly limestone one-third of the way down, *Ostrea acuminata* marls in the lower-middle sector.

La Tâche's soils are heterogeneous, varying considerably in profile from top to bottom of the vineyard. Their complexity was graphically illustrated in the summer of 2004 when trenches were dug in the upper, middle and lower sections during preparation for replanting a strip covering the entire vertical extent of the vineyard. These revealed multi-layered strata varying distinctively in profile according to location, which were studied and documented by various researchers (in particular Jean-Pierre Garcia from the Université de Bourgogne, Dijon and Dr Jerôme Brenot). Up to seven different soil types were identified within three principal profiles: at the base of the vineyard (near to the stone cross) soils are deep (1.5 metres) and very fine, which suggests erosion from the upper part of the vineyard. In composition they are clay-rich, with one metre of gravelly clayey silts surrounding brown-red clay overlaying the substratum, here composed of yellow *Ostrea acuminata* marls. A 25-centimetre layer of pebbles provides the topmost covering. Dating confirms that this gravel-clay-silt metre has deposited since the beginning of vine cultivation of the site between 540 and 980 AD. (Even rats' teeth were found in the deeper sections here.) In contrast, mid-slope soils are considerably thinner (40 centimetres), composed of brown-red silts beneath which is a layer of small, slate-like Prémeaux limestone blocks. At the top of the vineyard, the soil is equally thin and stone rich, comprising brown-red silts on clay and limestone with a significant yellow-ochre coloured sandy-clay content and around 40 centimetres of decomposed limestone scree. Here, Prémeaux limestone is apparent at around 50 centimetres below the surface.

These three profiles show a changing base-rock overlaid with a variety of soil types; Prémeaux dominates the upper part of the vineyard and *Ostrea acuminata* the lower sectors. Undoubtedly downward erosion has played a role as has the wall at the base of the vineyard which retains and accumulates eroded soil. The plant material used is a *sélection massale* from Romanée-Conti; now over 75% of La Tâche vines are of Romanée-Conti origin.

Harvesting in La Tâche

WINE: Reducing La Tâche or any wine of this stature to a verbal fruit-and-spice basket is futile. It is not that the wine defies description, rather that at this level of quality the tools available are woefully inadequate to the task. Scrabbling for ever-more extreme superlatives merely produces witless verbiage and fails to convey the totality in much the same way that a list of culinary ingredients bears pale relationship to the experience of the finished dish. This is a problem inherent in most wine assessment. The real impact of a great Côte d'Or *Grand Cru* is as emotional as it is sensorial so one can only hint at the magic and encourage people to pool resources and share a bottle.

What can be described with confidence are the broad structural differences between La Tâche and its peers. What sets it apart from both Romanée St-Vivant and Romanée-Conti is its depth and substance; La Tâche is a bigger-framed wine altogether, though perfectly in balance with its concentration of fruit. Richebourg, fine as it is, while of similar size and texture to La Tâche, seems a shade less refined. What first strikes one about a youthful La Tâche is its density and sheer class; this is

wine of abundant power and energy, a finely wrought vinous thoroughbred. Its potential, evident from the outset, is not a matter of alcoholic strength (13–13.5% by volume is the norm) or raw oak (although it is entirely matured in new wood) but comes from a dimension of richness and opulence combined with layer upon layer of flavour and finishing in a 'peacock's tail' of remarkable length. Neurophysiologists insist that there are no taste sensors beyond the back of the tongue – but something is clearly at work allowing us to sense this extraordinary aromatic explosion. As La Tâche ages it develops a sensational aroma spectrum of indescribable beauty. One senses notes of liquorice, even tar, spice, violets, cherry and other dark fruits, but it is the refinement, velvet texture and remarkable balance and power which make the synthesis stand above the mere listing of parts. Much as the emotional impact of hearing the B Minor Mass from a great ensemble in magnificent surroundings transcends anything that can be possibly conveyed by an analysis of the notes on paper, so does a fully mature La Tâche mesmerise and enrapture the senses.

RICHEBOURG

Richebourg is one of the finest of all the Côte's red *Grands Crus* and probably the most obviously opulent. It combines the elegance expected from Vosne-Romanée with a depth and substance which accompany exceptional suavity and refinement. The original part of today's Richebourg vineyard (Les Richebourgs) belonged to the monks of Cîteaux and to the Oratory at Dijon. Already known for its wine in the 16th century, as with most other vineyards it was confiscated from its religious owners at the Revolution and sold.

The vineyard is an amalgamation of two *climats* – Les Richebourgs proper and a reclassified Vosne Premier Cru Les Verroilles which was incorporated in the 1920s. The totality is separated from Les Echézeaux and Grands Echézeaux by the Premier Cru Les Suchots. The two Richebourg *climats* are contiguous, separated only by a vineyard track; they lie immediately to the north of, and march with, La Romanée and Romanée-Conti. To the east of Les Richebourgs proper across another track is Romanée St-Vivant. This is the heart of first-division vineyard land.

There is an interesting tale to the effect that one reputed Domaine obtained their Richebourg in remarkably curious circumstances. They applied for a legal determination for their vines located in the 'Richebourg-sous-Veroilles' *climat* not Richebourg itself though adjoining it, to be entitled to the designation 'Richebourg'. As the vineyard was clearly separate there seemed little prospect of the court ratifying a reclassifi-

cation. Fortunately, the two outside letters of '*sous*' mysteriously disappeared from the papers overnight turning the vineyard's designation into 'Richebourg ou Veroilles', suggesting that the names were alternatives. The court, so the story goes, duly approved the application and the Domaine had its Richebourg!

STATISTICS: *Area:* 8.03.45 ha. *Owners:* 10. *Average Annual Production:* 2,706 cases

PRINCIPAL OWNERS: **Domaine de la Romanée-Conti**: 3.53 ha (40–50); **Leroy**: 0.78 ha; **Gros Frère et Soeur**: 0.69 ha (1989–1995); **A F Gros et François Parent**: 0.60 ha (1945); **Anne Gros**: 0.60 ha; **Thibault Liger-Belair**: 0.55 ha (1936); **Méo-Camuzet**: 0.34 ha (1950s); **Jean Grivot**: 0.31 ha (1949); Mongeard-Mugneret: 0.31 ha (1964); **Hudelot-Noëllat**: 0.28 ha (1950); Bichot/Clos Frantin: 0.07 ha

TOPOGRAPHY/GEOLOGY: Richebourg lies mid-slope between 260–280 metres and inclines evenly towards the village of Vosne on much the same gradient as La Romanée and Romanée-Conti. The vines are planted on poor arable soil no more than 30 centimetres deep mainly composed of limestone scree deposits admixed with clay above hard rock. Even in this moderate-sized vineyard the geology is far from unitary. In places where the soils are slightly deeper they show accumulations of marine deposits. Although soils may be relatively shallow, lack of depth is not to be confused with lack of nutrient. Such paucity of soil forces the vine to develop deep roots to search for nourishment although root development will stop when the underlying impenetrable Comblanchien rock is reached.

The topography plays a role in wine quality here. At these altitudes on a relatively shallow slope ripening is likely to be retarded especially where vines reach into the Combe above which takes the road towards Concoeur. These higher sectors are relatively cold and thus require a longer period from flowering to reach equal ripeness with vines lower down. This often means harvesting at lower potential alcohol – i.e. less sugar – so chaptalisation may be required to bring the level up to the 13% considered acceptable for balance in a *Grand Cru*. The late Henri Jayer chronicled a noticeable difference between 'les Richebourgs' (5 ha) and 'les Veroilles ou Richebourgs' (3 ha). These latter are exposed east-north-east rather than full east so ripen marginally later. Fruit from this sector has around one degree less in potential alcohol but a lower pH which means

Engraved stone in Richebourg

better acidity and thus a slower, and potentially more interesting, evolution. Yields tend to be naturally low – especially in plots of old or virused vines. Availability of water is also a factor: according to an informal observation by one owner, a deep trench shows 25 centimetres of retained water after 24 hours, where a similar trench dug a short distance away will retain no water at all. The reason is that the second trench (lower down the vineyard than the first) drains into a geological fissure so any water runs off whereas the first has no such natural escape route. Another grower records that the deeper soils in his plot of Richebourg are impacted limestone which smells of petrol and for a brief period during vinification of this fruit he claims to regularly detect a distinct whiff of petrol. Such observations dramatically illustrate the complex geology of the Côte d'Or and the role it plays in the ripening of grapes and the development of trace aroma and flavour compounds. All part of Burgundy's magic.

WINE: Richebourg is among the greatest wines of the Côte. A firm-textured wine characterised by robustness and structure (*charpente*), the epithet most usually applied is 'sumptuous'. A great Richebourg is indeed sumptuous, but not in the sense of exaggerated extraction, heavy oaking or overripeness rather in the sense of natural concentration and richness, firm ripe tannins and above all, refinement of texture. Robustness does not quite describe Richebourg – although it is often robust – nor does the French term *de la sève*, which literally means 'sappiness', although the wine certainly has sap. Full, ample, velvety indeed and often almost flamboyant with a definite exotic dimension, it is generosity and intensity of flavour rather than any individual elements which makes Richebourg what it is. One can tussle with descriptors till the cows come home – plum, dark cherry, cassis, violets, leather, mocha coffee, chocolate – but again it is the harmony, the balance and overall mouthfeel, the freshness combined with ripeness which charm this wine with magic dust. Some Richebourgs (for example, Etienne Grivot's magisterial *cuvée*) start life with dominant acidity and strong minerality which needs forbearance and understanding. The soils make for the structure and contribute to the particular taste qualities; for a fine Richebourg is long-lived and needs ageing to give off its best. Nothing should be hurried; time must be allowed to release what is packed within. After ten or more years in a cool cellar Richebourg's glories start to emerge for contemplation and enjoyment.

Stone cross overlooking Richebourg

ROMANÉE-CONTI

Romanée Conti from the great 1990 vintage maturing in bottle

A visitor to Vosne-Romanée in search of the postage-stamp that is Romanée-Conti will need guidance to direct his steps to the stone cross and engraved corner-stone that mark the vineyard. Like the wine, and indeed its peers from this peerless Domaine, there is no advertisement, although recent times have seen the posting of a rather forlorn sign to dissuade visitors from wandering among the vines. Self-promotion – heaven knows their quality and consistency over the years amply justify pride – is not part of the Domaine de la Romanée-Conti's culture. This famous vineyard keeps a low profile, allowing its remarkable wines to speak authoritatively and eloquently to those lucky enough to taste them.

At just under two hectares, Romanée-Conti is indeed a micro-dot on the total vignoble that is Vosne-Romanée, let alone the Côte. It stretches most consumers' credibility to accept that this handkerchief of a vineyard produces wine of a quality that outshines those around it. The concept of such detailed terroir specificity, although gaining in understanding, bemuses people more used to buying well-made fruity, but essentially pedestrian Pinot. Few really believe Romanée-Conti merits fifty or a hundred times the price of a decent Vosne-Romanée village wine or two hundred times that of a perfectly palatable New World varietal and demotic opinion remains obdurately unconvinced by recitals of rarity or quality.

The history of the Romanée-Conti vineyard is well documented. Richard Olney (op. cit.) meticulously chronicles its changes of ownership, including a two-month spell under the proprietorship of Paul Guillemot who owned the station buffet in Dijon. Although deeds of sale confirm that wine has been produced in this place since 1580, the 'Romanée' denomination, affirming the site as known in Roman times, first appeared in 1651 under the stewardship of the Croonembourg family and the 'Conti' suffix when the vineyard was bought by the Prince de Conti on 18 July 1760 for 80,000 livres – over ten times the contemporary price for other 'distinguished neighbouring growths' (idem.). It finally came into the Domaine's ownership when it was acquired by M. Jacques-Marie Duvault-Blochet for 260,000 francs, in November 1869.

STATISTICS: *Area:* 1.80.50 ha *Owners:* 1 – *Monopole* of the **Domaine de la Romanée-Conti**. *Average Annual Production:* 462 cases

AVERAGE VINE AGE: The vineyard was grubbed up after the 1945 vintage and replanted in 1947. The first commercial release thereafter was the 1952 vintage. Fifteen ares were grubbed up after the 1993 vintage and replanted after several years fallow.

ORIGINS: See above.

TOPOGRAPHY/GEOLOGY: Romanée-Conti is indeed a jewel surrounded by jewels. At the epicentre of Vosne's nervous system of *Grands Crus*, Romanée-Conti is perfectly placed to produce fine wine. Its immediate neighbours from which it is separated by no more than the width of a path or narrow vineyard road – or in the case of La Romanée by nothing at all – are all *Grands Crus*: to the south, La Grande Rue; to the east, Romanée-St-Vivant; to the north, Les Richebourgs; to the west, la Romanée. It incorporates 20 ares of the southern sector of Richebourg, added by Croonembourg when he sold to the Prince de Conti as the extent was found to be deficient by that amount from the area contracted.

The vineyard is almost square rising an almost imperceptible 3–4 metres at a roughly even slope of six degrees. It lies mid-slope and faces east at an altitude of 260 metres. Geologically, there

is no great difference between Romanée-Conti, La Romanée, La Grande Rue and La Tâche, although the latter pair occupies a great extent of slope, making it likely that variation in soil and minutiae of situation account for differences in the wines. Vosne's soils are on a substratum of Jurassic rock layers, from top to bottom: Prémeaux limestone then marls rich in tiny oysters (*Ostrea acuminata*) giving onto crinoidal limestone (*calcaire à entroques*). Its subsoils are made up of white oolite and Comblanchien limestone, and Oligocene marls and conglomerates. It is believed, but as yet unverified, that Romanée-Conti lies on shaly limestones. These could either overlay the *entroques* or possibly form part of the *Ostrea acuminata* formation – the evidence currently available is unclear. Otherwise, its soils are relatively uniform – a brown clay-limestone mix with limestone scree in places and moderate stoniness; not particularly deep – around 20 centimetres of red-brown silts – giving onto limestone. The portion nearest to Vosne has more fossil-derived material from the deposition of oyster shells, while that in the upper section has more limestone. Soil analyses by Claude Bourguignon (see page 25) have shown the internal surface structure of the clay in Romanée-Conti to be markedly different from that of Richebourg which adjoins it to the north. It is from elements in this clay that the vine's roots feed and therefore its structure will certainly affect the uptake of nutrients and thus the individual qualities of the wine made from its grapes. The hollow or depression evident looking up the vineyard away from Vosne is almost certainly the location of an old stone quarry rather than the result of any removal of soil as has been suggested. However, despite a slope of only six degrees, the vineyard has suffered erosion and occasionally needed soil replacement. In 1786–7 Grimelin, the Prince de Conti's *régisseur,* ordered 800 cartloads of '*terre de montagne*' to fill in depressions. Today, any eroded soil is collected and replaced.

If its soils are unremarkable compared with those of its neighbours, what makes Romanée-Conti so special? Its location: the vineyard's situation and sloping aspect ensure maximum exposure to the daytime sunlight and heat. Exposed almost due east, Romanée-Conti generally ripens its fruit before its neighbours, allowing the ripening envelope to be pushed further while still retaining acidity. This, in part, is due to the central part of the *vignoble* being in the path of the *föhn*, a warm northerly wind. Although hail has occasionally hit the vineyard, Aubert de Villaine has never seen it affected by frost or mineral deficiency. In other words, the siting of Romanée-Conti is as near to perfect as it gets from a geological, topographical and climatic point of view. Differences from neighbouring vineyards, although almost impossible to define descriptively, are palpable in the wine.

The vines here remained ungrafted (pre-phylloxera) until 1947 when it was replanted with a *sélection massale* from La Tâche. The first post-replanting vintage of Romanée-Conti was 1952; this, though lighter than normal in tone and concentration, was nonetheless a remarkable wine.

WINE: Attempts to describe Romanée-Conti in specific detail entirely miss the point which is, above all, to convey an exceptional experience. Apart from the real risk of courting pretension, unpicking the essence of any great wine is no more achieved by a listing of aromas and flavours than would be the beauty of a rainbow by a spectrographic analysis of its component wavelengths. Nor is this a wine to be trivialised by scores which titrate pleasure as deductions from perfection. Those fortunate (and wealthy) enough to taste, even rarer drink, Romanée-Conti often come to it expecting more of everything – size, tannins, fruit. They are destined to be disappointed. The relationship between Romanée-Conti and La Tâche or Richebourg more or less mirrors that of Le Montrachet to its neighbours Bâtard-Montrachet or Chevalier in that, in each case, the greater of the pair exemplifies elegance and nuance above all rather than size or (perish the thought) hedonistic impact.

In aspect Romanée-Conti is less profound and obviously dense than either La Tâche or Richebourg. Often delicate, even deceptively light, in colour it is distinguished by its complexity and intensity rather than for any dimension of weight. Here one finds feminine elegance allied to exemplary purity and richness. Heresy as may be the description in these days of rampant egalitarianism, Romanée-Conti exudes nobility; not the result of contrived nobility – the vulgar ennobled – but the elite product of supreme breed and effortless class. Refinement, regality and reticence are its hallmarks. What makes this vineyard remarkable is its ability to fuse exceptional concentration to exceptional elegance. Although a seamless balance and elegant texture make it deceptively easy to enjoy young, it is with maturity that it really shines. Such is the quality of this vineyard that even the least promising of years is capable of delivering surprises. Vintages long since written off can confound the critics. A 1956 Romanée-Conti tasted at the Domaine displayed a profusion of perfume and, despite its light orange-tawny colour, a gentle caress of fully mature fruit. An indifferent vintage indeed but a complex and wonderfully ethereal wine nonetheless. Romanée-Conti represents the pinnacle of achievement in the panoply of Burgundy's red *Grands Crus* and an enduring testament to those who, over the centuries, have owned and tended this incomparable vineyard.

Romanée St-Vivant. The vines 'lick the walls' of Vosne-Romanée itself

ROMANÉE ST-VIVANT

At the point where it meets the village of Vosne-Romanée, Romanée St-Vivant touches the lowest point of all the Vosne/Flagey *Grands Crus*. As Henri Cannard (op. cit.) imaginatively noted, 'it almost licks the walls of the village'. In character St-Vivant contrasts markedly with all the other 'Romanée' *Grands Crus*, especially its westerly neighbour, Richebourg.

For a long period the vineyard, then known as Clos Saint-Vivant, belonged to the monks of the Abbey of St-Vivant de Vergy, a dependence of Cluny a few kilometres west of Vosne-Romanée, which pre-dated Cîteaux. In fact it comprised the Abbot's garden and part of the courtyard. A small parcel in the north-eastern corner, regarded as inferior in the early 19th century, was hived off as today's *Premier Cru*, Croix Rameau. The Romanée suffix was only appended to St-Vivant and indeed La Romanée itself thanks to their proximity to the original 'Romanée' vineyard, Romanée-Conti; and this term only made its first appearance in 1651 as a reflection of the Roman occupation of the site.

The lower section of the vineyard is known as 'les Quatre Journaux'; this denotes a measure of area, one journal equating to 8 ouvrées or one-third of a hectare. This section is owned by Domaines Dujac, Robert Arnoux, Sylvain Cathiard, de l'Arlot and Poisot and Louis Latour – this last markets their Romanée-St-Vivant *cuvée* as Les Quatre Journaux. Two individual parcels within the curtilage, Au Plans and Clos du Moytan, together with around three-quarters of the original Clos St-Vivant (the Clos des Neuf Journaux and the Prior's buildings plus courtyard), re-united as the Cros des Cloux, were farmed out to the Domaine de la Romanée-Conti by the Marey-Monge estate in 1966 and acquired by the Domaine in September 1988.

STATISTICS: *Area:* 9.43.74 ha. *Owners:* 11. *Average Annual Production:* 2,981 cases

PRINCIPAL OWNERS: **Domaine de la Romanée-Conti**: 5.29 ha (40–50); **Leroy**: 0.99 ha; Louis Latour (Domaine Corton-Grancey): 0.76 ha (14); Poisot: 0.74 ha (vinified by Antonin Rodet); Jean-Jacques Confuron: 0.50 ha (1929); **Hudelot-Noëllat**: 0.48 ha (1920); **Robert Arnoux**: 0.35 ha (1927); Follin-

Arbelet: 0.33 ha; **Domaine de l'Arlot**: 0.63 ha (35); **Sylvain Cathiard**: 0.17 ha (65); **Dujac**: 0.16 ha (60)

ORIGINS: The 'St-Vivant' suffix comes from the ownership of the Abbey of St-Vivant. The 'Romanée' prefix recognises its proximity to Romanée-Conti.

TOPOGRAPHY/GEOLOGY: The vineyard faces due east, spanning an altitude of 255–260 metres and slopes gently, almost imperceptibly, towards Vosne. Viewed from the north or south it can be seen that, far from being flat the vineyard is composed of a series of gentle undulations. It sits on three separate tiers from top to bottom. Two rocky bands traverse the *climat*, the lower one acting as a soil collector; so, unusually for Burgundy the soil in the upper sector is deeper than that lower down; it is also colder. The upper sector probably (though not certainly) gives onto crinoidal limestone – *calcaire à entroques.* The soil in the lower third of the *climat* nearest the village is Oligocene in type, deposited around 20–30 million years ago, comprised mainly eroded clays and marls of Jurassic origin (150 million years). This mixture has higher clay content than that further up-slope where it is separated from Romanée-Conti by a narrow road. The clays are water retentive and less well drained. The Domaine de Romanée-Conti generally excludes fruit from this sector from its St-Vivant *cuvée*. Elsewhere, good admixture of stones and pebbles makes for excellent drainage.

WINE: Romanée-St-Vivant is the most delicate and feminine of the Vosne *Grands Crus*. Tasted blind from a good source it is easily mistaken for Musigny. Though capable of ageing well, its delicacy comes to a certain degree at the expense of longevity. The aromatic intensity of a great Romanée-St-Vivant is thrilling – a cornucopia of exquisite scents, often floral in youth with notes of red cherry, raspberry and sometimes blackcurrant, transforming into a refined *sous-bois* character with age – complex and enticing, with a silken thread running across the palate and considerable length. This is Musigny-by-Vosne – perfectly poised, intensely delicate, but in no way dull or heavy. Ethereal and very special.

NUITS ST-GEORGES PREMIER CRU
LES SAINT GEORGES

This is the vineyard which, at the end of the 19th century, gave Nuits its present name. Les Saint Georges is undoubtedly the finest of Nuits' 35 *Premiers Crus* – including three partially planted to white grapes (the section of Clos de l'Arlot planted to Chardonnay, Les Terres Blanches and that of Les Perrières planted to Pinot Blanc). In Lavalle's 1855 classification, it 'occupies the first rank for conservation, colour, bouquet and finesse, given the necessary ageing – 10–20 years depending on the vintage' (Lavalle, op. cit.). There seems little doubt that the modesty of Henri Gouges, the town's most renowned *vigneron* in the 1930s, accounts for Nuits having no *Grand Cru*. Being closely involved with the establishment of the initial reglementation he may have felt it inappropriate to claim a *Grand Cru* for his own commune. Over seventy years later, an application for Les Saint Georges to be reclassified as *Grand Cru* is under discussion. However, local *vigneron* politics seem to have got it by the throat because the requirement for all members of Nuits' growers' *syndicat* to approve has led to competing demands for other *Premiers Crus* to be included in the application and for general upgrades throughout the commune. What started as a simple and perfectly reasonable undertaking seems likely to run into the ground, mired in vested interest and internecine wrangling.

There will doubtless be those who, while not disputing the supremacy of Les Saint Georges in Nuits, will argue that compared with for example, Cros Parantoux, Malconsorts or Boudots in next door Vosne-Romanée, it simply doesn't cut the mustard. While this remains a matter of personal judgement, it is important to remember that it is not just occasional brilliance but consistently high quality that is required in *Grand Cru* and in this regard the evidence is more clear-cut. Indeed, in the 19th century wine sold as 'St. Georges' claimed rank in the class with Musigny and Richebourg.

STATISTICS: *Area:* 7.52 ha. *Owners:* 10. *Average Annual Production:* 3,300 cases

PRINCIPAL OWNERS: Thibault Liger-Belair: 2.10 ha (1944); **Henri Gouges**: 1.08 ha (1961); Hospices de Nuits: 0.95 ha (45); **Robert Chevillon**: 0.63 ha (75); Michel Chevillon: 0.45 ha (1948); **Faiveley**: 0.23 ha (1933, 1959, 1974); Remoriquet: 0.19 ha (45); **Régis Forey**: 0.19 ha (1933); **Alain Michelot**: 0.19 ha (1978); Chicotot (n/a)

ORIGINS: According to Pierre Gouges' excellent study of the vineyards of Nuits, this is one of the oldest, being already planted in the year 1000. In 1023 it was given by Archdeacon Humbert of Autun to the Chapter of St-Denis at Vergy of which Nuits was a dependent diocese. It belonged to a brotherhood of St-Georges founded by the Barbier family in 1470.

TOPOGRAPHY/GEOLOGY: In Nuits, Les Saint Georges' main rivals are Les Cailles and Les Vaucrains. Why are these not *Grand Cru* material? Vaucrains is the more evident non-starter; it lies upslope from Saint Georges on very different soil – deeper, stony red clay – which gives a notably severe wine, somewhat four-square and comparatively lacking in finesse. Cailles, which adjoins Saint Georges to the north on the same soil band, gives altogether more 'feminine' wine. These differences are entirely soil-related, with elements in Cailles which are not in Vaucrains and vice versa. Vaucrains is stony on subsoil which is predominantly Comblanchien limestone whereas Cailles, located at the outlet of the combe, has a significant proportion of rounded pebbles in its soil. Les Saint Georges has the lot: it lies mid-slope, on a 6–8% inclination, reasonably sheltered by the forest above from stronger wind and ideally placed to ripen fruit. It combines oolite, Comblanchien and Prémeaux limestone with deep brown, limestone-based ferruginous soils with a significant fine clay component. The topsoil is relatively stony with a mixture of limestone pebbles of various origins; it changes in nature from south-west (stone-rich with finer-grained colluviums) to north-east (soil developed over alluvial fans).

WINE: As usual, soils provide the key to understanding why Les Saint Georges is the finest of Nuit's *Premiers Crus* and indeed its individual qualities. The supremacy of Saint Georges is not in doubt. It is always a step up on Vaucrains and Cailles, although in best vintages the differences are less pronounced. In lesser

Working in Les St. Georges

years, it is always the more complex and complete of the trio. In character, Les Saint Georges combines the qualities of its neighbours: the finesse and femininity of Cailles with Vaucrain's powerful structure. The finely divided clay promotes finesse while the iron content imparts the trademark southern Nuits' toughness and backbone. The 'femininity', however, is relative – Nuits doesn't really 'do' feminine in the way of Musigny or Romanée-St-Vivant although some in the Vosne sector, notably Boudots, come close. A great Saint Georges from the likes of Gouges or Robert Chevillon is unquestionably of *Grand Cru* quality. As with many *Grand Cru* aspirants, consistency across the *climat* remains debatable.

CORTON & CORTON-CHARLEMAGNE

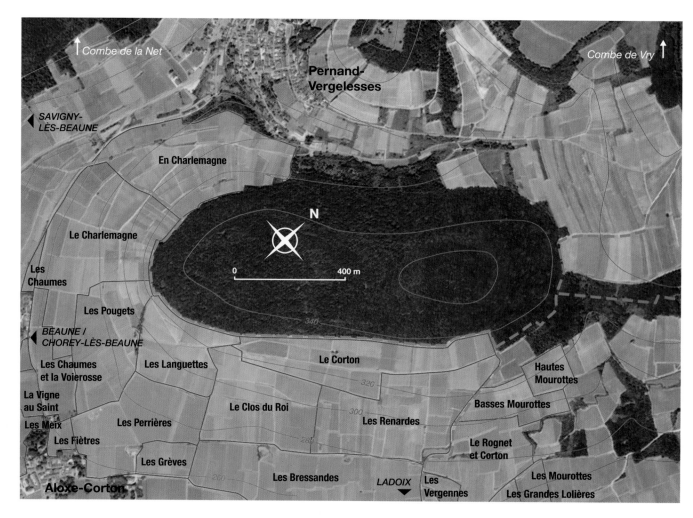

Of curiosity value, though of no wider significance, is the fact that just south of the border delimiting Côte de Nuits from Côte de Beaune at the Clos des Langres, on the hill of Corton both red and white wine are produced at *Grand Cru* level. Appropriately schizophrenic in character, the reds suggest a northern allegiance while the whites nod southwards.

The appellations encompass three villages: Aloxe-Corton, Pernand-Vergelesses and Ladoix-Serrigny which lie to the east, south-east and south-west respectively at the foot of the Corton escarpment. Topped by a protective fringe of trees – the Bois de Corton – this hillside is home to two of the largest and least tractable of the Côte d'Or *Grands Crus*: Corton and Corton-Charlemagne. Corton (Rouge) has the unique distinction of being the only red *Grand Cru* in the Côte de Beaune.

The AC designations are clear and logical if somewhat convoluted: the appellation Corton covers both red and white wine, while Corton-Charlemagne is for white wine only. The complication comes in determining what may be produced where. When the AC map was delimited certain *climats* were designated as most suitable for producing red wine (Corton) but where white wine is produced on them they are entitled to the appellation Corton Blanc (not Corton-Charlemagne). On the best sites for white wine production the reverse applies: whites have the sole appellation Corton-Charlemagne while red wine is designated Corton. In reality, little Corton Blanc is produced and this – white wine grown on essentially red wine soils – is generally of a quality which does not merit anything higher than *Premier Cru*. A third appellation – Charlemagne, comprising an area within the Corton-Charlemagne appellation – is no longer in use. So the real interest in these 232 ha of *Grand Cru* lies in red Corton and white Corton-Charlemagne. Both are capable of nobility but many offerings fall short.

Experience, and Dr Lavalle in his 1855 study, have

identified the finest of the Corton Rouge sites and these, not surprisingly, are to be found in the sunnier portions of the hill towards Aloxe and Ladoix where Pinot Noir is more likely to ripen fully. At the top of the tree, as *têtes de cuvée*, Lavalle put Les Chaumes, Clos du Roi, Renardes and Le Corton. He classed as *Premier Cru* vineyards which are now *Grand Cru*: Bressandes, Perrières, Pougets, Languettes, Fiètres, Le Meix and La Vigne au Saint. The official delimitation, finalised in 1936 after much detailed work, added the following to the *Grand Cru* roster: Les Paulands (upper part only), Les Maréchaudes (upper part only), Le Rognet et Corton (lower section – the upper part is Corton-Charlemagne), Les Vergennes and part of Les Mourottes. Red wine made from more than one *Grand Cru* site may be labelled Corton but not Le Corton, a designation reserved exclusively for wine from the Le Corton *climat*.

The Charlemagne sites are mainly found on the upper sections of the Corton hill which, having more limestone topsoil, are better adapted to Chardonnay than Pinot. These cover a reverse 'L' with the greatest concentration round Pernand-Vergelesses. The principal sites are Le Charlemagne (Pernand), Les Pougets, Languettes and Le Corton (all in Aloxe/Ladoix). In today's market Charlemagne generally commands a better price than red Corton, so many owners have replaced Pinot with Chardonnay where this is permitted – although these are not invariably planted on the most propitious *terroirs*.

To understand these complex appellations it is essential to familiarise oneself with the map.

Chardonnay grapes at Corton-Charlemagne

STATISTICS: *Area:* 232.07.60 ha –160.19.26 ha (Corton Rouge), 71.88.34 ha (Corton-Charlemagne) *Owners:* Corton *climats* – 200, Corton-Charlemagne *climats* – 75. *Average Annual Production:* 79,358 cases – Corton-Charlemagne 23,837 cases; Corton Rouge 35,299 cases; Corton Blanc 222 cases

ORIGINS: The name Corton is believed to be a contraction of Curtis d'Orthon. Curtis in old French means 'Domaines' rather like 'curtilages' in modern times, and Orthon was an early Roman emperor who owned land in this area. Charlemagne (= Charles the Great) was also a Roman Emperor, a remarkable man of considerable stature (both literally and figuratively), who held sway over vast tracts of what is modern Europe. Legend has it that he especially enjoyed the wines of Corton and that when these tinged his grey beard red, his (fourth) wife Luitgarde, clearly a forceful lady, objecting to this unsightly stain on his dignity, caused white vines to be planted on the Corton hill and persuaded him to drink white wine instead. The vineyards were gifted by Charlemagne around 775 and the wine thus became Corton-Charlemagne. The nomenclature of the various *climats* suggests historical reference: Clos du Roi for the Kings of France who owned land on the hill; topographical reference: Les Maréchaudes which roughly translates as 'warm marshes' which accords with its situation at Ladoix which itself means 'the source' – La Douix; and geological reference: Les Perrières (stones).

PRINCIPAL OWNERS CORTON-CHARLEMAGNE: **Louis Latour**: 9.64 ha (24); **Bonneau du Martray**: 9.50 ha (47); **Bouchard Père et Fils**: 3.67 ha (30–40); **Roland Rapet**: 3.0 ha (10, 25, 50); **Michel Voarick**: 1.66 ha; **Louis Jadot**: 1.60 ha; Bichot/Pavillon: 1.20 ha; **Domaine d'Ardhuy**:1.04 ha; Roux Père et Fils (1.00 ha); **Michel Juillot**: 0.80 ha; Dubreuil-Fontaine: 0.70 ha (1950, 1975); **Joseph Faiveley**: 0.62 ha (1961,1988); **de Montille**: 1.04 ha (incl. Corton Pouget holding); **Leroy**: 0.43 ha; Hospices de Beaune: 0.40 ha, sold as Cuvée Françoise de Salins; Follin-Arbelet: 0.40 ha; **Jean-Claude Belland**: 0.36 ha; **Bruno Clair**: 0.34 ha (1976); **Coche-Dury**: 0.34 ha (1960); **Joseph Drouhin**: 0.34 ha (1980); **Champy**: 0.33 ha; Charlopin-Parizot: 0.30 ha (1986); **Genot-Boulanger**: 0.29 ha; **Vincent Girardin**: 0.28 ha (50+); **Bertagna**: 0.25 ha (1975); **Tollot-Beaut**: 0.24 ha (1965); **Jacques Prieur**: 0.22 ha; **Christophe Roumier**: 0.20 ha (1968); **Simon Bize**: 0.20 ha (1939); Patrick Javillier: 0.17 ha; Nudant: 0.15 ha (30); Jean-Jacques Girard: 0.03 ha (55)

PRINCIPAL OWNERS CORTON: Louis Latour: 17.0 ha (34); Hospices de Beaune: 6.40 ha, contributes to two *cuvées*, Dr Peste and Charlotte Dumay, + 0.32 ha Corton Blanc; **d'Ardhuy**: 4.74 ha; **Comte Senard**: 3.72 ha (1943–2003) plus 0.46 ha Corton Blanc (1996); **Bouchard Père et Fils**: 3.25 ha (30–40); **Joseph Faiveley** (Clos des Cortons Faiveley): 3.02 ha (1936,1956–1977); Maurice Chapuis: 2.80 ha; **Domaine de la Romanée-Conti**: 2.27–1.19 ha Bressandes, 0.57 ha Clos du Roi, 0.51 ha, Renardes (all 40–50); **Chandon de Briailles**: 1.90 ha (30–60) plus 0.60 ha Corton Blanc (10–30); **Louis Jadot**: 2.10 ha; Pousse d'Or: 2.03 ha; Dubreuil-Fontaine: 2.10 ha (1929–2002); **Jean-Claude Belland**: 1.73 ha; **Tollot-Beaut**: 1.51 ha (1930, 1953, 1956, 1985); Roland Rapet:1.25 ha; Michel Gaunoux: 1.23 ha; **Michel Juillot**:1.20 ha; Michel Voarick: 1.00 ha; Baron Thenard: 0.90 ha; **de Montille**: 0.84 ha; **Jacques Prieur**: 0.73 ha; Follin-Arbelet: 0.70 ha; Ambroise: 0.66 (50); Nudant: 0.61 ha (60); Edmond Cornu: 0.56 ha; Bichot/Pavillon: 0.55 ha; **Leroy**: 0.50 ha; **Méo-Camuzet**: 0.45 ha (c. 1920); Bruno Clavelier: 0.34 ha (1950, 1980); **Champy**: 0.33 ha; Dupond-Tisserandot: 0.33 ha; Parent: 0.30 ha (40) plus 0.28 ha Corton Blanc (20); **Joseph Drouhin**: 0.26 ha (1971); **Bertagna**: 0.25 ha (1975); Philippe Bouzereau: 0.15 ha; Jean-Jacques Girard: 0.07 ha (55); Vincent Girardin (45)

TOPOGRAPHY/GEOLOGY: The most important topographical feature of the Corton hill which bears upon wine quality is its exposition. It is no coincidence that Pinot Noir is mainly confined to east, south and south-west expositions, where it has the most sun and thus the greatest chance of ripening fully. Many of the vineyards around Pernand are exposed south and south-west, even fully west, so enjoy much less early day heat and sunlight. Red wines from this sector often show underripe character in less good vintages and should be bought only after careful tasting. The soils also vary with location: with soils that are predominantly issues from the transformation of Upper Jurassic marls and contain more active limestone, the top section of the entire hill is ideally adapted to Chardonnay. The differences in soil type – whiter at the top, redder lower down – are very evident to anyone walking the vineyards. In the Pernand Charlemagne sector the subsoil is mainly marl but stony and well-drained. The heart of the slope, especially that north and east of Aloxe, is on Middle Jurassic Dijon-Corton and Ladoix stone with notably red, ferruginous, soils which impart depth and substance to the wine. The Bressandes vineyard is partly on an old quarry, so its subsoil is particularly rocky; in Perrières and Clos du Roi one finds more lava deposits. On the lower slopes – in Maréchaudes, Vergennes and Paulands for instance – eroded material has accumulated and the soils are much deeper than elsewhere, probably on hard Comblanchien limestone. With generally poorly nutritive soils, low yields are critical to wine quality. Humidity also plays a role, in that sectors where rivulets run – for example, near to the village of Ladoix and above En Charlemagne where a combe runs water down towards Pernand and Aloxe – may affect ripeness and favour rot. In this heart of the white appellation, soils are high in active lime with very little clay – this gives that attensive, tight minerality that differentiates Corton-Charlemagne from Puligny. Even such generalities mask a wealth of different soil-types. Bonneau du Martray, whose vines are all in En Charlemagne, has identified nine different soil profiles on their 11 hectares. Such topographical and geological subtleties play an important role in determining what ends up in your (expensive) bottle.

WINE: With such an extended vineyard, it is difficult to track typicity. This is certainly easier for Corton-Charlemagne which differs from both Meursault's and Puligny's finest above all in its structure. A tight, firm profile, characterised by acidity, which should however be ripe rather than bright and lemony, and strong minerality, are the hallmarks of a great Charlemagne. It has none of Puligny's open florality, Meursault's nuttiness or Chassagne's breadth. A characteristic youthful reticence makes tasting this wine something of a challenge in infancy. The overriding minerality is often, but should not be, confused with high acidity. With age the best develop great depth of flavour and an enticing aromatic spectrum – characterised by hints of spice, lime-blossom and hazelnuts, even a powerful hawthorn aroma in Jadot's bottling which comes from just above the Pougets *climat*. Look out also for notes of ginger and white pepper. The structure must be balanced by an adequate depth of ripe fruit and this is where many bottlings fall short. Corton-Charlemagne is opulence still but aristocratic and restrained rather than open and showy.

Red Corton exhibits a variety of personalities. The best from the likes of Faiveley's Clos des Cortons in the Rognet et Corton climat, Comte Senard, Chandon de Briailles, Leroy and Jadot and now Romanée-Conti – are rich, mouthfilling wines, firm and broad-shouldered, often with an element of gamey spiciness. The best reflect their origins – the finest *climats* being Le Corton,

Bressandes, Pougets, Clos du Roi, Renardes and Perrières. Many *cuvées* are blends of wine from several sites; none the worse for that, but an element of *terroir* origin is thereby lost. Corton ages well – and sometimes even magnificently. However, too many bottlings are clumsy, disparate in flavour, coarse-textured and unworthy of either their status or price. Experience suggests that, with a few unpredictable exceptions, Cortons rarely develop the aromatic complexity or interest that make the Côte de Nuits *Grands Crus* so compelling. Often good, sometimes very good, but only occasionally great.

Autumn vines at Aloxe-Corton

POMMARD PREMIER CRU LES RUGIENS

Pommard's wines are too often coarse and uninspiring. A few privileged *climats* among its 28 *Premiers Crus* stand above the rest, in particular Epenots and Rugiens and, on occasion, Pézerolles and Jarollières. There will probably be disagreement over the inclusion of any part of Rugiens as of *Grand Cru* potential and some will undoubtedly take up the cudgels for Epenots. Both are clearly capable of excellence, with Epenots on the Beaune side of the *vignoble* (including both Grands and Petits Epenots and Comte Armand's Clos des Epeneaux) often producing wines of considerable finesse combined with Pommard muscle and *puissance*. However, in my experience (and that of the overwhelming majority of top-class producers) it is the Rugiens du Bas – the lower south-easterly sector of Rugiens – in the Volnay sector which produces most consistently at the top level.

STATISTICS: *Area:* 5.83 ha. (Rugiens du Bas) *Owners:* 14+. *Average Annual Production:* Not available as wines sold as 'Rugiens' without designation of origin.

PRINCIPAL SOURCES: (*NB: Sources with holdings in only one sector are noted as such; where no location is noted holdings are in both Bas and Haut sectors*) **de Courcel**: 1.07 ha (65); **de Montille** (Bas): 1.02 ha (21, 36, 51); **Michel Gaunoux** (Bas): 0.69 ha (60+); Hospices de Beaune: 0.68 ha contributes to two *cuvées*, Dames de la Charité and Billardet; Fernand & Laurent Pillot: 0.65 ha (1964, 1971, 1980); **Faiveley**: (Haut) 0.51 ha (1953, 1986); Henri Boillot: 0.51 ha (1994); **Bouchard Père et Fils**: 0.41 ha (30–40); **Louis Jadot** (Bas) 0.36 ha; **Aleth Girardin**: 0.35 ha (1906); Joseph Voillot: 0.28 ha (50% 60; 50% 21); Richard Fontaine-Gagnard: 0.22 ha (1985); **Jean-Marc Boillot**: 0.16 ha (80+); Bichot/Pavillon; Billard-Gonnet (Bas) data n/a.

ORIGINS: The name 'Rugiens' derives from the red ('*rouge*') soils found here. These are high in red iron oxide which colours the earth.

TOPOGRAPHY/GEOLOGY: Rugiens Bas forms the lower section of the 12.66 ha Rugiens vineyard. It is situated just below the 300-metre contour which cuts the top of the Premier Cru Chanlis (Bas) and Rugiens Hauts vineyards. The slope is steep, rock-strewn and prone to erosion, with an Upper Jurassic soil type – dolomitic limestone – which is only encountered on the Côte in Pommard. There is a high proportion of active limestone in the soil, and the dolomite is rich in magnesium (dolomite = magnesium carbonate, whereas limestone only contains calcium).

WINE: The Michel Gaunoux, Billard-Gonnet, de Montille and Jadot *cuvées* apart, most Rugiens bottlings are from both Hauts and Bas so it is only possible to taste du Bas in cellars where fruit from this sector is vinified separately. In general Rugiens Bas has greater depth and finesse and is a more complete wine than that from Rugiens Haut. It differs markedly from Pommard's contending top-class Premier Cru Les Epenots, from the northerly Beaune sector, fine as this can be, both in class and intensity.

Pommard with Rugiens (note the reddish soil) and Volnay beyond

VOLNAY PREMIER CRU LES CAILLERETS

Volnay presents many contenders for *primus inter pares*. Champans, Clos des Chênes, Clos des Ducs, Bousse d'Or, Taillepieds and the anomaly of Santenots du Milieu (located in Meursault but entitled to the Volnay designation if red, otherwise Meursault) are all capable of excellence especially in the hands of the commune's handful of stellar *vignerons*. However, in this legislative pantisocracy, it is Caillerets alone which consistently fuses its structure to its elegance in a way which puts it above the pack and epitomises the finesse and class for which Volnay is renowned. The commune's history records that its wines were much appreciated in French royal circles and that many of the finest vineyards belonged to the monarchy in the 14th and 15th centuries, including Caillerets, Chevret, Champans, Fremiets, Bousse d'Or and Taillepieds. Indeed, in 1507 Louis XI sent an emissary to make an inventory of his Volnay vineyards. At the end of the 18th century, Thomas Jefferson noted that Volnay sold at a quarter the price of other far coarser *Crus*.

Les Caillerets comprises three *lieux-dits*: Les Caillerets Dessus (9.07.06 ha), En Cailleret (2.86.75 ha) and the Domaine de la Pousse d'Or's Clos des 60 Ouvrées (2.39.24 ha in the Caillerets Dessus).

STATISTICS: *Area:* 14.33.05 ha *Owners:* 12. *Average Annual Production:* 5,830 cases

PRINCIPAL OWNERS: **Bouchard Père et Fils**: 4.0 ha (30–40); **Pousse d'Or**: En Caillerets: 2.39 ha, Clos des 60 Ouvrées (1976 & 1989); Henri Boillot: 0.72 ha (1970); **d'Angerville**: 0.46 ha (1998 & 2003); Chandon de Briailles: 0.40 ha (25); **Lafarge**: 0.28 ha (51); Hospices de Beaune: 0.20 ha contributes to Cuvée Général Muteau; **Louis Boillot**: 0.18 ha (63); Jean-Marc Bouley: 0.18 ha (5); Bitouzet-Prieur: 0.15 ha (1981); Joseph Voillot: 0.14 ha (25)

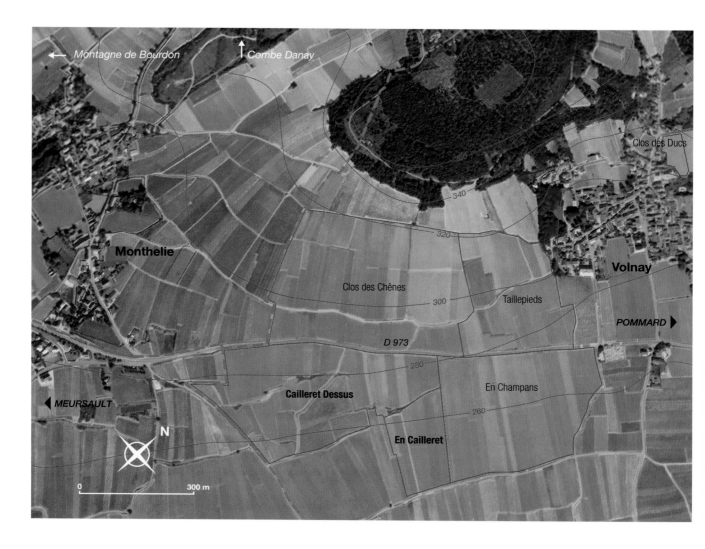

View towards Les Caillerets Dessus from Clos de Chênes

ORIGINS: The term 'Caille' appears often in burgundian vineyard nomenclature, most often as Caillerets (En Caillerets at Chassagne and Volnay, Le Cailleret in Puligny and Les Caillerets in Meursault and Volnay); also as Les Cailles in Nuits. Although '*caille*' also means quail (a small bird the French love to eat, especially as pâté or in tarts and pies), 'Cailles' here derives from *cailloux* which means stony. Marie-Hélène Landrieu-Lussigny (op. cit.) suggests that the '-ret' suffix is a corruption of '*roi*' (= king) and indicates royal ownership. On this construction Cailleret translates as 'king's stones/pebbles'. More plausible perhaps is her other explanation whereby '-ret' is a diminutive, translating Cailleret as 'little stones', in reference to the smallish round pebbles often found in these vineyards. There is also a geological derivation from *chailles* – a term which refers to small limestone plate-like stones and sandy kidney-shaped pebbles. Vineyards such as Les Cailles (Nuits) and Les Chaillots (Aloxe-Corton, Ladoix and indeed Cornas in the northern Rhône) share this designation.

TOPOGRAPHY/GEOLOGY: Les Caillerets is located below the RN 73 road from Volnay to Meursault – above it the Clos des Chênes, below it towards the RN 74 En Chevret and adjoining it to the north the Premier Cru En Champans. What makes this site special is both its situation – mid-slope and largely away from the influence of colder air from above – and its very thin topsoil which imparts the remarkable finesse which characterises the wine. The subsoil is mainly made up of Ladoix limestone, with abundant ancient quarries along the Route des Grands Crus in Les Champans and Caillerets, and also Les Champs Fulliot in Monthélie. Both Champans and Chevret, and indeed Santenots (which has an entirely different character) can produce excellent wine, but Caillerets has the edge in finesse, complexity and completeness, especially when it comes from a top source such as Pousse d'Or or Lafarge.

WINE: Caillerets is quintessentially finesse and delicacy – all red fruits, silk and lace. Its structure means that it often starts out with a slightly off-putting, almost angular, austerity, restrained on both palate and nose, but offset in good vintages by ripe, stylish fruit. Given a few years in bottle the best evolve to reveal the lithe finesse of which only aged Pinot Noir is capable. Volnay at its best is truly lovely and Caillerets in the right hands is Volnay at its best.

Meursault Premier Cru
Les Perrières

Old vine flowering in Les Perrieres

In the pantheon of Meursault's *Premiers Crus*, Perrières vies for top spot with Genevrières and the upper sectors of Charmes. Perrières' primacy is due to its position rather than to its soils, which gives it the edge on ripeness. It tends to both earlier and a shade more ripeness than either Genevrières or Charmes and yet retains the acidity essential for development in bottle.

This large vineyard extends to 13.72 hectares in a broad strip at the upper part of the slope adjoining Genevrières to the north and Charmes to the east. At its southerly extremity it is contiguous with Puligny-Montrachet, abutting the *Premier Cru* vineyards of (from top to bottom) Champ Canet, Combettes and Referts. As so often in Burgundy, the vineyard is divided into several sectors of differing quality potential. The Perrières Dessous sector – here to the south rather than downslope – and the adjacent 0.95 ha Clos des Perrières are considered the top locations. The latter, belonging to the Bardet family and produced under the Domaine Albert Grivault label, is itself a contender for promotion to *Grand Cru* in the eyes of its owners who have plans to apply for reclassification.

STATISTICS: *Area:* 13.72 ha *Owners:* 25 +/-. *Average Annual Production:* 6,030 cases

PRINCIPAL OWNERS: **Coche-Dury**: 0.23 ha (2005); **Albert Grivault**: 2.49 ha, incl. 0.95 ha of Clos des Perrières; **Comtes Lafon**: 0.77 ha (1953, 1983); **Bouchard Père et Fils**: 1.20 ha (30–40); **Yves Boyer-Martenot**: 0.69 ha; Jean-Michel Gaunoux: 0.59 ha; **Matrot**: 0.53 ha (56); **Pierre Morey**: 0.52 ha (1960, 1976); **Bouzereau**: 0.50 ha (1938, 1955); **Ampeau**: 0.57 ha (1958); **Château de Puligny-Montrachet**: 0.45 ha (1950); Potinot-Ampeau: 0.33 ha; Darviot-Perrin: 0.29 ha (1937); Vincent Dancer: 0.29 ha (1963); Bitouzet-Prieur: 0.28 ha (1983); **Jacques Prieur**: 0.28 ha; **Guy Roulot**: 0.26 ha (1964); Henri Germain: 0.16 ha; **Philippe Bouzereau**: 0.15 ha; **Latour-Giraud**: 0.14 ha (1963); négociant *cuvées* from **Joseph Drouhin, Louis Jadot** and **Vincent Girardin** are also excellent.

ORIGINS: As with its other burgundian occurrences, the name 'Perrières' indicates the presence of stones and suggests the presence of either an old quarry (as here, at Fixin Les Perrières and Vougeot la Perrière) or the result of erosion and deposition. Where quarrying has occurred, the soil has a human as well as a natural component.

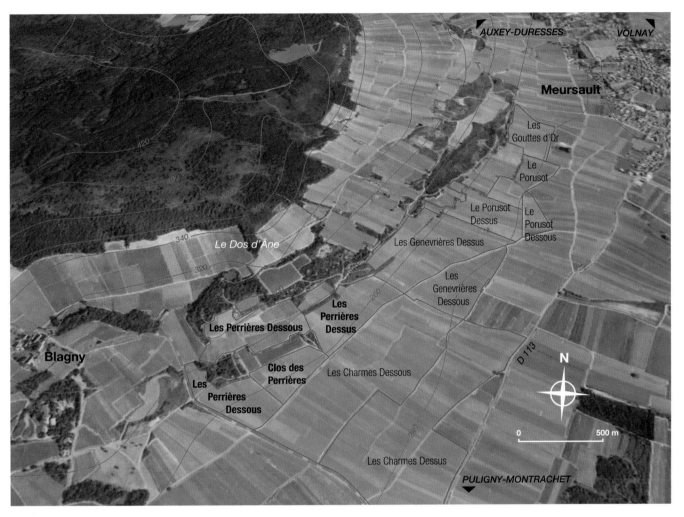

TOPOGRAPHY/GEOLOGY: The vineyard extends across a roughly triangular band of ground beneath a hill of rock and scrub (*chaume*) containing a variety of plants and wild flowers, including orchids, vegetation which is distinctly more Mediterranean than Alpine. On a moderate slope towards Les Charmes, Perrières' soil is typically redder than that of Genevrières which is lighter and sandier in appearance with a high proportion of gravelly scree. This is well-drained ground, filtering out excess water effectively, with a high percentage of active limestone (the highest in Meursault, in fact) which gives Perrières its particular power and presence. The subsoil is made up of Chassagne limestone, the southern equivalent of the white oolite and Comblanchien limestone that outcrop further north. This stone is an excellent material for house-building, and has been intensively extracted for wall-stone as it is still the case in the huge quarry in Chassagne-Montrachet.

WINE: Tighter in mouthfeel and structure and notably more mineral in flavour than either of its immediate neighbours, Perrières exudes elegance. It has race and complexity with a steely yet stony, peachy and sometimes rhubarb character that epitomises Meursault at its best. Charmes is generally the more powerful and obviously opulent of the trio, while Genevrières, although arguably the most complete of all Meursault's wines, is softer, more accessible and earthy in flavour with a tendency to lack acidity in riper vintages. A fine Perrières has depth and focus without being noticeably phenolic, with the structure for graceful ageing. Lafon's 1988, 1987, 1986, 1985 and 1967 Perrières tasted at the Domaine in 2009 were all in excellent shape – although the '67 (by no means a five-star vintage) was, not surprisingly, fading somewhat after 40 years in bottle. The others were holding up remarkably well; lovely, interesting old Meursault and ideal accompaniments to a subtly sauced piece of fish. Magic!

BÂTARD-MONTRACHET

This, the 'Golden Triangle' of Puligny-Montrachet, is where the 'genie of *terroir*' is demonstrated beyond dispute. From the stone entrance which marks the north-eastern corner of Le Montrachet, within two hundred metres one finds four *Grands Crus*, two *Premiers Crus* and several *Village*-rated vineyards. Bâtard-Montrachet lies directly to the south-east of Le Montrachet and extends along its entire length until it ends in Chassagne. In the unofficial classification of *Grands Crus*, Bâtard outranks Criots and is considered the equivalent of Bienvenues but below Chevalier and Montrachet itself. In truth, good, bad and ugly can be found even in such exalted appellations, so such comparative claims must be treated with caution.

STATISTICS: *Area:* 11.86.63 ha – 6.02.21 in Puligny and 5.84.42 in Chassagne. *Owners:* 49. *Average Annual Production:* 5,522 cases

PRINCIPAL OWNERS: **Leflaive**: 1.91 ha (1962, 1964, 1974, 1977, 1989); **Ramonet**: 0.64 ha (45); Paul Pernot: 0.60 ha (1976, 1982); Bachelet-Ramonet: 0.56 ha; **Faiveley**: 0.50 (1991); **Pierre Morey**: 0.48 ha (1965); Roger Caillot-Morey: 0.47 ha; **Jean-Marc Blain-Gagnard**: 0.46 ha (1939, 1943, 1986); **Jean-Noël Gagnard**: 0.36 ha; Hospices de Beaune: 0.35 ha sold as Cuvée Dames de Flandres; **Richard Fontaine-Gagnard**: 0.33 ha (1930–1978); **Jean-Marc Boillot**: 0.18 ha; **Vincent Girardin**: 0.18 ha (50+); **Etienne Sauzet**: 0.14 ha (1965); Jean Chartron: 0.13 ha (1960); Jouard: 0.13 ha (1941, 1996); **Marc Morey et Fils**: 0.13 ha (1954); Michel Morey-Coffinet: 0.13 ha (1997); **Domaine de la Romanée-Conti**: 0.13 ha – not bottled under Domaine label; **Michel Niellon**: 0.12 ha (1930); Louis Lequin: 0.12 ha; René Lequin-Colin: 0.12 ha; **Marc Colin**: 0.10 ha; Thomas Morey: 0.10 ha (1950, 1954); Vincent et Sophie Morey: 0.10 ha (1950–1963); **Joseph Drouhin**: 0.10 ha (1939); **Bouchard Père et Fils**: 0.08

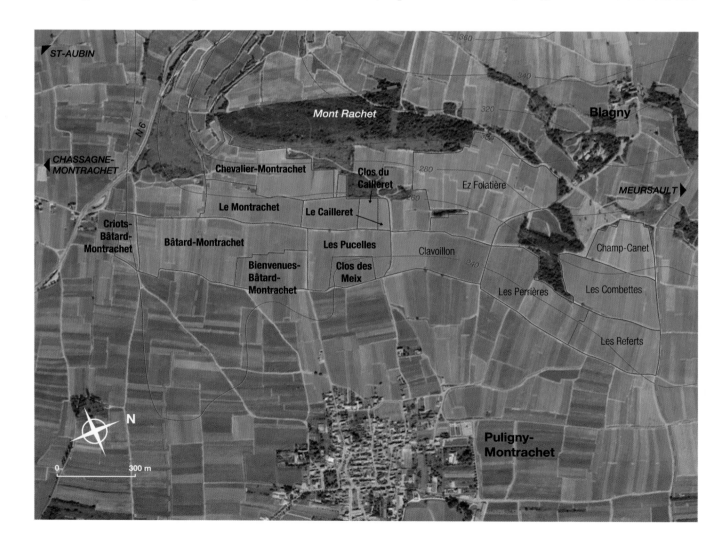

View from Bâtard-Montrachet with Le Montrachet, Chevalier-Montrachet, and the scrub of Mont Rachet beyond

ha (20–40); Château de la Maltroie: 0.08 ha (74); **Château de Puligny-Montrachet**: 0.045 ha (1976)

ORIGINS: See Chevalier-Montrachet.

TOPOGRAPHY/GEOLOGY: Bâtard is on a gentle slope towards the village and well-exposed east of south. The Puligny sectors of Bâtard have deeper soils than those in Chassagne which are largely composed of light-coloured limestone overlaid with limestone scree and stones in a brown limestone soil. In general, the lower parts of the vineyard are more iron-bearing.

WINE: With such fragmented ownership, defining typicity for Bâtard-Montrachet makes for an elusive quest. The best examples are plump and rich in character, in marked contrast to Chevalier's leaner profile. However, there should be no expectation of the super-ripe fruit of many New World Chardonnays, rather a touch of the grape's exotic side combined with a palpable tension, energy and puissance. Young Bâtard often tastes of hazelnuts and is quite spicy and sappy. In the best examples, the fruit is underpinned by a firm structure and ripe acidity; a supporting structural touch of tautness from skin and cask phenolics is sometimes no bad thing. Though not lacking in finesse, Bâtard often gives the impression of 'fatness' and is open-textured and somewhat obvious in comparison to either Chevalier or Le Montrachet which are more restrained and slower to unpack. Nonetheless, a well-constituted Bâtard needs at least five years to show its paces (few usually get that long) and develops attractively with further ageing. When fully mature Bâtard has a refined yet broad texture and exhibits all the nuance and palate complexity one expects from a top *Grand Cru*.

BIENVENUES BATARD-MONTRACHET

ienvenues adjoins the Bâtard-Montrachet vineyard at its north-east corner. Across the Puligny-Chassagne road to its immediate north-east is the Premier Cru Les Pucelles and across a vineyard track to its south-east are the Puligny *Village* vines.

STATISTICS: *Area:* 3.68.60 ha. *Owners:* 15. *Average Annual Production:* 1,793 cases

PRINCIPAL OWNERS: **Leflaive**: 1.15 ha (1958, 1959); **Faiveley**: 0.51 ha (1978); **Vincent Girardin**: 0.46 ha (50+); **Ramonet**: 0.45 ha (45); Paul Pernot: 0.37 ha (1966, 1995); **Etienne Sauzet**: 0.15 ha (1938); Bachelet-Ramonet: 0.13 ha; **Louis Carillon**: 0.12 ha (42); Jean-Claude Bachelet-Ramonet: 0.09 ha

ORIGINS: see Chevalier-Montrachet. It is also said that the name 'Bienvenues' reflects the non-burgundian workers who farmed these vines in the 19th century and were locally known as 'les Bien-Venues' which literally means 'welcome'.

TOPOGRAPHY/GEOLOGY: There is nothing exceptional about either the soils or topography of this *climat* and it should be considered equivalent to Bâtard in all relevant respects, with soils that developed over Jurassic limestone.

WINE: If there is any difference between Bienvenues and Bâtard, it can best be described as a class distinction rather than any real difference of flavour. Indeed, some producers with small holdings amalgamate both wines and sell the result under the Bâtard designation (perfectly legal). Apart from the producers listed above there are also *cuvées* from négociants such as Olivier Leflaive and Remoissenet. Perhaps the Bienvenues has marginally greater delicacy and femininity than its neighbour, although in truth, producer-to-producer variability far outweighs anything which might be ascribed to fundamental differences between the two *climats*. The fact that Bienvenues tends to be more expensive than Bâtard reflects its size and thus its rarity rather than any intrinsic quality factors. What therefore buyers should focus on is the reputation of the source rather than whether it is one or the other that is being bought.

Bienvenues-Batard-Montrachet

CHEVALIER-MONTRACHET

Of all Burgundy's white *Grands Crus*, Chevalier-Montrachet epitomises Chardonnay's potential for finesse and understated aristocracy. Its location, between the Puligny section of Le Montrachet and the top of the Mont-Rachet, and meagre, low-yielding limestone soils are the keys; here the ground favours finesse above substance and yields a wine of presence and refinement. In the pantheon of Puligny *Grands Crus*, Chevalier is superior to all but Le Montrachet – several notches above Bâtard, Bienvenues and Criots, fine as these undoubtedly can be. Within the vineyard's curtilage is the 1.03-ha enclave of Les Demoiselles. Bought during the Revolution in 1794 by the Jadot family, it was subsequently sold before being bought back in a joint effort by Maisons Louis Jadot and Louis Latour to whom it now belongs in more or less equal division.

STATISTICS: *Area:* 7.36.14 ha *Owners:* 16. *Average Annual Production:* 3,355 cases

PRINCIPAL OWNERS: **Bouchard Père et Fils**: 2.54 ha (30–40), including the Cuvée La Cabotte; **Leflaive**: 1.99 ha (1955–1958, 1964, 1974, 1980); **Louis Jadot** Les Demoiselles: 0.52 ha (60); **Louis Latour**: 0.51 ha Les Demoiselles (50); Jean Chartron, Clos des Chevaliers: 0.47 ha (1947, 1974, 1986); **Château de Puligny-Montrachet**: 0.25 ha (1981); Philippe Colin: 0.24 ha (1964); **Michel Niellon**: 0.23 ha (1962); **d'Auvenay**: 0.16 ha; **Michel Colin-Deleger**: 0.16 ha; **Vincent Girardin**: 0.16 ha (50+); Jacques Prieur: 0.13 ha; Alain Chavy: 0.10 ha (1976); Vincent Dancer: 0.10 ha (1952); **Ramonet**: 0.09 ha (40)

ORIGINS: The derivation of all the Puligny *Grands Crus* is encapsulated in a charming legend, redolent of the Middle Ages: the Seigneur of Puligny is depicted as the Chevalier (the Knight), who seduces Les Pucelles (the female twins) out of wedlock; in turn, they give birth to the Bâtards (bastards) who are welcomed ('Bienvenue!') by the populace. It would be a pity to look further than this fanciful little tale.

A note about the La Cabotte *cuvée* from Bouchard Père et Fils. A '*cabotte*' is burgundian patois for a small cabin-like building of dry-stone. This provides shelter for workers from storms and strong sun and somewhere for them to have their picnic lunch. Several *cabottes* remain in the vineyards of the Côte, but many are in disrepair. In 1990 a book appeared devoted to their origins and history: *En Bourgogne: Cabottes et Meurgers*, by Pierre Poupon and Gabriel Lioger d'Ardhuy.

TOPOGRAPHY/GEOLOGY: Chevalier-Montrachet is well-exposed east of south on a significant slope down towards the wall of Le Montrachet at an elevation of 265–290 metres. Its boundary here marches one-third of the way along that of Le Cailleret which adjoins Le Montrachet to the north-east. The vineyard consists of four terraces – one principal section and three smaller parcels to the north of the vineyard – each of which has a distinct soil type.

The upper part of the vineyard – that nearest to the Mont-Rachet itself – consists mainly of light-coloured marls known as *Pholadomya bellona*. This takes its name from the typical fossil frequently encountered in this layer; resembling a 5–10-centimetre heart shape and of the same family as mussels, it is known locally as '*coeur de gaulois*'. The lower sections are more ferruginous and progressively stonier. The soil overlays block-like stones of Chassagne limestone which are clearly visible, not least to the workers who found them appearing during ploughing when vines were planted. The fact that many rocks were broken down and rocks removed during replanting means that the vineyard is rather less stony than it might otherwise have been.

Chevalier is a low-humidity vineyard – dry, generally rot- and mildew-free though a touch of oïdium has been known. In general the soils are poor both in depth and vigour but being stony and thus heat-retentive they manage to ripen grapes well.

The most southerly corner, known by Bouchard Père et Fils who own it as La Cabotte, was originally part of the Montrachet vineyard. As it was unplanted when this was delimited and classified in 1935, it was forgotten and not included in the Montrachet *finage*. In common with the upper part of Montrachet, the subsoil is thin and made up of Chassagne limestone.

WINE: Chevalier does not just epitomise finesse but finesse allied to sublime purity and concentration. A great Chevalier combines Puligny elegance and florality with perfectly poised fruit and a backbone of what is best described as nervous energy. Although a shade less intense and compelling than Le Montrachet, its masculine leanness and athleticism give it a dimension of class above both Bienvenues and Bâtard. High initial acidity preserves even second-rank vintages and it is no surprise to find a well-cellared 20-year-old Chevalier expressive – nutty, mineral, complex, vibrant, energetic; entirely alert and utterly delicious.

Le Montrachet

Le Montrachet is the greatest dry white wine in the world, epitomising Chardonnay at its most complex, expressive and intense. The vineyard is unremarkable – nothing immediately stands out as exceptional with this narrow strip of vines mid-slope between Chevalier-Montrachet above and Bâtard-Montrachet below. Montrachet straddles the Puligny-Chassagne border, almost equally distributed between the two communes. Its wine is rare and expensive, sought out by collectors and the status-conscious wealthy world wide. As with much that is 'beyond price' it is not always fully understood or appreciated by those into whose hands it passes.

The superior quality of wine from this vineyard has been known since the 8th century, although it was only during the latter years of the 19th century that it was entirely planted to Chardonnay. In earlier times it was likely that the *encépagement* would have been a field mix of indigenous varieties rather than a single *cépage*. It would have been fascinating to taste the product of an ignoble grape (both Aligoté and Gamay were planted here) grown in this noble vineyard.

As might be expected, the French literati have gone overboard in their evocations of Montrachet: Alexandre Dumas suggested that the wine 'should be drunk on one's knees with one's head uncovered'; the poet (minor, presumably) Maurice des Ombiaux described Montrachet thus: 'it delights your stomach with a soft warmth, whilst your palate remains impregnated with its perfume, a Dionysian joy envelops you and opens for you the doors of Paradise.'

It is perhaps interesting to note that until Domaine Leflaive bought their original 0.08 ha holding in 1990 not a single vine of Le Montrachet was owned by a producer in Puligny. Leflaive apart, that still remains the case. The AC for all the Puligny and Chassagne *Grands Crus* was granted on 31 July 1937.

STATISTICS: *Area:* 7.99.80 ha of which 4.01.09 are in Puligny and 3.98.73 are in Chassagne. *Owners:* 17. *Average Annual Production:* 3,410 cases

PRINCIPAL OWNERS: **Marquis de Laguiche** – vinified and marketed by **Joseph Drouhin**: 2.06 ha; **Baron Thenard** – marketed by Remoissenet: 1.83 ha; **Bouchard Père et Fils**: 0.89 ha (30–40); **Domaine de la Romanée-Conti**: 0.68 ha (40–50); **Jacques Prieur**: 0.59 ha; **Comtes Lafon**: 0.32 ha (1933,1972); **Ramonet**: 0.26 ha (75); **Marc Colin**: 0.10 ha; **Richard Fontaine-Gagnard**: 0.08 ha; **Jean-Marc Blain-Gagnard**: 0.08 ha (1934);

Leflaive: 0.08 ha (1960); Lamy-Pillot: 0.05 ha; **Château de Puligny-Montrachet**: 0.043 ha (1970)

ORIGINS: Montrachet is an elision of Mont (= hill/mount) and Rachet (= bare/denuded/bald).

TOPOGRAPHY/GEOLOGY: Le Montrachet sits mid-slope at an altitude of 255–270 metres on an incline of 6–10%. Facing east it is well exposed to maximise heat and sunlight throughout the summer day. The higher section is drier, thanks to the two *combes* (St-Aubin in particular) which feed air downwards and minimise the risk of rot in much the same way as happens in the southern sectors of Corton-Charlemagne. The slope benefits from the protection of the Mont Rachet above from wind and hail which provides a beneficent microclimate for all the surrounding *Grands Crus*. If anything the Montrachet vines in the secteur Chassagne are rather less sheltered. The soil is poor in organic matter being mainly constituted of colluviums (silts and shales that slid along the slope) and fragmented limestone compounded with a notable proportion of iron oxide. It varies in depth from 0.5 metre (top) to 1.50 metres (bottom). There is a gross fault line, clearly visible at the top of the vineyard and highly striated in appearance, where two compartments have rubbed against each other before the lower portion faulted downslope. Chassagne limestone outcrops to the west of the fault line, whereas the ferruginous Oolite and Corton stone (as yet putatively) constitute the subsoil to the east. Generally, the faults are not marked in the present day landscape. It is the contrast between soft Upper Jurassic marls that have been eroded to the east and the Chassagne limestone to the west that generates this topographic step (1–3 metres high), not representative of the fault which is around 100 metres. The retaining wall of Chevalier-Montrachet above protects the vineyard to a certain extent from soil and rocks which might otherwise be washed down. Montrachet is the best 'scree trap' one can find in Burgundy retaining much of the finest-quality eroded soils; Chevalier, which has a more pronounced slope, retains less scree. The perfection of Montrachet is thus an amalgam of position (mid-slope), protection by the Mont Rachet above and advantage from drying and cooling air from the *combes* – all helping to ensure regular and even fruit ripeness from these ideal, well-drained soils. As so often with nature's great exceptions one finds nothing dramatically different – just a felicitous juxtaposition of critical elements.

WINE: The problem with understanding Montrachet is that expectations of it are too often misguided. Whatever the source, this wine is rare and expensive – double, treble or more the price of a Bâtard or Chevalier from the same producer – and those who can afford it often believe that more money should equate to more wine, which fashionable conceptions of quality parcel out as more fruit, more wood, more aroma and so on. In fact, the 'more' that one should be looking for, and which this great vineyard delivers abundantly, is measured in intensity and refinement. Montrachet is above all a wine of subtlety. What it adds to a fine Chevalier is an extra dimension of power and core intensity, but nothing that is obvious, superficial or overstated. It may be said to combine the richness and opulence of Bâtard with the grip, finesse and discretion of Chevalier in a wine which often gives a strong impression of tannicity – as if it had a red wine's constitution. The elements which make up any great wine appear in abundance and perhaps more importantly, in balance, in Montrachet – ripe fruit, ripe acidity, concentration, complexity, suavity of texture and balance. Whether or not it opens the doors of Paradise must be for others to decide.

View eastwards from the top of Le Montrachet vineyard

PULIGNY-MONTRACHET PREMIER CRU
LE CAILLERET

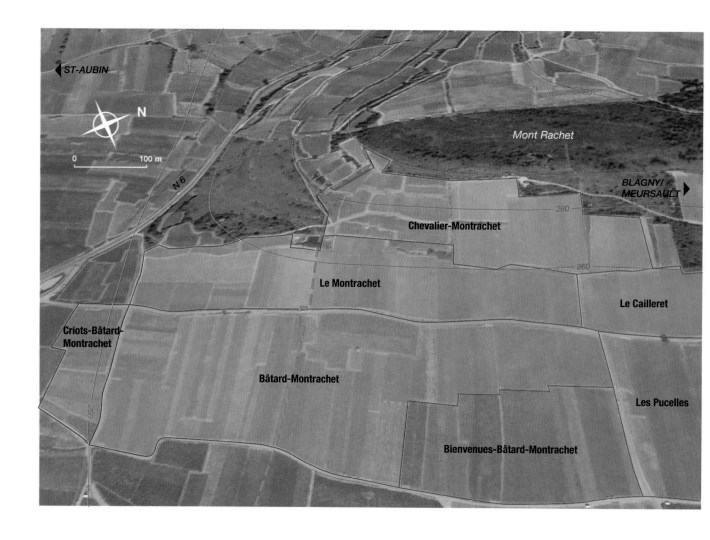

Cailleret forms the northern extension of Le Montrachet and is unquestionably of *Grand Cru* potential. The vineyard includes the Clos du Cailleret marked by a stone entrance portal at the north-east end of the vineyard, and the 0.63 ha *climat* known as Les Demoiselles (not to be confused with the Chevalier-Montrachet Demoiselles) owned by Guy Amiot and Michel Colin-Deleger. This latter consists of the parcel beneath the north-east end of Chevalier-Montrachet. In 1855, according to Lavalle, Cailleret – then at 5.41.50 ha – along with Pucelles and Clavoillon was planted to red grapes and merited top ranking. The 1.48.27 ha difference in size is probably accounted for by the adjoining section of Premier Cru Les Chaniots being then part of Cailleret rather than a separate *climat* as now.

Clos du Cailleret is not an AOC but a *lieu-dit* within Cailleret. Originally a trademark of Domaine Jean Chartron, wine under this designation is sold by both Chartron and Lambrays.

STATISTICS: *Area:* 3.93.23 *Owners:* 8+. *Average Annual Production:* 1,730 cases

PRINCIPAL OWNERS: **Jean Chartron** Clos du Cailleret: 0.86 ha white (1944–1990), 0.18 ha red (1946, 1957, 1972); **de Montille:** 0.85 ha (61); Pousse d'Or: 0.73 ha; **Yves Boyer-Martenot**; **Domaine des Lambrays** Clos du Cailleret: 0.37 (1947); **Michel Bouzereau:** 0.13 ha (1980); **Guy Amiot-Bonfils**, Les Demoiselles, **Michel Colin-Deleger**, Les Demoiselles

ORIGINS: see entry for Volnay Les Caillerets.

TOPOGRAPHY/GEOLOGY: Cailleret continues the gently sloping topography of Le Montrachet, if on a slightly different orientation (east not south-east). The underlying rock type is similar to its illustrious neighbour but the topsoil is stonier.

WINE: Cailleret is taut, elegant with a powerful concentrated core underpinned by strong minerality. Its structure and texture are often overlaid with a spiciness and notes of citrus – grapefruit in particular. Though lacking the power and sheer breed of Montrachet, these are wines of great poise and vinosity. Starting life with marked acidity and more or less opulence depending on the vintage, the best are designed for long ageing; a 1996 from Alix de Montille tasted in 2009 was still youthful, just beginning to show mature aromas, but with the depth and structure for another decade or more of development.

Le Cailleret; spraying in Les Folatières beyond

Puligny-Montrachet Premier Cru
Les Pucelles

Les Pucelles and Le Cailleret are *primus inter pares* among the Puligny *Premiers Crus*. The status of Pucelles is largely due to the consistently fine quality produced by Domaine Leflaive which owns nearly half the vineyard. In their hands the wine approaches the elegance and complexity of their Bâtard and Bienvenues with perhaps a touch more exoticism to add to its aromatic florality and mineral backbone. The vineyard's location, below Le Cailleret and separated from Bienvenues and Bâtard by the narrow D 113 road, is also a factor in Pucelles' quality potential. Les Pucelles incorporates the Clos des Meix which is part owned by Leflaive.

STATISTICS: *Area:* 6.66 ha; including Leflaive's 1.63.03 ha Clos des Meix and Jean Chartron's Clos de la Pucelle. *Owners:* 6+. *Average Annual Production:* 2,390 cases

PRINCIPAL OWNERS: **Domaine Leflaive**: 3.06 ha (1954–1985); **Jean Chartron** Clos de la Pucelle: 1.16 ha (1950, 1954, 1968, 1980); Paul Pernot: 0.40 ha (1967); Vincent Girardin: 0.27 ha (60); Philippe Chavy: 0.20 (1920, 1926); Marc Morey et Fils: 0.20 ha (1999); Morey-Coffinet: 0.20 ha (1999); Alain Chavy: 0.17 ha (1992)

ETYMOLOGY: 'Pucelles' means 'virgins' (see Chevalier Montrachet for derivation), though what this has to do with this vineyard is something of a mystery.

TOPOGRAPHY/GEOLOGY: The lower section – Clos des Meix – is the most productive, fed by an underground reservoir which collects rain spill-off; however it is not the best in quality potential – that accolade is reserved for the section nearest to Bienvenues and Bâtard. In general, Pucelles' soils are visually identical to those of Bâtard, Bienvenues and Montrachet, although deeper than those of Caillerets and Bâtard – logical, because of its position downslope – a factor which tends to increase yields. They are also much stonier. Within the entirety, soil depths vary widely – 1.5–2 metres around the Clos des Meix, to the much shallower part near the *Grands Crus* where maximum depth is 80 centimetres. This is in part the consequence of a rocky band which bisects the vineyard just below the Clos des Meix and acts as a soil retainer. As so often on the Côte, one sees part

Opposite: Clos de la Pucelle - an enclave in les Pucelles - with the village of Puligny-Montrachet beyond

of the vineyard giving body and another part finesse – neither exceptional alone but giving something special in combination. Pucelles is one of those vineyards where it makes eminent good sense to ask why, given its position, it is not already classed as a *Grand Cru*. There is no easy answer, but it is felt that because it is further downslope and in a shallow depression the quality is not quite as fine or consistent enough for the superior designation.

WINE: What differentiates Pucelles from its *Grand Cru* neighbour Bâtard-Montrachet? These are subtle – nuances of emphasis rather than gross differences in aroma or taste; indeed, the one is easily mistaken for the other. The commonalties are many: aromas of white flowers, acacia honey when young, rich nuttiness and a broad, fleshy palate sustained by that fine Puligny minerality. Bâtard is a shade more intense than Pucelles which is more reticent in that it gradually develops flavour complexity on the palate rather than being as obviously rich and plump as Bâtard. The wine tends to be soft and elegant in its youth with a fine natural balance; easy to taste, perhaps, yet deceptive in that there is much more to come. With age, Pucelles develops in presence, energy and muscle. In the best vintages, after a decade or so it shrugs off its youthful obviousness and blossoms into a wine of confidence and stature. There is always plenty of wine here, complex and complete but nothing out of place or overdone. Although perhaps more contentious than Le Cailleret, Les Pucelles is a more than credible candidate for upgrade to *Grand Cru*.

Winter work in Les Pucelles

CRIOTS-BÂTARD-MONTRACHET

At 1.6 hectares this diminutive white *Grand Cru* is something of a curiosity. First because it is the Côte's smallest white *Grand Cru* and among the smallest appellations in France; second because its limited production is rarely seen in public; third, because it is wholly in Chassagne-Montrachet. The rather forlorn patch which is Criots-Bâtard-Montrachet forms a roughly rectangular extension of Bâtard-Montrachet at its south-west end on much the same soils.

STATISTICS: *Area*: 1.57.21 ha. *Owners*: 7. *Average Annual Production*: 803 cases

PRINCIPAL OWNERS: Roger Belland: 0.60 ha (1979); Richard Fontaine-Gagnard: 0.33 ha (1930–1979); Jean-Marc Blain-Gagnard: 0.21 ha (1929, 1949, 1979); **d'Auvenay/Leroy**: 0.06 ha; **Hubert Lamy**: 0.05 ha (1975)

ORIGINS: Criots, also found in Meursault, is of similar etymology to Cras (Chambolle), Crais (Monthélie and Santenay), Aux Crais (Fixin) and the Echézeaux *lieu-dit* Les Cruots ou Vignes Blanches. It is generally accepted that *criots* is derived from *cailloux* which means 'pebbles'. Another, more fanciful explanation has it that a Seigneur of Puligny in the Middle Ages, having sired a son at the age of 70 was so disturbed by the baby's crying that he used to expostulate 'A crio l'bâtard' – 'how the bastard howls!'; hardly plausible but, as with that for the Puligny *Grands Crus*, evocative and perfectly charming.

TOPOGRAPHY/GEOLOGY: Criots is exposed east-south-east on a slight slope at an altitude of some 255 metres. Bâtard-Montrachet adjoins the full length of its north-eastern boundary. Its soil profile is broadly similar to that of Bâtard, with subsoil of Middle Jurassic origin, probably Chassagne limestone. It is

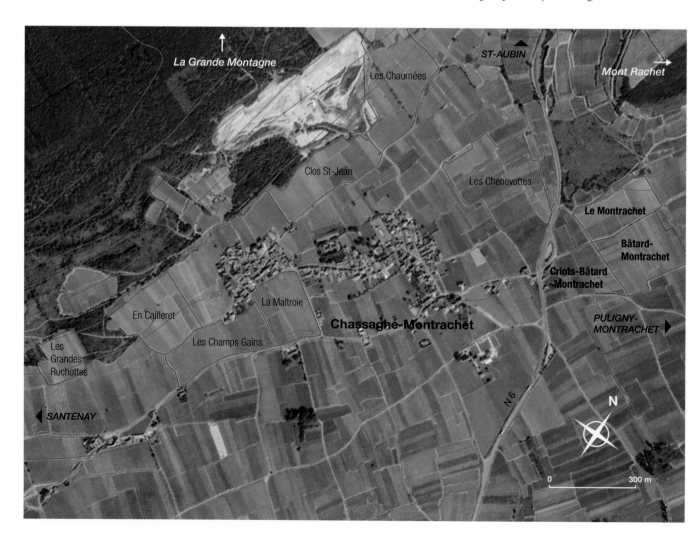

Criots-Bâtard-Montrachet with the village of Chassagne-Montrachet beyond

markedly stonier than Bâtard which accounts for its characteristic finesse, even ripening and fresh acid-based edge.

WINE: There are few offerings available from which comparisons can be made. The sources above are augmented by worthy negociants' bottlings (Louis Latour, Olivier Leflaive, Louis Jadot all have it on offer) from grapes or wine bought in bulk from those with insufficient fruit to make their own *cuvée*. My own experience of Criots suggests that it is rather more delicate than any of the other four Puligny *Grands Crus*, with a fine, almost steely backbone and mineral undertones but without the obvious opulence and body of Bâtard. Older examples, memorably from Hubert Lamy, have been most attractive.

PART 3

THE MAKING OF BURGUNDY

CHAPTER 6
PINOT NOIR

Pinot Noir is not idly dubbed the 'Heartbreak Grape'. Notoriously inconsistent yet capable of incomparable elegance, it fascinates and frustrates both drinkers and producers. Winemakers regard it as the ultimate challenge and however much it humbles them, they persevere in the quest for the elusive jackpot. In Pinot they find no compliant courtesan. Difficult to tame and highly sensitive to climate, siting, pruning and training, it demands care and attention from vine to bottle. In particular, it responds ill to rough handling in the cellar: leave it to its own devices and you court disaster. Consumers, nurtured on the easy opulence of other red varieties, find Pinot puzzling. Many who come to it reluctantly, often via a memorable bottle of Burgundy, undergo a kind of Damascene conversion, entranced by its clean lines, seduced by its finesse. In cases of serious infection, cellars are emptied of Cabernet, Syrah and Merlot to make space for the new idol. Pinot passion seems to inspire absolute devotion – a love affair which carries no shadow of a parting.

Pinot Noir's burgundian history is long. Archaeological work in 2008 by J.-P. Garcia in Gevrey-Chambertin has unearthed Gallo-Roman remains, including vine roots, confirming its presence on the Côte from the first four centuries AD. There is also documentary evidence: according to Dr Carole Meredith of UC Davis, 'Pinot Noir was already being grown in Burgundy when the Romans arrived there 2,000 years ago. The Roman agricultural writer Columella described a grape variety in the first century AD that was most likely Pinot Noir. So we're pretty sure that Pinot is at least 2,000 years old' (interview with David Graves at Saintsbury, Napa). The origin of its closer association with the Côte is unclear; some ascribe this to the influence of the Valois Dukes in the 14th century; others believe that Pinot is native to Burgundy and related, probably by successive mutation, to the wild vines found there; yet others suggest it came with invaders from Lombardy. In Carole Meredith's view 'Pinot Noir most likely came from northeastern France or southwestern Germany' (op. cit.). Take your pick!

Pinot is unquestionably the most expressive of all noble red grapes. No other variety comes close to its range of flavours and subtlety. It also comes with an alarming range of names – at least 240. It appears as Spätburgunder in Germany, Blauburgunder in Austria and Switzerland, Pinot Nero in Italy, and Chambertin, Burgundi Mic, Noir Menu and Raucy Male elsewhere.

Because it contains a higher percentage of flavour and aroma precursors in its pulp than any other red variety, it is also the grape best suited to express the nuances of Burgundy's *terroir*. Pinot, which derives its name from *pin* (pine), a reflection of the pine-cone shape of its clusters, has many variants. The Pinot Meunier, widely used in Champagne, is a mutant of Pinot Noir as is the Pinot Noir Blanc – a white grape which Henri Gouges found growing on his red Pinot vines in Nuits-St-Georges Clos des Porrets vineyard in the 1930s. The first year one branch bore white grapes, the following year the entire vine. He propagated 2.5 ha which now produces an individual Nuits-St-Georges Blanc, part from Les Porrets, part from Les Perrières. Pinot Noir is genetically unstable, mutates readily and is genotypically inseparable from both Pinot Blanc and Pinot Gris – they have identical DNA fingerprints but differing phenotypes; even clonal differences are so subtle as to be indistinguishable by DNA profiling. What differentiate these varieties are subtle mutations especially in pigmentation. Pinot Noir has recently been DNA sequenced, allowing the formation of a genetic map which in turn holds out the possibility of breeding for particular characteristics (e.g. disease resistance) without changing the grape's fundamental taste profile.

Worldwide Pinot plantings have increased dramatically in recent years, especially in Germany (11,800 ha) and the USA (16,000 ha). New Zealand has some 4,700 ha, with Switzerland and Austria at around 4,500 ha and Italy around 3,400 ha. Of France's total 26,500 Pinot hectares, the Côte d'Or has 6,116 and greater Burgundy 9,433. The variant most widely planted is Pinot Fin (= fine), also known as Pinot Tordu (= twisted) for its misshapen trunk. This is considered ideal for producing top-class wine. There remain patches of Pinot Droit (= straight) planted after the Second World War for its productivity and easily manageable upright growth habit. Well-known crossings of Pinot Noir are responsible for, among others, Aligoté, Gamay and Melon (Muscadet). Crossed by Professor Abraham Perold with Cinsault (aka 'Hermitage') in the 1920s, it became South Africa's Pinotage. Although there are some 50 French (Dijon) clones in commercial production, such is the genetic instability of Pinot Noir that the total worldwide clonal population has been estimated at over 10,000, many of which bear scant taste relationship to one another. In contrast there are around a dozen clones of Cabernet Sauvignon. New Pinot clones have been developed on the Côte from Raymond Bernard's early 1960s selections based on gathering material from various sites, evaluating their performance on factors such as yield, sugar, acid etc, and then making individual offerings available to producers.

GRAPE VARIETY FAMILY TREE

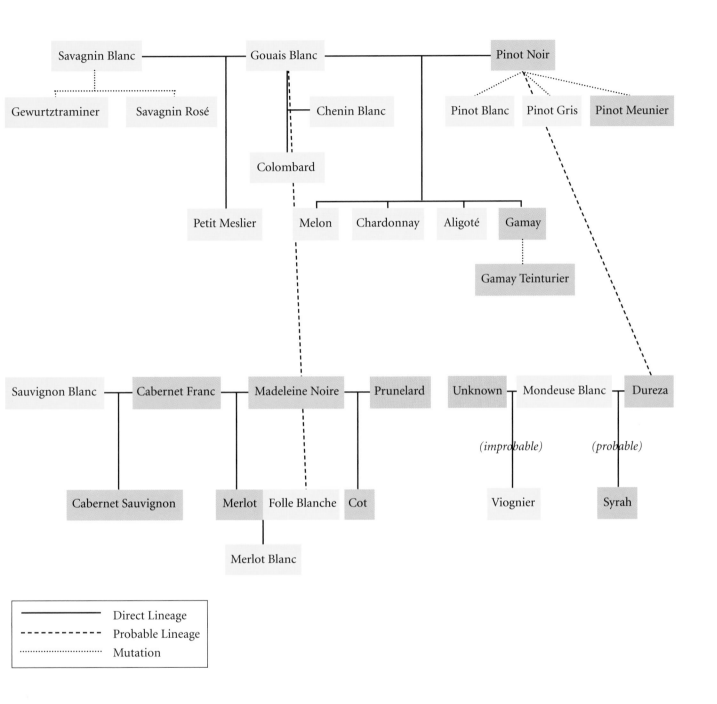

Harvested grapes in Grand Cru Corton (Perrières)

This was not strictly speaking clonal selection as there was no attempt at intervention in the natural process of the vine's genome. Bernard's process privileged production – the ability to accumulate sugar and to achieve naturally lower acid levels at ripeness. These early selections, from mother blocks of Pinot Fin in Ponsot's Clos de la Roche vineyard in Morey-St-Denis, are constantly being refined with a development emphasis on small berry size, open clusters to discourage rot as well as resistance to and freedom from disease. It is worth pointing out that what is considered 'best' for Burgundy reflects vines grown and wines produced in a different climate to most of the New World; the finest burgundian clones are therefore not necessarily those best adapted to conditions elsewhere.

It is also important to emphasise the difference between certified clean clones – usually those offered by official sources (ATVB, the Association Technique Viticole de Bourgogne, and ENTAV, the Etablissement National Technique pour l'Amélioration de la Viticulture, for example) and plant material such as many of the 'named' clones in the USA and elsewhere, which are essentially reproduced field blends, often heavily virused.

The current French and international favourite clones include:

Dijon 113: Irregular yielder; tight and somewhat austere wine, some smokiness, florality; elegance rather than substance; accumulates sugar readily which can produce high alcohols.

Dijon 114: Vigorous; good phenolics; high sugars; strong colours and good aromatics; susceptible to *millerandage*; well-textured wines suitable for keeping.

Dijon 115: Small, tight clusters, giving ripe fruit (blackberry/black cherry flavours) low in natural acidity and high in anthocyanins (tannins and pigment) with strong varietal character. Medium-structured wines, relatively soft and supple in texture.

Dijon 667: Below average bearer; fine colour and elegant aromatics; tannic wines with good fruit purity; built for keeping.

Dijon 777: A quality clone, planted across the world in quality sites. Early budding and ripening; low yielder; intense colour and aroma; round tannins; good texture (blackberry/blackcurrant); shows the elegant and feminine character of Pinot Noir. There are also new polyclonal selections of Pinot Fin and Pinot Très Fin offered by ATVB which comprise a mix of some 14 certified clones; these are considerably less productive than 115 or 777.

Recently Aubert de Villaine and Denis Fetzmann (of Maison Louis Latour) have formed the Association pour la Sauvegarde des Cépages de Bourgogne (i.e. to preserve the genetic inheritance of Burgundy's plant material) and they plan to select some 200 new clones in the next 15 years.

USA: Much of the early US work was done by Dr Harold Olmo at UC Davis in the 1950s and 60s. His selections were broadly for productivity as, at the time, yields were typically quite low and the potential for commercial success in the Californian wine industry far from bright. It was only with the growth of that industry and its ability to command higher prices that the concept of lower yields as a route to quality gained ground. UCD's Foundation Plant Services (FPS) currently lists 74 separate Pinot Noir clones of which many are cleaned up re-issues under new numbers which somewhat complicates the picture.

FPS 04, 05 & 06: 04 is the original Pommard Clone, from Ch. de Pommard; 05 and 06 are heat-treated versions of the same source material, as is FPS 91 which is the new Pommard clone. These are much favoured among Pinot producers in the USA although there is some confusion as to which of 04 and 05 is the one widely planted in Oregon. These clones are good all-rounders with small, tight-packed clusters and thick-skinned fruit. This results in intensely coloured wine, solidly structured with ripe, plush tannins and concentrated black fruit flavours – especially black cherry flavours and blackberry – coupled with notes of leather and spice. Pommard (04) is often meaty in character and somewhat Syrah-like but with good, if not spectacular length and nuanced aromatics. This older style of Pinot is losing favour to newer clones which trump on considerations of reliability, purity of flavour, growing habit, disease resistance/freedom, relative predictability of quality, cropping levels and so on.

The FPS list also includes the best California Heritage clones: the Swan clone (FPS 97), Chalone clone (from Chambertin, FPS 90), the Hanzell clone (E) and two Martini clones (FPS 75 and FPS 66). FPS 90 and 96 are reported as originating with the same source, Chambertin, as the Calera clone although there is some doubt about this last.

Swan clone: Propagated by Joseph Swan in Russian River Valley. Notably late ripening; gives bright fruit character with good weight and length.

Mount Eden clones: Several separate clones, reportedly introduced to California in the 1890s from Louis Latour's Corton vineyards. Similar in character to the Pommard clone, these give dark, rich flavours and work well as stand-alones.

Clone 828: Low-yielding clone originating from the Mâconnais with small berries giving intense skin pigmentation and deeply coloured wine with notably low pH and bright acidity. Flavours in the red cherry, blueberry end of the fruit spectrum. This clone has never been legally imported into the US as it had Red Globe, a leaf-roll-like virus. Much of what producers call 828 is AS2 – a selection from Archery Summit which somehow escaped into the wider world as 828.

'Calera' clone: Spicy, red fruits, good body and colour; mother block from cuttings from top Burgundy estates in the early 1970s. Reported as a 'suitcase clone' – stories abound of imported clones which somehow didn't go through the FPS. There is no statute of limitations on prosecution for plant smuggling, so US jail populations could be swelled by some of California's finest wine producers!

10/5: One of the first premium clones to be planted in New Zealand and still producing there (e.g. Felton Road block 3 and Ohmi Rise). Known as the 'Swiss clone', this needs plenty of warmth, a light crop and a long growing season to ripen fully. Its main failing is that it tends to produce a strong, often dominant, 'tomato leaf' character.

Abel clone: Also known as the Ata Rangi or 'Gumboot' clone, it is widely planted in New Zealand where it produces wine with an earthiness, substantial tannins, a lush, silky texture, often accompanied by dark cherry flavours and a noticeable savoury character. Its soubriquet reflects the story of its import into New Zealand, being apparently discovered in the gumboot of an incoming passenger (who it is said had jumped the wall at Romanée-Conti) by a zealous customs officer and winemaker, Malcolm Abel, who took it home and propagated it. It still forms the core of Ata Rangi's Pinot plantings, after Clive Paton worked a vintage with Abel at his Auckland wine farm and took cuttings back to Martinborough in 1982 from which he continues to produce one of NZ's finest Pinots.

Pinot's history in New Zealand has been particularly striking, having shot from almost nothing to become the country's flagship red variety in less than twenty years. Although the first plantings were made by Nobilo in the Auckland region in 1976, followed by a notable success with wine from St Helena in Canterbury in 1982, the revolution did not really start until Larry McKenna planted Pinot in his Martinborough vineyards in 1988. The grape now grips winemakers across the country, whose skill and dedication is evident from the excellent wines to be found in several geologically and climatically diverse regions; in particular Martinborough, Marlborough, Canterbury/Waipara, Wairarapa, Nelson and Central Otago.

It has taken off in Germany which now has 11,800 ha, with top-class quality being produced patchily, mainly in the Ahr Valley, Baden, Württemberg and the Pfalz. An early ripening variant, Frühburgunder, is planted in the Ahr alongside the traditional Spätburgunder. In the USA, Pinot Noir came to prominence when David Lett planted Eyrie Vineyards in Oregon's Willamette Valley in 1965. It is now the state's signature grape variety. Since then its American coverage has spread, with notable results on the Sonoma and Central Coast, in Russian River, Carneros, Anderson and San Luis Obispo. There are also reports of interesting Pinots from the Niagara Escarpment area of New York State. California now has some 25,000 acres (10,000 ha) of Pinot – evidence perhaps of its increasingly fashionable status than of its suitability for the region.

In Australia the finest Pinots are concentrated in the areas around the Mornington Peninsula and the Yarra Valley, with patches of excellence elsewhere – Tasmania for one. Chile has large-scale production, where it grows easily and disease-free, producing good crops of ripe fruit, but as yet only flashes of decent quality. Pinot Noir also does well, if patchily, in South Africa with plantings on a range of sites and soil-types: in the heat of Paarl/Simondium and Franschhoek and with notable success in the cooler climates of Elgin and Hemel-en-Aarde and promising early results from new plantings in southerly Agulhas. Austria, Switzerland, Italy and Spain all have plantings as does much of Eastern Europe, with patches of fine quality. It is Britain's most planted red variety and crops up in a minor role in many other countries, especially in sparkling wine production. Together with Chardonnay it is of course the backbone of quality Champagne. It also appears in the interesting guise of dessert wines, from the likes of Willi Opitz in Illmitz and James Downes at Shannon Vineyards in Elgin, South Africa.

Pinot is characterised by a natural colour deficiency compared with other mainstream red varieties. It is the only red grape not to have procyanidins – molecules which encourage the formation of colour compounds. Its composition is two parts red to one part yellow pigment which makes its colour appear more fragile, less dense and more oxidised than Syrah or Cabernet. In has the additional peculiarity of shedding colour if allowed to overripen, in contrast to other red varieties which intensify. Its thin, fragile skin is difficult to ripen fully, adding to a reputation for being light-coloured; this facilitates access for the grape-worm, a perennial nuisance on the Côte, and splitting which allows rot to develop. Pinot Noir is also unusual among reds in having relatively low levels of grape tannins, a peculiarity processing must take account of.

Pinot is susceptible to grey rot and mildew and highly vulnerable to the fan leaf (*court noué*) and leaf-roll viruses which ravaged the Côte's neglected vineyards during and after the Second World War. The former turns the leaves pale yellow or deep red and makes them drop prematurely spreading out their veins in a fan shape; the latter causes leaves to curl downwards late on in the season. Degeneration and death of the vine are the eventual consequences and the only solution is to grub up, disinfect the soil and replant with virus-free material. Both maladies are thought to be transmitted by root-sucking worms (*Xiphanema nematode* for fan leaf; mealy bugs or other insects for leaf-roll), through virus-infected plant material or grafting wounds though the route is conclusively proven. In the US Pinot has also been found to attract the sharpshooter family of insects which are vectors for Pierce's disease, a bacterial infection which kills vines by blocking their water transmission conduits.

Pinot Noir performs best in predominantly calcareous (limestone) soils with moderate nitrogen and clay content. Excess nitrogen promotes vigour and vegetative growth which result in problems with foliage and canopy control, also grey rot; nitrogen deficiency on the other hand (for example, on volcanic soils or gravel beds) tends to give undesirable hydrogen sulphide in the wine, a problem that is exacerbated as vines age and increase their nitrogen take up. In general, Pinot's minimum requirements appear to be: low to moderate vigour, well-drained soils and good exposure. As the progenitor of clones, Raymond Bernard, put it: 'we believe absolutely that Pinot Noir must grow in calcareous soils to express its true potential' (pers. comm.). However, it is not difficult to criticise this entrenched burgundian belief in the primacy of limestone as making a virtue of what you happen to have. Many in the New World have not been slow to make the same point.

Pinot is naturally relatively vigorous, requiring restraint by severe pruning and planting on low-vigour rootstock. Early budding makes it susceptible to spring frosts, always a risk on the Côte, which encourages growers to prune generously. It needs a long ripening season, preferably without extremes of heat. Winemakers in the hotter areas of California and elsewhere have realised that no amount of cool fermentation and careful handling will restore finesse once the sun has burnt it off.

The acid composition of Pinot Noir is an important factor in anthocyanin (colour pigment) development. It has significantly more malic (apple) acid than tartaric acid and it is this latter which lowers effective acidity (pH) and stabilises the wine's colour. The effect is indirect in the sense that acid composition affects the pH of a wine and thereby its anthocyanin state and thus its colour hue and density. This bears back on the vineyard as the amount of anthocyanin in a wine is an outcome of the vine's interaction with its site, management and plant selection. Malic acid concentration reduces sharply after *veraison* which, given its initial dominance, amounts to a diminution of overall acidity. This makes full tannin ripeness essential to stabilise inherently unstable colour to avoid premature browning. There is also evidence suggesting a correlation between depth of colour and wine quality. This does not necessarily mean that the one promotes the other; there may be a third factor promoting both, though the idea merits attention. In the cellar, it tends to ferment vigorously, making temperature control important, and has a habit of shedding youthful aromas and flavours rapidly, if transitorily, in bottle.

This snapshot of Pinot Noir highlights some of its complexities and susceptibilities. Not surprisingly it has brought strong men to the ground despairing. As one winemaker commented on receiving an award, 'It is the little moments that make it all worth it … but I'm sure I'll be on my knees with this grape again shortly.'

Its successes and failures are equally spectacular: weak Pinot is undrinkable; mediocre Pinot insipid; great Pinot transcends everything.

Chapter 7
Chardonnay

Chardonnay's capacity to produce attractive, eminently drinkable wine at every quality level has endeared it consumers and producers alike. It is malleable, versatile and food-friendly with a strong personality which balances fruit and alcohol but without the high-acid component which puts many off Riesling, though curiously not Sauvignon Blanc.

Although its origins are not well documented, there is now certainty that it was born in Burgundy. There is indeed a village called Chardonnay in the Mâconnais, but it is doubtful whether this has any relevance to the naming of the grape or indeed to its presence on the Côte. Frequent references to Pinot-Chardonnay reflect the widespread (and wrong) belief that it is a white mutant of Pinot Noir. Dr Carole Meredith's researches at UC Davis have revealed that Chardonnay is the offspring of Pinot (the varietal generic name for the genetically indistinguishable Pinots Noir, Blanc and Gris) and Gouais Blanc, a mediocre central European variety thought to have been introduced to France by the Romans. It was probably widely grown by peasants in north-eastern France for the production of ordinary wine.

The age of Chardonnay is more difficult to pin down. According to Dr Meredith, 'it must be younger than Pinot because Pinot is one of its parents. But it can't be older than the date at which its other parent, Gouais Blanc, was introduced to France, which was probably in the third century AD. Chardonnay has been confused with other varieties (e.g. Pinot Blanc and Melon) and has had many names, so it's not at all clear when Chardonnay first appeared. It seems to have been recognized as a distinct variety by the 1300s, but it might have already been around for a while before that. So the best we can say is that Chardonnay is probably at least 700 years old, but could be as much as 1700 years old' (op. cit.).

Its recent history on the Côte dates from the end of the 19th century when Louis Latour persuaded growers to replace Aligoté with Chardonnay. Aligoté was known to be planted in prestigious sites such as Corton and Le Montrachet as indeed was Gamay. Chardonnay now accounts for less than 30% of vines on the Côte and, despite its universal popularity, it is only the fifth most planted wine grape variety worldwide. The Côte d'Or's 2,388 hectares of Chardonnay represent 25.6% of its total 9,325 hectares of vines; greater Burgundy (including Chablis) has 15,421 hectares.

Chardonnay's character and growing habits are well-suited to the production of fine wine. Its particular attribute, which it shares with Riesling and probably explains its worldwide proliferation, is the ability to produce decent wine at high yields. Whereas 35 hl/ha is generally considered optimal for decent Pinot, Chardonnay will easily produce quality at 45 hl/ha or more. This may well have more to do with not having to balance liquids and solids finely as one must with red varieties than with any intrinsic characteristic. What is certain is that lower yields in general and smaller berried vine selections in particular produce more intense character in the resulting wines which suggests that yield components are in some way the critical issue.

Unlike Pinot Noir, Chardonnay vines are not designed for very great age. Vincent Leflaive used to grub up his at around thirty years and reckoned that the best fruit came at around ten. This may reflect the fact that Chardonnay is a more vegetative vine and thus burns out at an earlier age, although the variety's susceptibility to various forms of 'environmental insult' (leaf-roll, Pierce's disease or fungal malady) may play a role here.

Viticulturally, Chardonnay is an early budder and ripener, which makes its susceptibility to bud-burn from frost a particular problem in northern vineyards. This can happen either as winter kill, when buds or even the vine itself are damaged during dormancy, or more likely as spring frost damage to newly emerging shoots. Memorably severe winter frosts in 1956, 1985 and 1991 in Burgundy killed vines and necessitated widespread replanting of both Pinot and Chardonnay. Chardonnay is also susceptible to the *court noué* (fan-leaf) virus and to oïdium, the fungus that causes powdery mildew.

It is a notoriously vigorous and prolific variety, requiring severe pruning, low vigour sites, devigorating rootstock, high-density planting, reducing soil nitrogen and minimum fertiliser to control yields. This vigour easily dissipates energy in foliage, so careful canopy management is essential. Whilst high vine densities (10,000+ per hectare are normal in Burgundy) or close spacing can help reduce overall vine size, there seems to be an inherent yield 'capacity' of the vine-stock and site interaction mediated both by rootstock and clonal selection. Chardonnay prefers a longish growing season to short blasts of heat and is prone to shedding acidity as it ripens. In excessive heat it accumulates sugar faster than flavour ripeness and can thus be high in sugar yet unripe in flavours, which often makes harvest timing a tricky decision. It is also clear that excessive heat often causes grape berries to lose weight so that they appear to gain sugar; this is a concentrating effect that affects acids as well as sugars.

Underripeness is almost as undesirable as overripeness. This makes things difficult in the *secteurs tardifs* of the Côte, where site

or exposure pre-ordains late ripening. In cooler vintages these wines invariably require chaptalisation which detracts to some extent from their typicity. However, in good vintages a long, slow growing season produces excellent wines from the likes of St-Aubin, Auxey-Duresses, Pernand Vergelesses and Savigny, as well as the grander offerings from Corton, Meursault, Puligny and Chassagne.

Chardonnay appears in well-defined small patches in the Côte de Nuits, sometimes admixed with a field-planted dab of Pinot Beurot (= Pinot Gris) which adds a touch of palate breadth and an earthy richness. These wines are both unusual and individual – Morey-St-Denis Blanc, white Nuits-St-Georges from Gouges, Chevillon, Clos de l'Arlot and others, Vougeot Blanc, and Domaine Comte Georges de Vogüé's Grand Cru Musigny Blanc. These, Musigny included, are attractive curiosities rather than great wines; effectively white wines grown on red wine soils which impart a particular structure which mutes the minerality and finesse one looks for in fine Chardonnay.

Chardonnay is widely planted internationally. Among some 64 alternative designations are Rouci Bile, Shardone, Petite Sainte Marie, Sainte Marie Petite, Auxerrois, Weissburgunder, Melon d'Arbois and Beaunois. It has proved successful in the cooler climates of New Zealand, California, Orgeon and South Africa. In Australia it produces high quality in Margaret River (WA), Yarra Valley, Geelong, Mornington Peninsula (VIC) and Tasmania; it also does rather well, though in a different style, in warmer regions such as the Hunter Valley (NSW). It plays a major, often solo, role in Champagne.

A wealth of clones is now commercially available (over 30 in France alone) some emphasising the fat and oily side of the grape, others being dry and more mineral in character. As with Pinot Noir, Chardonnay clones have also been developed outside France, notably in the USA and Australia. However, the general preference is for the Dijon clone family which bud late and ripen early – ideal for cooler climates, such as Oregon. They are mostly small-berried and low yielding, many with a good proportion of shot berries, producing intensely flavoured wines. Some are more restrained in character, with an attractive stony minerality, others show lusher, tropical notes. The 'Dijon' French clones generally maintain acidity but are prone to shed it in hot sites, preferring cooler conditions.

Some of the current favourites are:
Dijon 76: Well-balanced, aromatic fine wines typical of the variety; good intensity and typicity although can become rather raw and phenolicky.

Dijon 78: Productive; need to restrain vigour; wines thin and neutral when overcropped.

Dijon 95: Full, rich and balanced wines with fine aromas; good in most situations; complete wines.

Dijon 96: Nervous, balanced and aromatic wines; regular and good production; complete wines.

Dijon 166: Noted for musk-like aromatics – not to be confused with the Chardonnay Blanc Musqué (see Dijon 809 below).

Tending young vines is back-breaking work

Dijon 277: Balanced and aromatic wines; vigour and yields require control to produce good quality.

Clone 352: The 'Espiguette' clone from southern France; shows a fine, high-toned creaminess with a delicate white-blossom perfume. Reference has been made to a 'woody apple character' from this clone planted in Russian River Valley in California.

Dijon 548: Early ripening clone – about 5–7 days earlier than 95/96 – so ideal for cool climates and higher sites; gives intense full-flavoured well-constituted wines.

Dijon 809: Good all-rounder, widely planted around Clessé in the Mâconnais; known as the Musqué clone, it produces notably aromatic wine with a floral Muscat-like scent. This character may benefit producers of (the increasingly popular) unwooded Chardonnay.

Most California Chardonnay clones after the Second World War originated from two primary sources: the Wente vineyard in Livermore and the Paul Masson vineyard in the Santa Cruz Mountains. (Strictly speaking these were vineyard selections rather than clones in the sense that the original material came from more than one vine in the mother vineyard and were most likely genetically different, whereas a clone is material from a single vine which is then propagated.) The Wente material itself originated from two separate French sources. Many other Chardonnay selections have been trialled, notably by grape-grower Larry Hyde and by Zelma Long at Simi. Mark Lingen-felder at Chalk Hill Estate, Healdsburg, has also been at the forefront of clonal development, with trials of no fewer than 17 Chardonnay clones including sponsorship of FPS 97.

Below are listed some of the best known from the 73 currently listed by FPS as available or provisional:

FPS 2A: Origins unclear, possibly German or from Wente vineyard; crops well but has large berries and can lack intensity. Much reported variation in flavour and aroma; main descriptors: pineapple, apple, Muscat and fruit cocktail! Resembles the 'Old' Wente clone, which references material from 1930s Wente vineyards pre-UC Davis certification. Budwood, originally from Montpellier, southern France, planted in Wente's vineyards in 1912. In contrast to FPS 2A, the 'Old' Wente clone is a shy-bearer and produces small bunches of intensely flavoured grapes

with many shot berries. It is favoured by Kistler vineyards for all their new plantings.

FPS 3A: Selection from commercial planting in Livermore Valley is widely planted, although not distributed since 1968 because of fruit set problems (shot berries). It balances good natural acidity and fruit weight though with a tendency to be a touch exotic.

FPS 04, 05: Known Martini clones from their origin in Martini's Carneros vineyard these are California's Chardonnay work-horses. Propagated in the mid-1960s, they are notoriously high yielders, producing fewer clusters but with larger berries and a heavier cluster weight. The grapes are naturally higher in acidity and have high levels of soluble solids which can contribute to full flavoured berries. Clone 4's ability to yield a large crop of reasonable-quality fruit has earned it the nickname 'Super Clone'. That might imply that it yields mediocre wines, but the opposite is true: grown on the right soil and balanced for low yield, it gives concentrated, complex wines, combining power and finesse, good grip and definition and with notes of tropical fruit and peach, qualities described as classic California Chardonnay. Together with FPS 05 this is sometimes known as Selection 108: A vigorous, high-yield clone that ripens late with a high pH. The result is a wine lower in acid with a fat, ripe and round texture – ideal for the warmer regions of California where volume is important.

FPS 06, 08, 14 are also of Martini (Carneros) origin as are their propagative offspring 09-13: High vigour, producing smaller, looser bunches with thick-skinned berries which inhibit rot. These also benefit from earlyish maturity. Crop levels are moderate producing reasonably concentrated wine. Since they are not well adapted to hot conditions (as in California) acidity may drop sharply around harvest.

FPS 15: Known as the Prosser clone, origin unclear, this clone yields erratically depending on siting, but generally in the low to moderate range, has loose clusters and is noted for *millerandage* (shot berries). Fruit composition is reported as good as are flavour qualities. It is considered 'ideal for cool climates and reserve Chardonnay programmes'.

FPS 16: Selected in Rutherglen, a warm area in the state of South Australia, and subsequently certified by UC Davis following a period of uncertainty as to its identity. The key to its distinctive personality is the acid balance of its fruit: relatively high in malic acid and low in tartaric. Malic acid is less stable than tartaric acid and decreases during ripening, especially in warm climates. Wine is therefore already low in acidity before being further reduced by malolactic fermentation. It earns its place in a blend, contributing a rich perfume and luscious fruit too, without throwing the total acidity out of balance.

FPS 17: Originally propagated Wente budwood planted in the Robert Young Vineyard in Alexander Valley. A moderate yielder, it is more subdued and less perfumed than either FPS 4 or FPS 16, yet it has a higher-toned nose and brighter palate, with a mineral undertone that tends to focus and define the lusher tropical fruit elements around it.

FPS 22: From cool-climate Friulí region of northern Italy. Its wine is on the lean, herbaceous end of the Chardonnay spectrum. Clone 22's virtues in a blend are brightness and a firm, even weight on the palate.

There is still interest in some of the better older US clones. For example, Kistler Vineyards think highly of the Masson clone (aka Mount Eden clone) which dates from the mid-1930s. Chalk Hill's winemaker, Bill Knuttel, believes: 'It's unfortunate that nobody looks at the old clones; it's a mistake, because they have their places in the right vineyards.' He refers to its low yields and to its 'intense, varietally true flavour qualities'.

Mendoza or McRae: Its tendency to *millerandage* or shatter, giving bunches with irregularly sized berries but low yields, gives this clone appeal. It is widely planted in Australia and New Zealand (notably at Kumeu River). It gives fullish, intensely flavoured, attractively perfumed wines often a touch exotic.

In the cellar, Chardonnay is a winemaker's delight – it practically makes itself. Because it attains relatively high sugar levels, even in less warm, sunny vintages, it needs little chaptalisation. However, where it has overripened, the resulting low acidity requires adjustment, which is best avoided. Chardonnay that is very ripe tends to be fat and flabby, often with a tropical fruit component to its character – pineapple, guava, candied fruit, and so forth. Otherwise, it tolerates a variety of vinifications without losing its interest; skin contact, fermentation cool or warm, in cask or bulk, *bâtonnage* or not, all work well. It can be matured in old or new wood, but is easily marked by coarse-grained or heavy-toast oak which makes it tight, noticeably phenolic and dominated by wood flavours. Unwooded Chardonnay is increasing in popularity as alternatives for those who dislike overtly oaky wines and can be exceptional: Chablis from Louis Michel, for example. Contrary to popular belief, the best unwoodeds age superbly. Particularly memorable was a 1981 Chablis Grenouilles from Michel enjoyed in 2009.

As with most fine white varieties, acidity and flavour intensity are the keys to longevity. With Chardonnay this makes yield critical as inappropriate fruit-load dilutes both acidity and flavour. For top class, precision harvesting is essential to retain an optimum balance of sugar for alcohol and acid for freshness and flavour/aroma development. Chardonnay is reasonably resistant to oxidation, an attribute which allows reduced use of preservative sulphur and makes for a slow, even evolution.

What matters supremely in Burgundy is that Chardonnay faithfully expresses *terroir* without sacrificing varietal identity. One only has to contrast Chablis, Puligny, Corton and Mâcon to appreciate this. It performs well on a variety of soils, from Chablis' Kimmeridgian clays, to the high pH, relatively acid-neutral soils of the Mâconnais and of course spectacularly on the clay-limestones of the southern Côte d'Or. Contrary to popular belief, it dislikes pure limestone.

Burgundian Chardonnays can be enjoyed early on for their youthful florality and mineral freshness or late for their mature qualities. Received wisdom, even among knowledgeable consumers, insists that white wine is not for laying down, a view that is shared by the majority of drinkers. While most are indeed designed to be drunk young, the finest Côte d'Or whites age beautifully. Unfortunately, much is consumed in the first flush of youth and therefore never gets the chance to show its paces. The spoilage risks attendant on the relatively recent phenomenon of premature oxidation (see Chapter 12) has made consumers understandably reluctant to buy top class white Burgundy for laying down. Discounting this risk, the *Grands* and finest *Premiers Crus* should be kept for a minimum of 3–5 years while the best will continue to develop attractively, given good storage, for much longer. Taste a 30-year-old Chevalier-Montrachet, Corton-Charlemagne or Grand Cru Chablis, and marvel at the diversity of aroma and flavour – complex, rich in nuance, yet still restrained and profoundly aristocratic.

Harvested Chardonnay grapes in Meursault

CHAPTER 8
THE INFLUENCE OF CLIMATE

Frosted vines in Corton-Charlemagne

Burgundy is the most northerly region for fine red wine production in Europe. Here grapes grow at their marginal limits of ripening and as such are vulnerable to the vagaries of weather to a greater extent than regions with more consistent climates. This is both an advantage and a disadvantage: advantage, because the long growing season required to ripen fruit here is key to finesse and flavour development, so in years when grapes do ripen fully the resulting wines are elegant, seductively perfumed, well-structured and long-lived; disadvantage, because in less propitious years a lack of heat or light or an excess of rain delivers fruit deficient in the constituents for balance. In such circumstances the *vigneron* must work hard to produce something attractive and typifying its origin. Climate is therefore a major driver of quality in Burgundy.

In descending order of scale, three broad levels of climate are recognised: macroclimate covers regions and sub-regions (Côte

d'Or, Côte de Nuits and so forth); mesoclimate breaks down the influence of topographical features (for instance, slope, exposition) and covers vineyards or sections of a vineyard to an extent of tens or hundreds of metres; microclimate refers to the area immediately round the vine (for example, distinctions between inner and outer canopy). Each plays a part in growth and flavour development and collectively they determine vintage variation and vintage character.

While the wider weather pattern determines the overall character of a vintage, significant local variation superimposes on the seasonal envelope. From Dijon to Santenay, factors associated with site, elevation and exposition differentially influence how grapes ripen. Different soil-types and clones respond in different ways to heat and rainfall, so how a grower conducts his vineyards influences balance and ripeness in fruit: skilful canopy management can amortise excesses of heat and provide additional light and aeration in cooler, wetter years; ploughing soil allows heat to be retained and reflected back onto the vines and promotes drainage. Practitioners of biodynamic viticulture report that this can advance fruit ripening by a week or more on the Côte – invaluable when harvest carries the risks associated with equinoctial storms – and improves overall ripeness. It is clear that while a producer must live with the vintage, intelligent vineyard management can do much to ensure that the fruit he picks is as balanced and well-constituted as possible. Weather is thus not immune from human influence and it is in the vineyard, not the cellar, that the vagaries of vintage should be addressed. With today's techniques, the skilled *vigneron* can produce something profound, even in a 'poor' vintage.

The Côte lies on the 47th parallel and has a temperate, continental climate with cold winters, hottish summers and dry autumns. Its situation opens it to several influences: maritime from the west, continental from the east and Mediterranean from the south. It is fortunate in that most of its vineyards are protected from the rigours of its northerly latitude by the barrier of the Vosges to the east and the plateau of Langres to the immediate north, while the Morvan hills to the west take much of the rainfall which limits excess. The Côte is fortunate in its situation: at Autun, some 54 kilometres (34 miles) due west of Beaune, the annual average rainfall is 200 millimetres greater. Comparatively, the Côte has a similar climate to Bordeaux but somewhat cooler (because of colder winters rather than colder summers) and drier; Dijon has about the same sunshine and relative humidity – 50% annual average.

THE REQUIREMENTS FOR RIPENING GRAPES

Vines need many elements to produce ripe, well-constituted fruit: sunlight, heat, water – enough, but not too much, and at the right time. A gentle rise in heat is preferable to a sudden heatwave interspersed with periods of cold, and several small showers to a torrential rainstorm; enough rain to keep the photosynthetic process going is equally preferable to either torrid heat or drought (as in 1976 and 2003). A critical factor for the vintage is the amount of sun in the month or so before harvest. Around 170 hours generally presages mediocre quality, 180–200 hours good and more than 200 hours exceptional quality. Flavour is a function of ripeness so within the overall envelope distribution of these elements is more important that total quantity.

The minimum requirements to fully ripen grapes are met on the Côte: 1400 hours of sunshine from budburst to harvest, 685 millimetres of rainfall, an average temperature of 15°C during flowering, 22°C during summer, 3°C during winter and an annual average of 10.7–10.9°C. Average rainfall exceeds 700 millimetres and sunshine averages 2,000 hours providing some compensation for a lower than optimum average summer temperature of 19–20°C. The lowish rainfall in February/ March means that the soil is not waterlogged, which speeds up vine growth and thus ripening; it also allows pruning away the previous year's wood to take place in dry conditions with the sap rising, both of which minimise the risk bacterial and fungal diseases infiltrating through open pruning wounds. May and June, in contrast, are high rainfall months which can disrupt flowering – the all-important emergence of embryo bunches. In May the temperature can rise rapidly, helping the vine's buds to swell; in June the average is 16–18°C. To a certain extent this strong continental influence compensates for Burgundy's northerly position.

There are broad gross differences between the two Côtes. While the Côte de Nuits faces due east, the Côte de Beaune is broadly oriented south-east so receives more of any ambient heat and sunlight, essential energy for photosynthesis and for the development of colour and flavour compounds. The maritime influence of the Mediterranean is greater in the Côte de Beaune which is drier and less affected by northerly winds. The net result is that the Côte de Beaune is slightly warmer than the Côte de Nuits and generally harvests up to a week earlier, giving a better chance of escaping autumnal storms.

Burgundy's winds come from many directions, most notably the strong, cold, northerly *bise*. Moderate winds are beneficial in that they dry fruit after rain and sanitise vineyards but they also disrupt pollination, spread airborne fungal spores (downy and powdery mildew in particular) and increase leaf transpiration which may cause vines to shut down in exceptional heat. Wind also promotes 'spray drift' which in Burgundy's highly fragmented pattern of ownership means one plot cannot be isolated from those around it. Being biodynamic or organic is difficult when your neighbour is spraying systemics on a regular basis.

A simple rain gauge – not all is high-tech

SEASONAL HAZARDS

Each season brings risks of weather-borne disaster. In winter and spring there is the risk of frost – which can have a serious impact as in 1957, 1965 and 1991. Late frost can kill buds and fewer buds mean less crop (not always a bad thing); severe frost (as etched indelibly in growers' memories from 1985) may split and kill the vine which is capable of surviving temperatures of −25°C but not for prolonged periods. Pinot Noir shares with Chardonnay the trait of budding early, so frost is a particular risk. Further north in Chablis, elaborate measures are taken to counter frost outbreaks, especially in the precious *Grands Crus*. Fortunately for the Côte, severe frosts are rarer here than there.

In most years the vegetative cycle is reasonably even, but irregularity at either end of the season frequently gives the weather a decisive influence. The critical periods – bud burst, flowering, fruit set, *veraison* and harvest – are all susceptible to adverse weather. Uneven or unduly extended flowering means uneven ripeness between and within bunches at harvest which influences quality potential. Two results of disrupted flowering are particularly important: *coulure* and *millerandage* – the first a total aborting of flowers which reduces crop size, the second a partial abortion which forms small berries intensely rich in sugars and polyphenols, making for wines which have greater colour, concentration and aromatic expression. *Millerands* contain less potassium, an element which reduces acidity, so *millerand*-rich wines have fresher acidities and lower pH levels which make for a longer more interesting evolution in bottle. Heavily *millerandé* vintages in Burgundy (e.g. 1992) often produce fine quality. June also sees the maximum rainfall on the Côte at a period when the vine is particularly thirsty, increasing the risk of both *coulure* and *millerandage*. In general spring conditions determine the size of the vintage, autumn its quality.

Hail is also a significant risk. It can arrive at any time between April and August and devastate vineyards, destroying flowers, scarring leaves or rupturing the grape berries and provoking rot. In the worst cases it splits the wood and kills the vine. Hail storms tend to be highly localised, often just a few hundred metres across, cutting savagely through any vegetation in its path. Sheltered sites are far less hail-prone than more exposed vineyards on open plains or hillsides. Although cloud-seeding rockets help, they are of limited efficacy; in the face of hail, the *vigneron* is virtually defenceless. Curiously, some vineyards are particularly vulnerable whereas others seem miraculously immune (Comte Armand's Pommard Clos des Epeneaux is one such fortunate site). Susceptibility may have to do with differential air-flow from the *combes* nicked into the Côte's escarpment.

Provided there is sufficient heat, sunlight and rainfall to keep the vine working, summer is less critical to wine quality than many suppose. What matters is the distribution of these three critical parameters. An evenly warm summer with periodic small bouts of precipitation is far better than weeks of cool dry conditions interspersed with short periods of intense heat or violent storms. As in cooking, although searing gives a powerful decadent taste, a gentle simmer better promotes flavour subtlety.

With autumn comes the harvest and the weather instability associated with the equinox. Here, rain is the chief risk: heavy falls may cause the vines to pump water thereby diluting the juice, and storms can split the berry skin encouraging rot when anti-rot sprays are prohibited. Pinot Noir, with its thinnish skin, is particularly susceptible. New anti-botrytis products which may be safely used up to and post harvest have been developed and are coming onto the market. Brave growers delay harvesting in the hope of better weather to dry out bunches and it is a matter of record that recent years have favoured those prepared to wait.

Right: A chlorosed vine

Opposite: One of the vigneron's nightmares: an approaching storm

MICRO- & MESOCLIMATES

The Côte is a vast patchwork of micro- and mesoclimates which have a significant bearing on wine quality and are an integral part of defining *terroir* differences between communes and even *climats*. Many factors influence how grapes grow and ripen in any particular vineyard.

Burgundy's vineyards are mainly exposed due east, south-east, south, or in a few cases face west (for example, parts of Pernand-Vergelesses). Exposition, to morning, afternoon or evening sun, obviously affects the amount and strength of heat and sunlight a vine receives; it also affects wind exposure. The Côte's exposition in relation to the rising sun is generally favoured over land which faces it directly. Vines just below the Côte's western escarpment benefit to a limited degree from the wind-shelter it provides.

The Côte's vineyards lie at an altitude of 100–395 metres. Higher ground will have a lower average temperature than lower ground, adjusted by a lapse rate of 6.49°C per 1,000 vertical metres and often greater exposure to wind, both of which retard ripening. Slope acts to spill off both water and cold air. The latter means that upper sectors are less prone to frost, as demonstrated in 1985 when severe winter weather destroyed many lower-lying vines.

The physical characteristics of soil bear on the effects of climate. Reflectivity of topsoil influences the heat reaching the vine and its heat-retentive properties can even out day–night temperature variation. The importance of diurnal temperature difference is emphasised by producers in many regions where Pinot Noir and Chardonnay are planted, as it is felt to increase complexity. The soil's compactness and granularity influence water penetration – water percolates easily through gravels but not through heavy clay – and thus the uptake of essential nutrients, especially in hot, dry years when the roots need to tap water from deep reserves. Soil compacted by heavy tractor traffic loses permeability.

Forests trap cool air and act as frost inhibitors. The recurrent *combes* which bisect the Côte laterally on an east–west axis are a major macro element in the climate and exert a profound influence on vineyards. They act as conduits for rain, humidity and for small rivers as well as forming efficient wind tunnels which accelerate air-flow, catching exposed vineyards in their path. Some are wider than others, but all play an important part in modifying air and water flow. Vineyards near the south-facing sides of these *combes* tend to produce wines of greater elegance perhaps because of receiving more sunlight – e.g. Les Cras and Les Fuées in Chambolle and the Clos St-Denis in Morey. Both La Romanée-Conti and Le Montrachet lie between two *combes* which influence fruit ripening through the movement of air.

Around each vine various influences combine to produce a localised climatic environment. These include the extent, height and distribution of the foliage canopy which impact on the maturity and quality of fruit at harvest. For example, removing leaves to expose bunches to direct sunlight near to harvest is thought to ripen tannins and pigments and to increase fruit concentration; equally, shading in hotter vintages protects the fruit from scorching. Heavy, less well-aerated canopies retain moisture and can promote rot or facilitate disease.

In considering weather and local climate, what matters is how the variables affect the building blocks of wine quality – the development of sugars, acids and enzymes and of tannins, pigments, flavour and aroma compounds. These processes depend upon a complex mix of factors. Research shows that the optimal temperature for enzymatic systems is 20–22°C and around 25°C for the growth and retention of volatile compounds. However, the chemical messengers (cytokinins) which play an important role at various stages of vine growth appear to require much cooler temperatures while the vine root zone needs an average temperature in excess of 30°C to function optimally. It is clear that with Pinot Noir and Chardonnay retention or loss of many aroma and flavour compounds is temperature sensitive; too cool and they lack aroma, colour and flavour; in excessive heat they disappear through the berry wall. Anthocyanins and tannins are stable and non-volatile and therefore not at risk from unduly high temperatures, although they do alter in character and concentration. Evidently a multiplicity of climatic factors bears upon the growth and development of a bunch of grapes and that in the Côte d'Or these are subject to subtle local variation.

The burgundian climate is thus a major determinant of outcomes, as the severity of excessively hot and dry final stages of the growing season will easily compromise quality – as indeed will cool and wet. A mild final two months is the ideal. What is equally true is that, despite being a region of marginal ripeness for Pinot (if less so for Chardonnay), barring natural disasters viticulture sensitively adapted to prevailing conditions will produce fruit which can then be transformed into wine which is both attractive and reflective of its *terroir* identity. Climate is not just a natural phenomenon that growers must accept, but an ever-present challenge to which, within obvious constraints, they must actively respond.

Drainage conduits - here in Romanée-Conti - help discharge excess water

CHAPTER 9
THE SIGNIFICANCE OF VINTAGE

Vintages have captured the imagination. They mesmerise critics and consumers alike and have become the focus for judging not only the wines of Burgundy but most others besides. Buying decisions are often based entirely on the reputation of the vintage and it is this more than anything that determines price and saleability. On the Côte, the quality potential of any given vintage is a complex amalgam of weather, local climate variation and vineyard topography. Generalities may capture the character of a vintage but inevitably gloss over significant differences between one village, *climat* or producer and another within the broad envelope.

In one sense a vintage is the summation of a single growing season from bud burst to harvest. This, the weather, differs from year to year. The amounts and distribution of light, heat, wind and rainfall produce important variations in the accumulation of the multitude of substances needed to produce ripe, balanced grapes. In Burgundy's irregular northerly climate fruit composition varies from season to season, from vineyard to vineyard and even from one row of vines to another. Weather leaves its imprint on wines – both in terms of quantity, overall quality level, and particular taste qualities. Some years produce naturally riper, more powerful wines while others are less opulent, leaner and more elegant. Some vintages are marked by more obvious tannins (1988), others by more obvious fruit (1985, 1989, 2002), others by a lack of concentration (1987, 2004), others by heat (1976, 2003). Within the overall pattern variations are often determined by extreme weather disasters – for example, storms, hail or frost; these tend to be localised impacting more on quantity than on quality. Abnormal events often strike in one place and not another hitting one commune or vineyard but not its neighbour. Weather is far from even-handed!

Burgundy's producers understand these variables and prefer to discuss individual *cuvées* rather than a vintage en bloc. For them, the primary focus is not to make the best wine possible from the material available but to achieve maximum expression of *terroir*; to give voice to the individuality of specific plots within the framework of the vintage. This perspective, which defines the finest wines as those which maximise typicity, does not always chime with vintage. Naturally riper years may produce attractive wines but not necessarily better Burgundy.

In another sense, vintage is the 'year' on the label. As the stated year need only contain 85% of wine from that particular vintage there is no guarantee that the wine will be 100% from a single crop. In times past inter-vintage blending routinely enabled a

grower to use a stronger vintage to bolster a weaker one and there is nothing to prevent a *vigneron* doing this today. That no-one will admit to this doesn't mean they don't. However, the rule is open to abuse as it obscures the destination of the 15% siphoned off to be replaced by 15% of other wine.

The idea of 'vintage' as a simple marker of a season's wine quality is a gift to traders and journalists. Each year wine-writers work up a piece (or several) to offer their assessment of the current crop. These judgements become definitive, defining the wider perception of the year, and once published are rarely revised. Thus does the reputation of a vintage become fixed – 'buy' or 'avoid' – with little room for nuance. Making vintage the main perceived determinant of quality glosses over differences in *terroirs*, growers' styles and local conditions. A pity, and indeed a distortion, because many attractive, even great wines are produced in most years and there is plenty to avoid in the 'must-buy' vintages. Vintage assessments are useful style guides, but less valuable as pointers to individual success and failure. If vintages weren't such convenient pegs of assessment there would undoubtedly be a much greater inclination to look at individual wines.

The distinct preference for 'big' vintages – the riper the better – reflects years of conditioning the market to accept that size, power, opulence, extract and concentration are the rightful hallmarks of quality. In such circumstances there is understandably less interest in leaner vintages. This polarisation is irrational and steers consumers away from much that is fine. While, up to a point, heat concentrates fruit flavour, it also concentrates tannins while reducing acidities in all but old vines whose deep roots seem to assure them of balanced fruit whatever the weather. Riper vintages certainly produce excellent wines – generally well-balanced, approachable, fruit-laden, with ripe tannins and acids – but unless vineyards are carefully managed, excessive heat risks hardening and thickening the skins of Pinot Noir and concentrates sugars to the point where *terroir* identity is submerged under alcohol, extract and tannin; Chardonnay becomes fat and frowsy, lacking in either grip or finesse. Opulence blurs the purity and definition which makes great Burgundy so exciting. This reinforces the view that the vintages best positioned to express *terroir* are not always the biggest, richest or ripest.

Cooler vintages, in contrast, have a longer, slower ripening profile which produces wines with more elegance, higher acidities, brighter tannins and often a more attractive balance of natural constituents. Such conditions preserve aroma and flavour nuances which readily burn off in great heat. Alcohols are more moderate and can, if necessary, be fine-tuned by chaptalisation. In less ripe vintages, Pinot Noir is however vulnerable as its relatively thin skin exacerbates the difficulty of producing concentration without excessive extraction. For example, the best 1991s were lovely, full of depth and expression but many misread their fruit producing harsh wines with a bitter, tannic edge. Such years also suffer from a lack of consumer understanding that wines with high tannins and acidity need time to resolve. 'Poor' vintages often produce remarkable surprises – not all the 1983s were dilute or rot-tainted; 1986 was generally excellent for whites, if uninspiring for reds and there are some truly delicious 2004s in both colours. Not perhaps vintages to buy blind or indeed drink young but, given patient cellaring, ones which often hide delightful secrets. After all, the individuality of *climat* often only starts to speak once the ephemeral seasonal influences of weather and vinification are out of the way.

Individual harvest policy also makes for style and quality variation within the envelope of the vintage. When, what and how grapes are picked affects fruit balance in terms of acids, pigmentation, tannins, polyphenols, sugars and so forth. The last days and weeks of the growing season are critical in Burgundy, a period of unstable autumnal weather – and a little more or less heat, light or rain can make the difference between an excellent and a merely good result. Many years have been blessed with late September sunshine and warmth which have effectively saved the vintage (in recent times 1991, 2001, 2008).

Yield also plays an important, though not decisive, part in a vintage's quality. It used to be thought that there was an invariable inverse relationship between the two – the greater the quantity, the lesser the quality – but this article of faith has been exploded by many fine vintages which combined high crop volume with high quality: among them 1990, 1996, 1999. What does hold good is that there appears to be an optimum charge of grapes that a vineyard or block of vines can ripen and this varies from site to site and from year to year. Forty hectolitres per hectare may be consistent with *Grand Cru* quality in Chambertin in 2005 but not in 2007 when 30–35 hl/ha is all the vineyard could ripen successfully. This ideal level may not be reached because of poor fruit set or adverse weather, or exceeded by heavy rain causing vines to pump water and thus dilute the crop. This to some extent makes nonsense of the AC system of pre-determined maximum yields with blanket percent-

age increase in the event of a big crop, and a compelling case for annual revision, site by site, to take account of prevailing conditions.

Several conclusions suggest themselves: first, given the primacy of *terroir* in burgundian thinking, preference should be for vintages which maximise this potential; second, no two vintages in Burgundy are alike; third, there is no straightforward correlation between weather conditions and wine quality; fourth, that in any given vintage, significant differences exist between communes, vineyards and producers which seriously limit the value of broad brush-stroke assessments (and scores), and fifth, that while highly acclaimed vintages undoubtedly produce some magnificent wines it is not always these which best express the Côte's typicities. Difficult as it might be to accept, there is no obvious correlation between the quality of a message and the volume at which it is delivered; indeed, generally the reverse.

Vintages clearly matter, but the abundance of quality in almost every vintage dictates a less dogmatic approach from critics and consumers. For the latter, the message is that in Burgundy their value as indicators of quality has been greatly overplayed.

Vintages matter in Burgundy - but not to the extent that many believe

Chapter 10
Understanding &
Managing Vineyards

Quality begins in the vineyard. In Burgundy, as elsewhere, the realisation that if the potential for flavour, aroma, concentration and typicity are not in the fruit at harvest, no amount of winemaking wizardry can restore them has radically altered the mindset of many producers. Time was when the winemaker's pitch was 'bring me some fruit (preferably ripe) and I will turn it into great wine'. Like the master chefs of the past, the secret was in the recipe, the skilled combining of ingredients that turned often mundane raw materials into something magical. No longer: while today's chef expends much time and energy sourcing produce for maximum purity and flavour, his winemaking counterpart, if he is not graphically stupid, is superintending the care of his vineyards to ensure that his vines are healthy and primed to produce optimally ripe, concentrated fruit containing the best possible balance of constituents. Nowadays, viticulture is a noble profession and an estate's viticulturalist is at least as important as its winemaker, arguably more so. The advantage of the Côte's small family-run domaines is that they are often the same person or close family. Good *vignerons* develop a close affinity with their vines, knowing the characteristics and difficulties presented by each plot; they cultivate, treat and harvest appropriately, a skill well beyond even the most sophisticated machine.

The essentials of vineyard management are common to all good plant husbandry. Any amateur gardener understands the necessity for healthy soils and plants and sensitivity to both for best results. Producing *vin de terroir* imposes its own require-ments: *vignerons* must 'read' their land, observe how vines grow and behave on it in order to understand and respect its individu-ality and thus enable the vine to best express its origins through its fruit. This requires viticulture which is both precise and cerebral, eschewing products and practices which cause long-term damage, and developing a fine sensitivity to the balance between plant and environment. In addition, the *vignerons* must adapt to the conditions and vagaries each season brings.

Over the years, the Côte's vineyards have suffered lasting damage from five major sources: overfertilisation, virus infection, overproductive clones, use of the inappropriate SO4 rootstock and planting of the productive Pinot Droit vine. Considerable effort has been devoted to correcting these problems, but they continue to influence wine quality. Potassium, heavily used after the Second World War to promote growth, remains in soils reducing acidity in wines. Viruses, particularly *court noué* (= fan-leaf), are endemic, degenerative and diminish productivity. Inferior material (especially the productive Pinot Droit) remains even in important *Grand* and *Premier Cru* sites. SO4 still exists but is in decline. It takes time to reconstitute a vineyard, but as these problems work themselves out, yields will naturally decrease and quality increase.

Unfortunately, in the recent past the prevailing perspective has been that of preventive medicine with chemicals used to eradicate undesirable insect, bacterial and microbial activity. The realisation that this was no long-term solution as these strong systemic and contact prophyalxes were broad spectrum, killing both good and bad micro-organisms indiscriminately and weakening many desirable ones in the process, refocused *vignerons* on promoting conditions which increased the vine's natural resilience. As the agronomist Claude Bourguignon put it, milk has become bad for health not because it contains too many microbes but because it contains too few. Today's approach is less interventionist: where the prophylactic approach sought to dominate the land, this listens to it. Technology is not excluded but repositioned as a resource to be used only when it improves on traditional practice. This shift of emphasis has made a signal difference both to wine quality and to the long-term viability of the Côte's vineyards. An evolution rather than a tipping point, but significant nonetheless.

The intimacy of working with small plots of vines taught a new generation that there is no unique recipe for vineyard management. Different *terroirs* behave differently and often need bespoke regimes. Because *terroir* can change significantly within a few metres on the Côte, the conduct of vines here is inherently more complex than would be the case for a larger vineyard on relatively uniform soils. Burgundy's fragmented pattern of ownership is perfectly designed for the *vigneron* as winemaker. What follows sets out the more important consid-erations that should exercise his mind.

Man made drainage channels (here at Aloxe-Corton) help minimise soil erosion

WHAT TO PLANT

efore a vineyard can be managed, it has to be planted and decisions taken here will profoundly influence quality of wine produced. There are two main areas of concern: what to plant and how to plant it. The plant is the interface between the earth and its wider growing environment. To express *terroir* at maximum level it needs maximum vitality and this requires minimum interference with this interface. Today's vine is a two-part graft: the upper part – the scion – is the variety (Pinot, Chardonnay); the lower part – the rootstock – links the vine to its growing medium. Each part comes with a selection of attributes. In the pre-phylloxera era, before the Comte de la Loyère, owner of Château de Savigny-lès-Beaune, started experimenting with vine training as we now know it (*palissage*) in the 1850s, vines were planted '*en foule*' on their own roots (*franc de pied*) and propagated by *provinage* – layered, hedge-like, one onto the next. While phylloxera put an end to 'own-roots' planting, Pinot Noir's naturally tendency to mutate

Newly planted young vine next to a well-established vine in Chevalier-Montrachet

and growers' capturing these in individual selections led to a great diversity of plant material.

CLONES

Today, the decision on the upper part of the vine (the scion) lies between bought-in clones or material propagated from individual vines, often from the same vineyard (= *sélection massale*). A grape variety is a large family sharing the same genetic make up but exhibiting a variety of different characteristics. This is reflected in the enormous selection of scion material since clones were introduced in the 1960s. The first commercial clones were bred for productivity and resistance to the fan-leaf and leaf-roll viruses which ravaged Burgundy's vineyards after the Second World War, particularly in the Côte de Beaune. The best of today's clones are quality-oriented, preference being for lower yield, looser bunch configuration (tight bunches assist the spread of rot and disease), small berry size and good bunch weight; some produce more colour, others higher sugars, better acidity or structure which further complicates the planting decision. The range continues to expand and improve with burgundian selections preferred worldwide for quality Pinot and Chardonnay plantings.

Is a single clone or mix of several best? The arguments range around wine quality, purity of *terroir* expression and vine health. The evidence is inconclusive as both systems produce excellent, even great wines. Some believe that single clones give one-dimensional flavours whereas a mix increases complexity, others that a single clone gives better delineated *terroir* expression. On these, the jury is still out. The founding father of clones, Raymond Bernard, insists his trials show no significant differences between single clones and a mix and indeed, many excellent non-burgundian Pinots come from single clone plantings. However, as each single clone carries the same attributes and defects as the mother block from which it came, a mix has the advantage of providing an element of insurance if one clone succumbs to disease. For this reason, most new plantings in Burgundy use a clonal mix. As far as yield goes, somewhat against conventional wisdom there seems to be no simple correlation between a clone's productivity and wine quality – the best recipe being a mix of higher and lower yielding clones. What is indisputable is that while clone selection can improve quality and assist in expressing site identity it is no compensation for inappropriate site selection, excessive yields or inept winemaking. Provided harvest fruit quality is balanced in terms of phenolic ripeness, sugars, pH, acid and so forth, a judicious clone selection can add interest and complexity. This idea is being extended by some (notably in the USA) who are working with field blends of different clones.

The use of clones is not universal: several top quality Domaines (Romanée-Conti, Dujac, Gouges among others) eschew (or more accurately distrust) clones preferring to select scion material from their own vineyards by a screening process which marks the best individual vines and propagates budwood from them (*sélection massale*). Mass-selected material is felt to be better adapted to, and thus more expressive of, its origins. Others prefer it on the grounds that, if done intelligently, yields are reduced without the need for artificial concentration. In this they look for colour density, skin thickness and tannin development in red grapes, acid retention and dry extract in whites. *Sélection massale* is criticised for being less disease resistant; however, choosing the healthiest plants from which to propagate is also to select those that have proved best adapted to their environment.

There is also an historical element to the planting decision. The undoubted excellence of Burgundy's greatest wines depended on the quality of early vine selections. Aubert de Villaine refers to the historical value of '*plants fins* and *très fins*' which were planted on the Côte pre-phylloxera and which undoubtedly contribute to the quality of a *Cru*, propagated by *provinage; 'un patrimoine sans prix'*. He stresses the importance of maintaining diversity in the plant population and adds that many clones were selected for quantity or for convenience of working. Others point to the importance of retaining and perpetuating 'memory' by selecting the best plants – those that regularly produce ripe, balanced fruit, small berries, *millerands*, and well-aerated bunches. Such historical references are part of the experience and judgement of those who work the Côte's vineyards and, as such, deserve attention and respect.

ROOTSTOCKS

It is widely believed that to the extent that they influence growth patterns, rootstocks also influence *terroir* definition. For ultimate *terroir* expression, vines would be grown on their own roots; although this is seen as impractical, some experts are now advocating own-root planting and then managing the inevitable infestation – not a realistic proposition for a grower with a few precious rows of *Grand Cru*. Since phylloxera devastated most of Europe's vineyards in the 1870s it is accepted that the

Immature Pinot Noir grapes in mid-summer

only way to prevent recurrence of the malady – which remains in the soil – is to graft scions onto phylloxera-resistant roots. Not just any roots, but those best adapted to prevailing conditions, particularly those of site and soil. The choice of rootstock is hugely important, influencing as it does such attributes as; lime tolerance, vegetative growth habit, tendency to increase/decrease scion vegetative growth, budding dates, tolerance to drought conditions, pest and disease, etc. On the Côte this means low vigour and tolerance of active lime. Preferred root stocks are 3309, 161/49, Riparia, 5BB, 125AA. SO4 has high vigour and can burn out after around twenty years, so is best avoided; 5BB appears to work well as does 125AA which has good tolerance of active limestone, adapts to a wide range of soils, especially poorer sites with heavy clays, and is more devigorating than 3309.

Managing for Quality

Having selected the plant material, the *vigneron* has to choose how to plant it. The important considerations here are planting density and row configuration. Until relatively recently in Burgundy, vines were planted 10,000 per hectare (one vine per square metre in a 1 x 1 metre configuration). This is now on the increase with densities reaching 12,000 or even 13,000 vines per hectare. The thinking behind this is that denser planting encourages root competition, thereby forcing vines to delve deeper for moisture and nourishment. This extends the belief that *terroir* character is best expressed by nutrients and trace elements found at depth rather than on the surface. Deep roots also give a vine a better chance of surviving drought than surface root systems in ground which may easily dry out in hot spells.

Planting configuration includes row orientation. In Burgundy vines are normally planted on the vertical axis with the slope. However, in places (particularly in sections of the *Grands Crus* in Morey St-Denis) vines have been oriented along the contour to minimise soil erosion, a constant problem on the Côte even in relatively shallow-sloping vineyards. Whatever the configuration, the *vigneron* has to be aware that one side of a row may receive more heat, light or shade than the other and thus may require different treatment to ensure even ripeness.

Planting decisions remain part of a vineyard's character for its lifetime and the naturally enhanced quality of older vines provides a strong incentive to promote longevity. Old vines are a precious resource for any *vigneron*, being more resilient and lower yielding; age also brings greater flavour concentration and complexity, better structures and an indefinable dimension of old-vineyness. In Burgundy a 20–30-year-old Pinot vine is still considered young – an apprentice fruit provider which has yet to reach maturity and thus become of real interest; old vines are anything from 30–130 years old and are an essential component of most great wine. Age in Chardonnay vines is less important as the limited skin contact it generally receives means that phenolics play a relatively minor role. However, extracting maximum concentration with such vinification requires that the fruit is fully physiologically ripe.

It is not clear precisely why vines age to produce wines of character and expressiveness. Indeed, whether a vine is good because it is old or old because it is intrinsically good (survival of the fittest) is debatable. Older vines often have small berries

Winter pruning beneath the Corton hill

which impart greater concentration of aroma and flavour, but the precise path to reduced berry size is critical – selection of plant material and dehydration will produce completely different qualities. The superior quality of older vines may merely reflect their better adaptation to site.

YIELDS AND FRUIT QUALITY

Where fruit quality is concerned, the fashionable mantra is that low yields are the only honest way to make great wine. Domaine Leroy is the arch exponent of this philosophy. Lalou Bize-Leroy reports a 20-year average yield of 15 hl/ha across her vineyards and is certain that by concentrating flavour you thereby concentrate *terroir* expression. A contrary view, expressed by Dominique Lafon among others, is that you must neither artificially stress vines to diminish yield or push them to increase it but keep each plant in balance with its environment where it will naturally ripen the right amount of fruit. His wines (mainly Chardonnay), from an average yield of 40 hl/ha, are rightly considered among Burgundy's finest as are those of Jean-François Coche (Coche-Dury) from yields reaching 48 hl/ha for Meursault *Village* and 40–45 hl/ha in *Premier Cru*. There is clearly no *a priori* incompatibility between quality and a decent yield nor is the relationship the simple inverse that is often claimed; big crops do not always mean indifferent quality or vice versa. Nor is there credible evidence that reducing yields beyond a certain point increases wine quality; the reduction *ad absurdum* of one drop per vine would not necessarily produce exceptional wine. The word that tends to be forgotten is 'optimum' – each vine is capable of ripening so much fruit and that quantity varies from season to season. In general, great Pinot is incompatible with yields over 35 hl/ha in any circumstances, and great Chardonnay in excess of 45 hl/ha; this 10 hl/ha differential between them is maintained year on year. What growers strive for is balanced fruit: in reds this means two-thirds liquid to one-third solids – with sufficient grape sugar to produce 12–13.5% alcohol and tannins that are ripe, not green or bitter. At 10,000 producing vines per hectare, this equates to 5–7 small bunches per vine. Improved fruit quality means not just better overall ripeness, but more consistent, even ripeness and, with reds, finer tannins.

PRUNING

The vine is a weed which will proliferate wildly if left unchecked. Pruning controls its natural vigour, area of foliage and reduces crop size. Potential yield depends both on the vineyard (vine age, soil nutrients and general vigour), on the vines themselves (clone and rootstock) and on the vintage conditions. The *vigneron's* challenge is to work out how to optimise yield without sacrificing quality. His main weapons are: short pruning and severe debudding to reduce the potential number of bunches per vine and, if necessary, crop thinning later in the season.

Pruning is a key operation to remove last year's wood and to prepare the vine for the coming season; it is best done in the late winter or early spring when the sap is rising and spore populations are at their lowest to discourage the take-up of airborne fungal diseases. There are many considerations involved, not the least of which is vine age: sap has difficulty in passing through hard, old wood whereas the 'pipework' is less restricted in a young vine. Fertility is not even throughout a vine – the buds furthest from the stem are the most fertile; some growers report that in young vines the fruit at the end of the cordon gives around one degree more potential alcohol than that near the stem. Pruning must also adapt to the size of the last harvest, possible diseases and whatever climatic accidents (hail, frost) it may have undergone. The best *vignerons* prune severely – a calculated risk as it leaves no insurance for aborted flowering or low fertility. Timing also matters as it influences the stimulation of the vines and thus bud burst, flowering date, harvest date and crop levels. As the old burgundian saw has it: 'Prune early or prune late, nothing beats March's date'.

During the growing season, further measures are taken to control yield and promote quality: excess buds and shoots are removed (green pruning) to concentrate energy in the remaining bunches and later, foliage is periodically trimmed and thinned to balance leaf and fruit. The vine has two cycles – the first, vegetative, lasts until around the end of July and accumulates sugar in leaf development, particularly in the last three months; the second, after the grapes change colour (*veraison*) directs energy away from leaf development into seed and berry growth. If the potential crop still seems too large, there is always the option of crop thinning (= *vendange en vert*) This is very much *à la mode* but the reality is that it is a skilled operation which needs careful timing; overdoing it risks compensatory activity producing too high sugars before the grapes are fully ripe. Most regard this as a last resort, in naturally abundant vintages and realise that it has to be drastic to have any real effect. Too regular crop-thinning suggests less than rigorous use of the pruning shears.

Chardonnay vine in flower

TRAINING

As well as being pruned, vines are trained rather than being allowed to grow wild. As Paul Draper of Ridge Vineyards, California explains, this affects 'yield and the exposure of fruit to sunlight, factors that affect maturity of the grape and its flavours, which in turn affect texture'. Recent years have seen a change in thinking in Burgundy on how this is best done. The traditional Guyot system uses one cane tied horizontally off the vine stem, with 6–8 buds for the current crop, plus a separate short stem pruned to 2 buds for next year's cane. At 10,000 vines per hectare this gives 80,000–100,000 buds per hectare – considered ideal for balanced fertility. This system, developed by Dr Guyot in the late 1800s during reconstruction of vineyards after phylloxera and oïdium, was designed principally to promote yields to help struggling *vignerons*. Now the prevailing feeling is that Guyot is maladapted to quality Pinot Noir production and many have switched to the Cordon de Royat system, already used by tradition to reduce yields on heavier soils in Santenay and Chassagne-Montrachet. This has one or two branches run either side of the stem from which canes are trained upwards. According to Domaine Dujac, whose vines are now all Cordon trained, 'moving to Cordon was key to extra stuffing in wine'. They report improved fruit quality all round: more even ripeness, less vine vigour, better airflow, cleaner canopies and healthier grapes. Although the benefits are not universally accepted, Cordon training is spreading to the Côte de Nuits, particularly with new plantings where it is seen as a valuable expedient for calming the vigour of young vines. There are even experiments with the Gobelet system which brings canes upwards directly from the vine stem in a goblet-shaped configuration.

SMALLER BLOCKS

Any *vigneron* serious about quality works individually with smaller plots. He will notionally divide one block into different 'sub-blocks' – reflecting vine-age, clone, rootstock, soil differences, changes in drainage or exposition. As a row's orientation to sun and wind affects how its fruit ripens, it makes sense to treat the shaded side differently from that which isn't; old vines need different viticulture to young vines, dry soils to damp soils etc. Attention to such details marks out the great from the merely good.

CANOPY MANAGEMENT

As well as being pruned and trained, each vine needs to have its leaf canopy managed during the growing season. Until recently many burgundian *vignerons* probably thought canopy management referred to where to pitch your beach umbrella on your Caribbean holiday; most now take this very seriously. A well-managed canopy helps optimise fruit quality: it provides a balance between leaf and fruit and allows the penetration of sunlight and heat; it also facilitates airflow through the foliage to dry off excess moisture which both counters Botrytis and disperses airborne infestations. A few centimetres higher summer pruning, more thoughtful leaf thinning to take account of plot siting and exposition, and encouraging low hanging canes to allow more radiated heat all pay worthwhile dividends.

One notable area of progress has been the practice of regular deleafing to expose bunches (and flowers) to direct sunlight, especially in the lower 'belt-line' areas of the canopy. This helps both to even out flowering and later to ripen tannins and wood. However, there is some evidence that direct sunlight acts selectively on phenolics – not always on those most desirable characteristics. Increasing canopy size can generate high sugars in suitable conditions, but does not of itself increase fruit ripeness. So a fine balance of light and shading is required.

It was thought that once autumn defoliation had occurred there was no advance in fruit ripening. Now growers such as Domaine Rousseau in Gevrey actively encourage leaf drop and find that a few days of direct exposure to the sun at the end of the growing season add to tannin ripeness and flavour complexity. Conversely, in hotter sites of the United States, for example, growers will use shade cloth to cover the fruit zone and reduce insolation.

Tying vines - essential early season work

SOIL

Soil is a living entity whose microbial life provides the interface between mineral and vegetal; its flora and fauna take ingredients necessary to the plant and render them assimilable. Being specific to the type of soil/subsoil and also climate sensitive they are a critical vector for the expression of *terroir* in wine. Soils differ physically, chemically and biologically all of which influence vine growth, making active soil management an integral part of quality wine production.

Burgundy still suffers to a limited degree for decades of treating soil as little more than a convenient growing medium and a collective disregard of critical importance of its living inhabitants. Excessive use of ever stronger industrial pesticides, herbicides and acaricides severely diminished microflora and beneficial insect life to the point that soils became virtually inert. Up to the 1980s, artificially stimulating vine vigour by additions of nitrogen, phosphorous and potassium in pursuit of increased yields led not only to phytosanitary problems and product resistance but, critically, to impoverishment of taste and quality from grapes lacking flavour, complexity and acid–sugar balance. This has taken decades to reverse. Healthy soil contains microflora, such as yeasts and other organisms including worms, parasites and nematodes which can support or hinder the vine. Indeed, vineyards are thought by many to have specific populations of micro-organisms which play a role in *terroir* expression. Recognition that soil vitality is as important as vine health now drives the top end of the Côte's viticulture.

Good soil management involves keeping the earth aerated to maximise water drainage and encourage root penetration. While heavy tractors compact the topsoil making drainage difficult and stifling aeration, working the ground increases the chance of erosion but brings essential oxygen; reduced oxygen diminishes the formation of oxides which in turn limits the vine's access to nutrient sources. *Vignerons* also recognise that different soils respond differently to heat and rain: some warm more slowly which means later bud burst and a delayed vegetative cycle, others are more heat-retentive or better-drained.

Roots, another important vector for fruit quality, also need care. Vines have two types of roots: laterals, which spread out near the soil surface, and tap roots, which nourish the vine from deep water and nutrient sources. Good vineyard practice encourages the development of deep rather than shallow roots by ploughing to cut surface laterals. Unfortunately, the advent of convenient machinery and sprays led many *vignerons* to stop working their soil, preferring herbicides to ploughing in weeds and grasses, giving vineyards the appearance of manicured English gardens.

The assimilation of nutrients and trace elements are regarded as essential to *terroir* expression. Although imperfectly understood, the mechanisms seem to involve natural weathering of the rock substratum – i.e. the limestone is dissolved – giving matter which the vine then assimilates and converts into olfactory and gustatory compounds. Vines will nourish themselves from surface nutrients if these are readily available rather than using their pre-programmed genetic processes to seek out the mineral complexes which are essential for more elaborate flavour development. Research indicates that soil management can alter the availability and uptake of these complexes, so the minerals need to be present in suitable form and the soils such as to encourage their absorption. Too much organic matter and poor drainage are known limiting factors. The value of deep roots is that they expose the vine to a larger potential reservoir of water and mineral nutrients.

Soil erosion is a continuing problem in Burgundy; heavy rains wash away topsoil even in gently sloping sites which over time changes their character unless it is collected and replaced. One means of limiting erosion, much favoured in the 1970s and 1980s, is to plant selected grasses between the vine rows. While grasses both exclude alien vegetation and retain moisture, they compete with vines for nutrition and water. For many, the experience is that wine made from 'grassed' vines, while having more body tends to lose focus, luminosity and purity; for others the reverse holds true. Pierre Gouges, whose Domaine pioneered the use of grassing, tells of a plot of Chênes Carteaux, immediately above Nuits' Les Saint Georges, replanted in 1955. The early wines were only of *Village* quality, but once grasses were interplanted quality improved to *Premier Cru* level, a circumstance he ascribes to the promotion of more and deeper root development.

Stony soil and Cabotte above Clos des Lambrays

Leaf roll virus in Clos de Vougeot

PESTS AND DISEASES

How to handle pests and maladies is no longer a controversial subject. Up to the late 1980s synthetic sprays were in regular use, whether or not there was a problem – this was preventive medicine and contributed significantly to soil impoverishment. Thereafter, one either worked on a 'treat as required' basis or else converted to an organic regime, using only permitted non-synthetics. Disaffection with chemicals has spread, greatly assisted by the development of means to stimulate the vine's natural tolerance of disease and of selectively destabilising pests' reproductive cycles. Improvements in application – including precision sprays – have also had manifest benefits, reducing quantities required and limiting covering neighbouring vines with unwanted chemicals. Viruses are not the problem they once were and moderate infection can be managed or even (as biodynamic adherents aver) eradicated. Some believe that up to a point virus-infected vines are a positive influence in that they naturally reduce yields; however viruses can also cause a reduction in quality and, in the long term, a virused vineyard is not sustainable.

BIODYNAMICS

By far the most significant development in burgundian viticulture has been the uptake of biodynamics. This involves elements of both homoeopathy and astrology with the overriding aim of restoring the soil's trace and base elements, natural fauna and micro flora (especially yeasts) and reinvigorating the vine's vitality and natural defence mechanisms. Treatments use some nine principal compounds, prepared from natural ingredients – silica, nettle, yarrow, chamomile, valerian, oak bark, dandelion and the like. Some are sprayed directly; others contribute to bespoke compost, while a *materia medica* provides remedies for specific problems. The principle is to treat different parts of the plant at precise times determined by the lunar cycle's influence on leaves, flowers, roots and grapes. The treatments, prepared by 'dynamisation' on homoeopathic dilution principles and matured in cow horns, work by stimulating what is naturally present in soil and plant.

Not surprisingly, biodynamics has polarised expert opinion. As with mainstream homoeopathy, there is vehement scepticism from those who consider it untestable and thus unverifiable. Others, such as agronomist Claude Bourguignon, while admitting that the mechanisms may be imperfectly understood with no demonstrable cause–effect chain, find mensurable differences in biodynamic and non-biodynamic soils in terms of improved vine root depth and thickness, increased populations of beneficial organisms and greater biodiversity. Yeasts, which form as a bloom on grapes and are seen by many (including the likes of Jean-François Coche-Dury) as an integral part of site specificity, are reported as being strengthened both in number and vigour by biodynamic viticulture. Tangential benefits come in significant cost saving from using low doses of non-toxic preparations.

For producers the perceived benefits of re-establishing the integrity of the vine within its environment on both wine quality and vine health are beyond doubt. Many Domaines, now with years of biodynamic experience under their belts, report: better overall maturity, in particular higher sugars; earlier and better physiological maturity, important in marginal regions such as the Côte d'Or; smaller berries and thus lower yields; more even ripeness; more regular year-on-year maturity, and significantly improved disease resistance. This latter is particularly striking: at least two five-star Burgundy Domaines report that plots of terminally *court-noué* virused vines were restored to full health and productivity following biodynamic handling.

Eschewing conventional treatments brings its problems. In particular, the treatment of rot and mildew causes concern for biodynamic operations. The usual remedy, copper sulphate, is only usable in very small quantities in biodynamic regimens so an element of 'pray and hope' rather than 'spray and cope' is called for. However, as biodynamically treated vines tend to develop strengthened natural resistance, the need to pray is counterbalanced with a diminished need for hope.

The benefits follow through to the cellar with reduced amounts of spray residue in juice giving cleaner and more predictable, ferments. Pierre Morey, a first-division Meursault *vigneron*, finds that bought-in fruit from non-biodynamic viticulture requires more attention, more *bâtonnage* and shows a greater likelihood of stopped fermentation than that from his own biodynamic vines. As to the wines, tasters repeatedly pick out biodynamic samples from non-biodynamic controls in blind tastings, reporting them to have more energy and finer acidity; fruit aromas are better defined and minerality more profound. In general, *terroirs* show greater precision and transparency in wines of finer purity and distinction.

The fact that the science remains unresolved does not mean that biodynamics is akin to necromancy as some detractors claim. The quality of Domaines who, after considerable experimentation, now work biodynamically – Lafon, Leflaive, Leroy, Romanée-Conti among many others – is powerful testament to its credibility. As with mainstream homoeopathy, 'unproven' does not mean 'chimerical'.

Phacelia cover crop in ground to be replanted in Romanée-Conti

HARVEST

Timing the harvest is among a burgundian *vigneron*'s most critical decisions. The window of opportunity is narrow as autumn equinoctial storms can disrupt fruit balance through rain dilution or rain/hail-induced rot. However, when your annual income depends upon having wine to sell, it takes guts to wait for rain-soaked fruit to dry out. In seasons where flowering is early, in late May rather than June, an earlier harvest allows more flexibility in timing, allowing *vignerons* to fine-tune picking plot by plot, rather than having to rush to beat bad weather. The overriding aim is to pick properly ripe fruit, but determining ripeness is far from an exact science. Under- or overripe grapes produce inherently unbalanced wine which, up to a point, compromises *terroir* expression, so attaining proper maturity assumes prime importance at Burgundy's northerly latitude.

The background to the enigma that is fruit ripeness lies in understanding two important propositions: first, that analytically equally ripe grapes may disguise completely different patterns of development and thus produce completely different wines; second, that even within a single bunch of grapes ripeness is often far from homogeneous. It is likely that vines are programmed not to ripen all their fruit simultaneously – an extended ripening period has obvious survival value. In addition, there is a particular problem with Pinot Noir which is known for its compactness, one clear causative factor. What the grower seeks is even ripeness, both through the vineyard and within bunches; otherwise he has to go to inordinate lengths to remove over- or underripe berries.

A ripe grape contains the summation of a season's weather. Sugars and acids in the pulp, tannins and colouring pigments in the skins develop at different times and rates, often in trace quantities. Many of these compounds are precursors of flavour – untasteable until transformed into wine. As the concentrations and balance of these constituents determine the aromas and flavours of wine made from them, it is essential that all the necessary components are present at harvest as, apart from a few crude adjustments, they cannot be added later.

The most common problem with Pinot Noir in Burgundy is achieving 'physiological ripeness'. This occurs when enough sugar has accumulated in the grapes at the same time as the skins and tannins are fully ripe. The converse, underripe phenolics, means that colour, flavour and aroma compounds are not fully developed at sugar ripeness which generally results in unbalanced wine with raw, often bitter tannins and limited aromatic potential. In Burgundy, in general, phenolics are ripe and the wait is for sugars to catch up. There is, however, no doubt that better, more age-worthy and structurally sound Burgundy can be salvaged from an underripe grape than from an overripe one although elsewhere style preferences may dictate the reverse.

The burgundian *vigneron*'s dilemma is whether to wait for the sugars to catch up, or pick under-ripe fruit and attempt to rebalance in the cellar. Some growers deliberately harvest early to avoid acid loss and rot (and for security) and rely on technology to correct deficiencies. Despite the *imprimatur* of an appellation certificate, these wines, while pleasant and with decent varietal character, lack *terroir* definition. This problem bedevils not only Burgundy but Pinot growers worldwide. Red wines made so far north tend in any case to a marked vegetal character and lack the warmth and opulent fleshiness of those from more southerly climes; in compensation, Burgundies have longer maturation potential than their southern brethren and develop greater interest and expressive nuance as they age.

Even given ripe fruit, how do you pick: all your vines in each entire appellation at a time, or in smaller blocks; and in what order? There are no easy answers. Some understandably pick their most valuable lots – *Grands* and *Premiers Crus* – first, to ensure these are not lost or damaged. The best Domaines harvest sequentially as each plot reaches ripeness and accept the risk of rain. If rain comes, does one pick and remove any rot or wait for the sun to return to dry and concentrate the berries? Provided skins are sufficiently thick, the rot risk is reduced although the juice may be diluted. In pursuit of perfect fruit, top-class Domaines have increased their harvesting budgets to have more, better trained and sober pickers, giving the flexibility to pick with maximum speed, block by block, at optimal ripeness. Larger Domaines with multiple appellations run the risk of not harvesting a vineyard at the ideal date, a problem which smaller estates are better placed to avoid. Few in the Côte mention mechanical harvesting; Pinot with its relatively thin skin and the sloping, parcelled nature of the vineyards are ill-suited to it. Even the best machines are undiscriminating, picking second-generation fruit (= *verjus*), unripe fruit and of course, no stalks. Mechanical harvesting also seems to give a slight, but noticeable, green element to wine.

Conscientious winemakers spend much time walking their land, working with their vineyard personnel, observing how each vine, row and block develops and fine-tuning detail to maximise fruit quality. Top-class wine demands precision viticulture. There is no short cut.

Acrobatic harvesting keeps you fit

CHAPTER 11
TURNING GRAPES INTO WINE

While quality certainly begins in the vineyard, it all too often ends in the cellar. This highlights the importance to the interested consumer of knowing something of the broad processes by which wine is put together. Visiting Domaines and walking vineyards develops a feeling of place, but it is impossible to taste critically without this additional background. This chapter provides a glimpse into the decisions involved in vinifying grapes, the choices that *vignerons* must make and their consequences. Winemaking is at least a skill but at most an art and it is the indefinable artistic element, the feel for the individuality of grapes and how to turn them into fine wine, which distinguishes great winemakers from mere technicians.

In Burgundy of course, one does not vinify Pinot Noir or Chardonnay, but this or that vineyard, the aim being the maximum *terroir* definition in a wine of purity, intensity and elegance. *Terroir* is the core and soul of wine – a belief

that, although varying in intensity from season to season, the constants of site identity are there, to a greater or lesser extent, irrespective of vintage conditions. This puts the vineyard at the heart of the winemaking process. The task of extracting these constants into wine, preserving them through *élevage* and finally delivering them into bottle informs every stage of burgundian winemaking. In this project the desires of the winemaker are tangential and on no account, except perhaps for higher volume generic wines, should there be conscious manipulation of style to suit this or that market. If you are lucky enough to have great *terroir* then it makes no sense to compromise it. Understanding a site's characteristics is slow and intellect-consuming; it takes years to assimilate a vineyard's subtleties and to work out how best to vinify its produce. Experiencing each growing season at first hand and observing the pattern of ripening in individual vineyards and blocks fine-tunes how each batch of fruit is handled. These thought processes start long before harvest.

Domaine Rousseau's Clos St-Jacques - note the yeast bloom on the berries

Interpreting the Grape

s any of the Côte's stellar winemakers will confirm, there are no great secrets or tricks – just the careful treatment of first-class raw material. Indeed, most mediocre wine is more likely to be at least in some measure attributable to deficient fruit rather than inept winemaking. There is no recipe for *Grand Vin*, rather a multiplicity of subtle variations within generally accepted guidelines to be adapted to the vineyard, vine age, vintage and sometimes even the time and space available for the job. For example, a *climat* that naturally produces higher tannin will not be vinified in the same way as one which gives less, or fruit from young vines in the same way as that from old vines. In general, hot ripe years tend to mask typicity while cooler ones give them greater expression, so flexibility is the key. In short, it is not a matter of how you cook chicken or salmon but of how you cook this particular chicken or that piece of salmon. This is the antithesis of the approach which turns wine into a commercial item where the winemaker 'produces'; in Burgundy, above all, he 'interprets'. However, this approach is not universal. There are some (for example, Frédy Mugnier) who are more formulaic in their winemaking from year to year on the grounds that by duplicating the process with every wine in the cellar you remove yet another source of variation, leaving *terroir* as the remaining variable in the mix.

Top-class fruit needs minimum manipulation to translate it into fine wine. Aubert de Villaine of Domaine de la Romanée-Conti puts the point concisely: 'You must be rigorous, exigent, and allow yourself not even the slightest diversion to this rule, of which the key words are: restraint, selection, mastery of methods, care for detail, minutiae, patience and, above all … humility. Nothing great will come from Burgundy without this rigour. The quality of man's decisions and the discipline with which they are implemented are so important' (in Jacky Rigaux, 2006, op. cit.). He also famously said that 'the ideal is to do nothing'. The late Henri Jayer, one of Burgundy's most famous winemakers, put it another way: 'You have to learn how to be lazy' – meaning that once the grapes are in the vat interference should be kept to a minimum. What they are saying is that *vignerons* should work with what the vintage provides and that well-constituted fruit will turn into balanced wine without undue manipulation. None of this denies the *vigneron*'s influence on what ends up in the bottle; rather, that inappropriate or excessive interference traduces *terroir*.

Understanding how to make fine Burgundy starts from the observation that its hallmarks are elegance and minerality

Automatic punch-down in traditional oak vats

coupled with an intense purity. Profoundly unscientific language this may be, but it will strike a chord in anyone who has ever been knocked sideways by a great Côte d'Or *Grand Cru*. Wines of such pedigree are distinguished by scintillating aromatics and, whatever textural or flavour qualities may accompany them, it is these that are *terroir*'s surest markers. This makes vinifying great *terroir* a fine balancing act and reinforces the inappropriateness of directing wine towards a predetermined style.

Preservation of subtlety is infinitely harder to achieve than destruction. Aromas are fragile and easily submerged under excessive oak, tannins or alcohol. Overworking red grapes to increase extraction makes wine taste good at the start of its evolution but produces an imbalance later on. The elements defining texture and mouthfeel may be refined in the cellar but are easily wrecked by rough handling. Fine-tuning structure and establishing a satisfactory acid and tannin balance are the hardest things to achieve in any wine. Pinot and Chardonnay are no exceptions.

Hands-on: Sorting tables are essential for ensuring that only ripe fruit finds its way into the vats

Within the general guidelines, much is elective. Consider a few of the variables for red grapes: whether to destem the fruit and if so how much; pre-fermentation cold soak or not; 100% natural yeasts or 100% inoculum or anything in between; punching down the cap or pumping over juice and how frequently; 10–40 days maceration on skins; malolactic fermentation in bulk or in cask; how often to rack; the appropriate amount of new oak for each wine and how long remains in cask. The permutations are limitless. The critical parameters are as follows:

SORTING

The *vigneron*'s first decision is what to put into his vats. In the Côte d'Or's northerly location, grapes are rarely perfectly or uniformly ripe making it essential to remove anything underripe, rotten or damaged and any second generation berries (*verjus*, *conscrits*) that may appear. Underripeness adds jarring acidity and green tannin, and even a small percentage of rot-infected fruit can contaminate a whole batch. Best practice starts with rigorous *triage* in the vineyard and continues in the cellar where grapes are run across a high-tech sorting table with a moving belt and ultra-violet lighting to ensure complete elimination of unwanted material. Sloppiness here is invariably punished.

CONCENTRATION VS. EXTRACTION

Even producers often fail to distinguish wines made from pure, ripe fruit from those from grapes manipulated to ape this style. The distinction is critical in Burgundy where the character of individual *terroirs* matters more than concentration per se. Of course, some vintages produce naturally rich and concentrated wines, but this is not a style actively sought by *vignerons*. Indeed, though much praised and highly priced, overt opulence often exhibits more of the character of the vintage than the underlying *terroir*. As Thierry Brouin of Domaine des Lambrays puts it: 'heavy extraction merely produces extract of Pinot Noir, not extract of *terroir*.' Real concentration comes without manipulation from old, low-yielding vines. The more one accentuates the tannic and extractive elements, the more the myriad of subtle sensations which exist naturally in the grape are obliterated. Heavy pressing certainly adds an impression of concentration in the form of strong tannin, but at the expense of *terroir* definition. Big, super-ripe, lusciously fruity wines are not what Burgundy is about however highly the market may value them. As Einstein put it: 'Any fool can make things bigger, more complex and more violent. It takes a touch of genius – and a lot of courage – to move in the opposite direction.'

Making Red Wine

The important factors differentiating red from white winemaking lie both in the composition of the fruit and in process differences. Red grapes contain colouring and tannin material in their skins that white grapes to a large extent, though not entirely, lack. These are essential for reds but undesirable in concentration in whites, so red grapes are vinified on their skins and whites off them.

STEMS

The role and value of stems is one of the most controversial questions among Pinot Noir producers in Burgundy and beyond. Stems are composed of woody vegetal material and their presence during fermentation can markedly alter a wine's character: they absorb colour, heat and alcohol, the latter probably no bad thing, but can also add an unwelcome vegetal astringency. So whether to partially or completely remove stems and just vinify berries or to use a proportion of whole clusters, stems included, is an important decision. For the majority on the Côte the consensus is that stems bring little, so they destem completely; others, including Leroy, Romanée-Conti and Dujac, believe that whole bunches are beneficial and since their viticulture is directed at getting both ripe fruit and ripe vine wood the negative aspects of stems are rarely a problem; if there is a risk, there is always the option of destemming. Their decision to vinify with 100% or near whole clusters is not for any positive qualities stems bring but to avoid premature oxidation which prolongs fermentation and delays its onset; this also reduces the need for sulphur throughout. A further major benefit is that fermentation takes place, at least in part, within the berries. This results in wines which are both more aromatic and more complex than those from extra-berry fermentation. The entire extraction profile is different with whole bunches as the cap has more air spaces allowing the must to flow more easily through it during punch downs and less heat retention which moderates the overall temperature. Technical stuff indeed, but of cardinal importance to the finished product. This 'whole bunch' vinification should be distinguished from the Beaujolais process of carbonic maceration where whole bunches vinified in a closed vat without punch downs tend to produce soft, early-drinking fruity wine which lacks structure and ageing potential. In Burgundy the vats are open – traditional vinification producing well-structured long-lived wines.

A general increase in destemming has undoubtedly contributed to the rise in overall quality in Burgundy. This is attributable to Henri Jayer, a tireless advocate of stemless vinification. Before he started campaigning, many Burgundies had an irremediably green herbaceous streak which came through as rusticity, particularly from second-division villages or less well-exposed sites. In his experience, fewer stems meant softer, mellower wines with a shade more richness. Some have noticed that not all *terroirs* are suited to whole bunch vinification – Dujac for example find their Charmes-Chambertin is better with fewer whole clusters, so here only 50–70% are used.

For many, the decision is not clear-cut as stems vary in quality – sometimes but rarely fully ripe (that is the wood is brown and fully lignified) sometimes not. Unripe stems contain tannin and harsh acidity (try tasting some) which are released during punching down, crushing or in the press, and are detrimental to overall wine balance. A proportion of ripe stems may be added back to help the fermenting mass drain, as pulp without them tends to become jammy and difficult to work. There are no rules, but it is generally accepted that the riper the stems the more that can be added and vice versa, and that vintages where *veraison* is abnormally prolonged or there is a rapid end of season ripening, a higher level of destemming is merited. Others destem and then add back ripe stems to have more cinnamates which impart a spicy, cinnamon character to wine. In some vintages stems can make a significant contribution to quality; in 2008 their potassium content helped lower acidities and restore balance.

Blind tastings with pairs of wines made from the same fruit either destemmed or not, suggests that whole cluster vinification gives a much richer, smoother mouthfeel whereas destemming imparts more emphatic fruit character. The textures of whole bunch wines are softer, more cohesive and compelling. The downside of including stems is an increased risk of green, vegetal aromas and flavours (asparagus, green bean and so forth). Many misinterpreted the 'no-stem' philosophy, failing to make the distinction between whole cluster and stem addition, destemming then adding back stems to the vats. There is no correct answer: stems vary in quality and ripeness. The rule, as Josh Jensen of Calera Winery in California points out, is to treat the stems as gently as you treat the grapes. As on much else, the good *vigneron* will remain flexible.

CRUSHING

In red grapes, all the colour, most of the tannin and many flavour and aroma compounds are concentrated in or beneath the skins. These must be extracted and breaking the skins by gentle crushing starts the process. This is not pressing, which comes later. The usual practice is to pass the fruit, post destemming, through rollers which break the skins to a greater or lesser extent. The narrower the rollers the more juice is liberated. However, this practice is on the decline in Burgundy.

DEALING WITH DILUTION

With rainy vintages or wines from large-berried clones dilution is a risk which will cause the *vigneron* to contemplate rebalancing his wine. There are two main ways of doing this: extracting water by one of various new(ish) methods or else by simply bleeding a proportion of juice from the crush (a process known as *saignée*). Either way, the aim is to end up with two-thirds liquid to one-third solids in the fermentation vats. Even in great Burgundy vintages where the skin-to-juice ratio seems close to ideal many Domaines bleed off 10–20% of the juice for added concentration. Others disagree, believing that however early you turn the taps, you are shedding the best quality juice. Many of the less quality-conscious see this as pouring money down the drain and refuse to *saignée* whatever the circumstances. There is no doubt that, in less than ideal vintages, the practice has turned many a weak-kneed wine into something more than respectable.

Technology has come to the aid of the 'dilute' *vigneron*. Reverse osmosis, a process that extracts water under negative pressure through the grape's skin, was trialled at Pousse d'Or in Volnay in the early 1990s. The results were so promising that the technique is now widely used … in Bordeaux. There have since been further essais on the Côte, at Domaines Roumier, Méo-Camuzet and Armand Rousseau – but with no great enthusiasm for the results. Although illegal on finished wine, reverse osmosis can also be used to remove excess alcohol, elements of volatile acidity and the spoilage yeast brettanomyces ('brett'). However, removing water from underripe fruit concentrates the green tannins as well as flavour and aroma. Cryo-extraction, which removes water in the form of ice crystals from the grape, has much the same flaw, although it works respectably for 'ice-wine' styles. There are justified fears that these technologies will encourage habitual overcroppers to believe they can rectify in the cellar as a substitute for conscientious viticulture and as too often in Bordeaux, deliver massive,

hugely concentrated wines as a matter of routine. As ever, there is no substitute for ripe, well-balanced fruit.

COLD SOAKING

The initial stages of red winemaking extract colour and tannins from the grape's skin. With intact, unbroken berries the yeasts have difficulty getting at the sugars in the pulp to start fermentation, so the process takes longer. The normal practice in Burgundy is to crush the fruit, cool it (to prevent fermentation starting) and then leave it for several days to macerate. Some Domaines (Rousseau, for example) seek as short maceration as possible; others prefer longer.

The value of cold-soaking red grapes is debatable. A few hours maceration allow an extraction of aroma and a fine colour which is retained thereafter. There are those (notably the late Gary Andrus, founder of Archery Summit in Oregon) who maintain that tannins require heat above 23–27°C to polymerise, so cold maceration is pointless. Others (Liger-Belair) will tell you that the purpose of cold soaking is not primarily for colour and tannin extraction but to add aromatics and elegance. All agree that prolonged cold-soaking of unripe fruit is likely to extract precisely the phenolics you are anxious to avoid.

Tannins leached out in cold soaking are simple and 'monomeric' in structure and inherently unstable becoming fixed (stabilised) to a greater or lesser degree as maceration progresses. This is a problem as stable tannins are needed to 'fix' colour which will otherwise wash out. It is important to start fermentation without delay after cold-soaking to avoid sour flavours, especially from native yeasts. Many who involuntarily cold-soaked before fermentation now do so as a matter of course, having bought cooling equipment or installed jacketed tanks. The days of lowering grandmother into the vats, weighted-down with bags of dry ice, are thankfully over.

Tannin research suggests that the picture is not quite as simple as many portray it. Some believe that pip/seed tannins – which comprise 3.5–5.0 mg per berry as opposed to 0.5 mg for skin tannins – are not as destructive as widely believed as their initial astringency soon disappears. The longer chain skin tannins are far more astringent and durable, neither of which are desirable properties. Cold maceration may well increase 'softer' pip tannins – which runs entirely counter to conventional wisdom on this subject (cf. James Harbertson, oenologist at Washington State University).

During the late 1980s and early 90s many top Domaines

consulted the Lebanese oenologist Guy Accad who touted a scheme (originally pioneered at Montpellier University in the 1950s and rapidly abandoned) consisting of 5–10 days cold-soaking heavily sulphured crush designed to maximise extraction and minimise sulphur use later. His influence, which caused much brouhaha at the time, still pervades the Côte.

The main objection was that massive sulphur doses neutered the natural yeast population and thereby risked compromising typicity – the cardinal sin. The evidence does not support this in that wines made under his aegis showed as great a variation between vintages and vineyard sites within a single cellar as elsewhere although many lacked precision. Some of his erstwhile clients continue to work along modified Accadian lines.

Precious La Tâche fruit before fermentation. Note the undestemmed whole bunches

YEAST

Once you have sorted out a policy on stems, crushing and cold soaking you must decide how to ferment your fruit. Grapes from each *climat* will be kept separate as will smaller blocks from within a vineyard if they have different qualities and requirements – young vines from old, one clone from another. Fermentation requires yeasts to transform sugars into alcohol and much besides. As the process continues weaker yeasts die, deactivated by alcohol, leaving stronger ones to carry on. Most Domaines use 'natural ferments' – yeasts which exist naturally on grape skins and airborne in wineries. A few, notably the Carillons in Puligny and Maume in Gevrey, prefer non-indigenous yeast cultures, mainly to avoid incomplete fermentations and the attendant risk of acetic bacteria transforming unconverted sugar into volatile acidity (vinegar). This is controversial in Burgundy where it is believed that each vineyard organises itself around the grapes, yeasts and other micro-organisms and that these form part of the expression of *climat*. While the jury is still out on this question, imported yeasts are regarded as industrial products which have nothing to do with *terroir*; by altering the natural course of fermentation they are seen as distorting character and degrading a wine's flair.

An experiment some years ago provided limited support for the idea of site-specific yeasts: a Gevrey grower exchanged a tonne of grapes with a Vosne grower. The Gevrey fruit vinified in Vosne had a noticeable 'Vosne-ish' quality about it and *mutatis mutandis* for the Vosne fruit vinified in Gevrey. Sadly, the experiment has not been repeated. Nonetheless, there is anecdotal evidence for yeast site-specificity: Bruno Clair in Marsannay notes that, whatever the character of the vintage or ripeness of the fruit, the grapes of his Savigny Dominodes ferment more rapidly than those of his Clos de Bèze, a fact he attributes to differences in yeast population. On a practical level however, it is reasonable to suppose that yeast populations in a winery are shared by all the *climats* being fermented there which would counter the idea of site-specificity.

FERMENTATION

This is a complex chemical and physical process the detail of which is far from well-understood. What is generally acknowledged is that its speed and temperature range are critical to wine quality; in particular that long, slow fermentation produces more and more complex aromas and flavours than shorter vinification. Although cask fermentation of red grapes has been tried, they are usually fermented in bulk – in vats – because of the difficulty of getting grapes, skins and stems in and out of a narrow barrel bung-hole.

The conduct of fermentation matters because important flavour elements under the grapes' skin (precursors) need the right conditions to maximise release: too low a temperature and you miss them, too high and the wine becomes fragile and unsubtle and risks oxidation. High temperatures also increase volatile acidity (vinegar) requiring more sulphur which is a potent destroyer of finesse. Pinot Noir's composition contains many amino acids which are powerful yeast nutrients, so that temperatures can increase rapidly producing an undesirably ebullient fermentation. That is not to say that the permissible temperature range is narrow: Jadot's Jacques Lardière is content to let his vats rise to 40°C, whilst others prefer to vinify cool. What matters are an even temperature distribution through vats and avoiding sudden peaks or troughs – a gentle simmer rather than a violent boil. Many growers express concern at loss of aroma during fermentation – 'if you can smell it in the cellar, then it's not in the wine'. In Burgundy, 30–34°C is regarded as a normal maximum and Jacques as a mild, though respected, eccentric who happens to produce superb results. Many, including the late Henri Jayer, believe that to be solid a wine must pass through the entire range up to about 34°C as each yeast works at its optimal temperature and at its appropriate moment. Missing that important peak risks a serious loss in purity and possibly a stuck fermentation later on. Jayer ascribed the aromatic complexity of his wines to the fact of '*laisser faire la nature*'.

Tannin management is crucial. As well as being part of a wine's texture, tannin is essential for 'fixing' colour by 'bonding' to it. The balance is important: colour without sufficient tannin simply precipitates out early on, while tannin with insufficient colour won't bond. This makes it essential to maximise colour without overdoing the tannins. As both are contained in the cap of skins, pips and stems which floats to the top of a vat of fermenting red wine, this is worked to increase extraction, either by *pigeage* – punching the solids down into the liquid mechanically, by hand or by foot, or by *remontage* – removing juice from the bottom of the vat and pumping it onto the solids. While both operations increase extraction, *remontage* is gentler than *pigeage* which needs particular care: in weaker vintages (e.g. 1994) some is essential, in naturally firmer ones (1988, 1993) less or none is advisable. Neither process should be overdone either in frequency or force. While Pinot Noir's natural lack of colour and tannin make additional extraction desirable, this must be adapted to the character of the fruit: skins, texture of the stems and density of the berries. Skins thickened and hardened by heat contain rough tannins which age awkwardly.

TIME ON SKINS

A slow even rise in fermentation means longer vatting which is generally considered desirable for top-class Pinot. A couple of burgundian estates who fermented their *Grands Crus* (both Corton, as it happens) for around ten days discovered their wines improved dramatically when they were persuaded to lengthen this by around 5–7 days. Organoleptically, there appears to be what might be termed a migration of tannins: they start being focused, almost bright and, as maceration proceeds, start to broaden and spread around the mouth as well as softening somewhat. What is certain is that if you pick at high yields and macerate short you have no chance of getting a decent, let alone concentrated, wine. There used to be a school of thought that great Burgundy only came from short *cuvaison* and that new wood meant a loss of fruit. Then the reverse became fashionable: longer *cuvaisons*, prefermentive maceration and new wood everywhere. The forests rather than the vineyards were being expressed in the wines. In general, more delicate vintages require shorter fermentations. Prolonging the cycle to increase substance is likely to increase extraction of the less desirable elements. However, there is no universal rule: longer maceration with fewer punchdowns and shorter macerations with more

The cap of skins, pips and stems in a cuvée of Pinot Noir

punchdowns can produce excellent wine. In 1969 and 2005 Domaine Dujac recorded some of their shortest macerations ever – nine days from picking to pressing – and neither vintage was short on extract.

Each stage of vatting thus plays its part in extracting substances from the grape and transforming others. Prefermentive maceration maximises extraction of highly water-soluble colour pigments, whereas aromatic compounds are mostly extracted during fermentation. Although there is a risk of extracting bitter pip tannin by excessive skin contact, leaving new wine on its solids after fermentation generally produces finer tannins which, being soluble in alcohol but not in water, are not leached out in earlier stages. These tannins fix inherently unstable colour compounds extracted during maceration before fermentation starts.

CHAPTALISATION

Despite advances in viticulture designed to promote ripeness, much fruit is picked early, often for security against inclement weather, with insufficient natural sugar and cane sugar routinely added (chaptalisation) to correct the deficiency. This process is legal but often overdone in pursuit of added opulence or to hide deficiency, especially lack of fruit. M. Duvault-Blochet, a 19th-century owner of Domaine de la Romanée-Conti, considered great Pinot incompatible with less than 13% alcohol. Today around 12.5–13.5% is regarded as optimal for *Premiers Crus* and 13.5 for *Grands Crus*. Some disagree: Domaine de Montille in Volnay has long regarded 12% as entirely satisfactory for balance and ageing potential and have not chaptalised for many years to increase that level. The longevity and evolution of their wines is eloquent vindication of their viewpoint. For many today, chaptalisation is not primarily to gain alcohol but to prolong fermentation. This is made possible by the (now legal) process of adding sugar in several small additions rather than all at one go which favours better extraction of colour, aroma and other trace compounds.

OTHER ADJUSTMENTS

Many deficiencies are correctable; much of this is deep technical stuff, but it is worth mentioning the most common adjustments:

Acidification: Something which causes unduly twitchy concern is acid deficiency. Winemakers often react to low acidity by adding acid to both red and white wine, in the form of tartaric or, heaven forbid, citric acid. Achieving a good acid balance for both red and white wines is complicated by the fact that their natural acid composition – mainly malic and tartaric acids – changes during vinification. Harsh-tasting malic (green apple) acid degrades to softer lactic (milk) acid during the secondary (malolactic) fermentation. Normally high malic acid indicates lack of ripeness but this is not always the case. Some Burgundy vintages (e.g. 2008) show abnormally high malic levels because of a lack of sunlight to transform malic acid in the berries into tartaric acid which bonds with other elements and precipitates out as clear crystals visible in wine or on corks. Provided a red wine has sufficient tannin and balancing alcohol, a modest technical acid deficiency or excess really doesn't matter. Tartaric acid is generally adjusted at fermentation but can precipitate out later so determining the correct addition is glorified guesswork making the end result uncertain. Nor is tartaric acid addition good news for drinkers as it adds a hard nerve to wine which integrates poorly; citric acid's bright lemon juice flavours are even worse, so both are best avoided. Winemakers of nervous disposition should take comfort in the fact that some of the finest, longest lasting Burgundies have come from acid-deficient vintages – prime examples are 1947, 1953, 1959, 1971 – and that many high acid years have blossomed from virtually untasteable (1972) or awkward (1991) into delicious, complex bottles. Many interventions, acidification and chaptalisation included, affect texture as well as flavour, so a technical deficiency is generally preferable to a clumsy adjustment.

Sulphur: Sulphur is widely used as an antiseptic in processing fruit of all sorts. Its primary function in red and white wine making is to prevent air from reaching fruit, juice or wine and starting oxidation prematurely; it is usually used as sulphur dioxide (SO_2 gas dissolved in solution) or divided elemental sulphur in powder form, on whole fruit, before crushing/pressing, on freshly pressed juice (white), in cask, at racking and at bottling; sulphur candles are burnt inside casks to sterilise them. Sulphur occurs in two forms in finished wine: free (still active) and bound (inactive). While most jurisdictions impose limits on both free and bound sulphur in wine, conscientious growers work to minimise sulphur usage during winemaking and at bottling. In young wine (especially whites) sulphur is noticeable both as a pungent smell (free) and as a flat, cardboardy taste (bound); it distracts from a wine's purity and transparency and dulls both aroma and flavour, hence the desire to avoid it. The downside risk from low sulphur levels is that a wine will start to referment (if it contains any unfermented sugars), spoil from undisciplined bacteria or simply

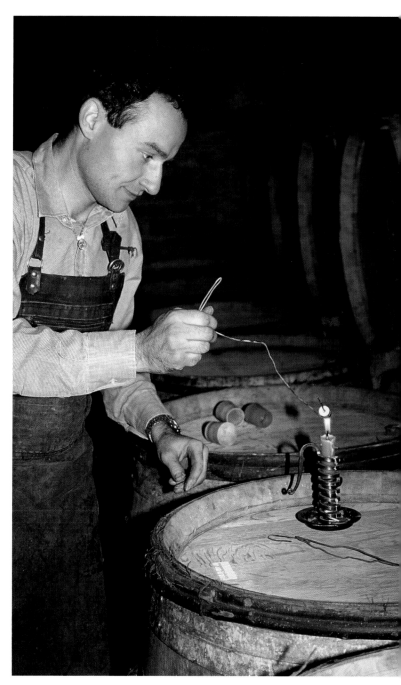

Candles are used to check sediment when racking wine off its lees

oxidise prematurely (as has so prominently happened with white Burgundy) so a balance must be struck between purity and protection. Some domaines have been working sulphur free, which risks problems stability later and also eschews the benefit of 'good' yeast selection that SO_2 can deliver at the start of fermentation.

PRESSING

After fermentation, the new (free-run) wine is run off its grape solids and the residue pressed. This yields additional wine but often of a higher tannicity and extract which the *vigneron* can either blend back with the larger free-run fraction or retain for blending or not later on. The dilemma is that in naturally well-constituted vintages the press wine's additional structure is not needed whereas in weaker vintages pressings can be harsh and distort balance. As each generation of presses becomes gentler – many *vignerons* tell you that their press is hardly more than a 'nudge' – *vin de presse* is more often than not re-incorporated. In Burgundy, most is – *Grand Cru* pressings are still *Grand Cru* wine. Some consider this should be done immediately – getting together early makes for a more harmonious marriage; others that the decision should wait until after malolactic fermentation to better assess how much pressings to add back.

MALOLACTIC FERMENTATION AND RACKING

'Malo' occurs naturally after the primary (alcoholic) fermentation and involves natural bacteria transforming malic acid into softer lactic acid. Longer vatting has led to some new ideas about this: malo is now often in cask, rather than in bulk; the old, almost indecent, rush to rack immediately after malo is out, the trendy tendency being to leave wine on its lees – provided they are clean – for a few weeks or longer to flesh it out a bit. A few are even trying lees stirring (*bâtonnage*) and report increased complexity and richness.

The decisions here revolve around length and speed. Some prefer to have malo start as soon as possible after alcoholic fermentation and for its duration to be short. Some add an inoculum to induce it, others prefer a natural delivery. In Burgundy, where cellars are cool and winter is winter, many leave the wines to their own devices – using a touch of heat if malo really won't start. In general, opinion favours late, extended malos, early onset and shorter durations attending more tumultuous fermentations which are considered to produce less well-constituted wines with reduced life spans. Dujac, for example, find that longer, slower malos result in finer and better structured wines. These different views may simply reflect degrees of risk aversion as wine on lees can become heavily reduced (reversible) or spoil through the production of sulphur-derived mercaptan off-odours (irreversible). Provided the lees are healthy and the wine is monitored regularly there is little to be feared from extended contact.

In general, provided the wine is not becoming unacceptably reductive, rackings (a process whereby wine is transferred from cask either to aerate it or to remove it from its lees or both) have been reduced to a minimum. Wine left on lees or in a tightly stoppered container for too long at this stage is likely to develop off-flavours, making periodic aerobic racking a necessity although sufficient oxygenation occurs through normal cellar operations to limit its frequency. In this respect Pinot contrasts strongly with Syrah or Mourvèdre, which are both notoriously reductive (stinky) grape varieties and require plenty of aeration. In Burgundy and elsewhere, one aerobic rack after malo and another, anaerobic, racking before bottling is more or less the norm; the first racking can be avoided with a light dose of sulphur to extend lees contact which is felt further enriches the wine.

Racking is an important and precise operation

Cleaning casks with high-pressure water

OAK AND ÉLEVAGE

No less than elsewhere, in Burgundy the subject of oak has attracted more, and more sustained, comment and controversy than any other winemaking topic. Debate ranges round the appropriate amount of new wood, which oak origin is best adapted to which grape variety, how casks should be coopered and how long wine should spend in them. Years of discussion and experiment around these topics have refined thinking but produced no golden rules.

What needs to be emphasised is that grape tannin differs markedly from oak tannin: first, fruit tannins reflect the subtleties of *terroir* whereas oak tannins carry no *terroir* component; second, wood adds elements not derived from grapes and marks wine to a greater extent; third, fruit tannins resolve and integrate into wine faster and more completely than the fruit itself, unlike wood tannins which are highly durable and can remain tasteable long after the fruit has disappeared. Both Pinot and Chardonnay are easily marked by oak, so maturing wine in a high percentage of new wood or leaving it in cask for a long time is likely to be detrimental. More new wood equals more wood impact. For these reasons top winemakers prefer structure derived from fruit rather than from wood.

The 228-litre burgundian cask is the ideal format to provide Pinot Noir and Chardonnay with the gentle oxidation it requires as it evolves, rather than a rapid, destructive, oxidisation. Its size and shape promotes even maturation and allows impurities to settle by gravity in a smallish footprint which facilitates their removal and minimises loss. This takes longer and is less efficient in containers of other shapes which often require additional filtration to clean and brighten the wine. Wood, like no other material, permits the gradual contact between wine and air but contrary to popular belief, new casks do not let external air through their staves; tests show that as available oxygen is absorbed by the wine a tightly stopped barrel develops a progressive vacuum. Recent years have seen increasing use of larger cooperage (500- and 600-litre casks in particular) for maturation with promising results.

The wood–wine interaction provides a controlled oxidation enabling red wine to evolve at its own pace in harmony with its own needs; this reduces the natural astringency of tannins, promotes colour stability and develops a wine's aromatic complexities. It also allows hard short-chain tannins to polymerise and phenolics to become more complex, producing long-chain molecules which are more stable and softer tasting.

This is what happens on a smaller scale in bottle. In short, judiciously used oak refines a wine's aroma and flavour.

Conventional wisdom has it that new oak leaches tannin into wine. This undoubtedly happens, but to a lesser extent that generally believed; research has shown that its main flavour contribution is to enrich wine through degradation of the oak component 'lignin' – giving nuances of coffee, vanilla, grilled almonds. For most Burgundy producers, the value of wood contact is not to add oak flavours but to promote the micro-stability of the wine through the gradual interaction with oxygen. The balance between oxidation and reduction in cask is a fine one requiring constant vigilance. Reduction is reversible – simply rack in the presence of air – oxidation is not. Given too much oxygen a wine sheds colour and freshness, too little and it becomes unpleasant and even rubbery.

There are two schools of thought on the importance of oak origin. One maintains that there are noticeable differences from one forest to another. Etienne Grivot, for example, considers that Nièvre gives a distinctly more oriental, spicy character to wine than, for example, Allier. Others find that after 5–10 years in bottle, wood origin has little influence on flavour. What is generally agreed to matter is the quality of the oak – the finer the grain the better – and how the timber has been seasoned. It takes around 200 years of tree growth to obtain suitable

Corton-Charlemagne and Corton ageing in barrels in Pernand-Vergelesses

wood for casks; as yet, the role of tree age and different forest *terroirs* is not officially recognised. Wood varies in character and composition from one place and tree species to the next, so talking loosely of Tronçais (Allier), Bertranges (Nevers), Darney (Vosges) or Cîteaux (Côte d'Or) oak is not particularly helpful. Those in Burgundy who have tried Baltic oak have been pleased with it, not just because it is significantly cheaper than French wood. There is a pressing need to research specific sites and define criteria for classifying oak with a view to the development of an Appellation Contrôlée. This would bring some order and control to the cask market and, in some opinion, enhance *terroir* expression. At present this seems a distant prospect.

How wood is dried and coopered is arguably as important a determinant of its behaviour in contact with wine as its origin. Exposing staves to several years air 'drying' slowly leaches out undesirable heavy tannins and works subtle transformation on tannin compounds vanillin and eugenol to influence wine aromatics. Three to five years used to be considered ideal but this is not universally accepted; drying beyond a certain point appears to produce more, not less, tannic barrels. Kiln drying is an entirely different process which adds another spectrum of flavour and aroma compounds. To secure wood quality and retain control of every stage of the cask-making process, many top Domaines buy trees at auction and have them felled (when the sap is descending) and dried outdoors before being bespoke coopered. Even with properly seasoned wood, cask preparation is critical: firing staves to a heavy toast changes the wood's composition and increases the grilled, mocha coffee components. Some coopers now char the cask heads, adding a further burnt dimension. Burgundy's general preference is for low or medium toasting ('M' or 'MT' on casks) for both Pinot and Chardonnay. 'HT' is a warning of strong, burnt flavours.

Some mediocre producers see oak as an improver, the philosopher's stone that transforms wine into something special, and an essential part of the 100 point recipe. Properly ripe fruit has enough tannin and structure of its own without undue addition; wine lacking natural concentration often emerges from new wood as hard and hollow. Even the most addle-headed Burgundian now realises that stuffing a weak wine into new casks is not the answer: it merely produces dull, over-oaked wine. At top Domaines and for the more naturally powerful *Premiers* and *Grands Crus* oak is being reined back; some estates use none. Talk to the de Montilles! Those who generally use 100% – Leroy, Romanée Conti, Dujac for example – do so from considerations of hygiene and prudence rather than to add structure. Tasting their wines from the most powerful *Grand Cru terroirs* shows the oak to be imperceptible after a year or so in cask. The conventional recipe is for more new oak in naturally richer vintages; in fact, these vintages are lower in malic acid – a great integrator of oak; so in very ripe (low malic) vintages such as 2003 and 2005 growers should logically consider using less new wood.

Thinking has also changed on the length of cask ageing. Markets now expect to taste fruit in wine and the die-hard belief that young wine was only destined for greatness if it tasted like chewing railway sleepers is long gone. Adapting the period of *élevage* to the style of a wine has made for better

balance, although many wines are still ruined by crude oaking – desiccated fruit and hard tannins from poor quality oak, inept cooperage or too long in cask. *Grands Crus* will generally support a higher percentage of new oak for longer but even here one finds significant variations: Rousseau's Charmes- and Ruchottes-Chambertin have 40–50% new oak, their Chambertin, Clos de Bèze and Premier Cru Clos St-Jacques 100%. *Villages* and lesser *Premiers Crus* and intrinsically weaker vintages merit less oaking. There is thus no settled wisdom on wood and wine. A grower's oak regime is part of the art of wine. As usual, a fine sensitivity to the individualities of each *cuvée* marks out the five-star *vigneron* from the competent journeyman.

Oak staves seasoning in ideal conditions in the open air

FINING AND FILTRATION

Preparing a wine for transfer from bulk to bottle is treacherous ground. However robust or fragile a wine, the operation is a shock from which it is likely to suffer. The accepted guideline is not to intervene unless necessary for stability (to remove microbial spoilage agents), clarity (a wine must be and remain bright in bottle) or taste quality (harsh tannins and heavy phenolics can have their rough edges knocked off by fining). Fining and filtration are manipulations which should depend on the wine's needs and nothing else. Ideally these are best avoided but this is not always possible and in such circumstances, dogma makes no sense.

Unfortunately, a critic-driven campaign has led to what amounts to an obsession among some consumers and writers with unfiltered wine in the mistaken belief that filtration is invariably destructive. The impact of either fining or filtration depends entirely on the nature of the wine and on the type and severity of the process used. Filters can be coarse, to catch gross impurities such as old boots and false teeth, or fine, to remove the minutest of spoilage organisms. They can also remove colloids, aromas, fragrances, bacteria, yeasts and structurally important long-chain tannins. The materials used and pressure across the filter medium make the difference between a gentle operation which preserves the wine intact and one which strips out its guts. Until meddlesome European Union bureaucrats outlawed the use of fresh eggs on the absurd grounds of salmonella risk (despite there being not a single recorded wine-related case) the preferred fining agent for fine reds was fresh egg white which passes through wine without perceptibly altering its taste. *Vignerons* are now forced to use reconstituted powdered egg white which alters the character of fining.

Fining and filtration are indispensable tools in the wine maker's armoury and it makes no sense for either producers or consumers to condemn their use as a matter of dogma. The opposite extreme, that you make wine at 110% then sacrifice 10% in the filter, as a justification for routine filtration is complete nonsense. Label statements on the lines of 'no fining, no filtration' should be distrusted as should those who routinely fine or filter for no other reason than their own peace of mind. There is probably a good deal of ethical double-speak on this; it takes little to imagine those who publicly forswear filtration rolling out their machines on rubber wheels on a quiet Sunday afternoon in some peaceful burgundian backwater and filtering away in the hope that their neighbour, slumbering righteously after his weekly gastronomic blow-out, won't hear the noise.

Those who drone on about superior delights of unfiltered wine should perhaps be reminded that cellar processes cannot be tasted, only the results of bad handling. In any case, as what matters most is what ends up in the glass, the controversy is largely academic. Blind tastings have repeatedly demonstrated both that it is difficult to tell filtered from unfiltered wine and also that over time any perceptible differences tend to vanish. As the 'no filtration' obsession applies mainly to wines intended for bottle ageing such evidence makes its rationale even less comprehensible. Those who pay high prices for wine rightly expect winemakers to take risks to maximise quality and see avoiding undue manipulation as one such risk. However, no-one faced with an aggressively tannic or dirty wine after a decade of cellaring will thank the producer for such senseless dogma. If Burgundy buffs really want to campaign, they should direct their energies to unnecessary spraying, excessive yields or poor quality control. At least here their protestations could really make a difference.

BOTTLING

Choosing when to bottle is critical: poor timing risks losing some of the quality painstakingly nurtured through vinification and preserved through cellar maturation. A winemaker who has lived with his wine for a year or more should have a feel for the right moment. He must also decide whether to bottle cask-by-cask and face consumers confused by the inevitable bottle variation or else to rack all the wine from each *cuvée* into a tank first. Some (e.g. Faiveley) bottle their top wines by hand cask by cask; others (e.g. Romanée-Conti) equalise six casks at a time; most prefer to rack into bulk to ensure complete homogeneity. There are arguments for each method but in the end it is a matter of personal policy. Many producers now consult the lunar cycle, preferring to bottle when the moon is on the wane to limit disturbance in the wine.

High-speed bottling

MAKING WHITE WINE

Wile red vinification seeks structure from tannins for ageing potential, white winemaking focuses on preserving acidity, which is its life-blood. Many of the general considerations outlined above for red wine apply equally to making white wine.

SKIN CONTACT

White grapes are not generally destemmed (machine harvested fruit being the obvious exception). The first decision is how much skin contact to allow – whether to press immediately to separate the juice from the skins to avoid discoloration or to leave the fruit on its skins for a few hours before fermenting in tank or in cask. Skin contact extracts aroma and flavour compounds but also tannins which can give an undesirable phenolic structural element to the wine. Extended skin contact or harsh pressing increases the amount of lees and also protein instability in the wine which may then require filtration later on. After whatever period of skin contact is chosen, the grapes are pressed and the resulting juice generally chilled and left for 12–24 hours to settle out gross impurities (*débourbage*) before being fermented. Some – among them Roulot and Dujac – prefer to crush before pressing; this allows them to increase the juice yield at lower pressures as well as extracting more tannin – a useful buffer against premature oxidation.

Sampling the freshly pressed must from Chardonnay grapes

FERMENTATION OPTIONS

Some estates ferment in tank and then mature in cask; others prefer fermentation in cask which is widely believed to favour wood–wine integration. Most Domaines use natural yeasts, although this practice is by no means universal. There is debate over ideal fermentation temperatures, which tend to be much cooler for whites than reds. One major Rhône producer, but as yet no-one in Burgundy, has exploited the fact that the flavour and aroma precursors in white grapes appear to unlock in sequence by fermenting three fractions then blending the results: low temperature for fruit and elegance; mid-range for flesh and warmer for depth and structure.

Malolactic fermentation is particularly important to white winemaking as a method of preserving acidity and freshness. Most burgundian whites go through malo either totally or partially to reduce acidity and for stability; where acidity needs to be retained malo is stopped with a shot of sulphur dioxide or microfiltration. Maturation for white wines is shorter than for reds, the interval depending on the wine's style and quality. As a white wine's constitution is not as robust as a red's, particularly clean and careful handling is needed; 'three times as much water as wine' is the cellar rule for scrupulous hygiene.

Harvesting Chardonnay direct to stainless steel tanks

BÂTONNAGE

Rousing the lees of white wine to enrich texture and flavour by stirring has long been practised on the Côte. This needs care as overuse or rousing of dirty lees adds an unpleasant 'leesy' character to the wine. Some (for instance Dominique Lafon) use *bâtonnage* to control reduction rather than to enhance flavour. Others prefer the gentler practice of rolling the casks which promotes freshness although the wine sometimes becomes unduly 'fat'. Some – e.g. Ramonet and Pierre-Yves Colin – practise very little *bâtonnage*.

FINING, FILTRATION AND BOTTLING

As tannins are not involved to any significant extent, preparing a white wine for bottling is more concerned with clarity and stability. Various fining agents are available, depending on specific requirements, and much the same risk considerations apply to whites as to reds. Here also, overprocessing can flatten or eviscerate a wine, so similar care is needed. Bottling for white wine comes anything from a few months after harvest for a fresh, sappy Aligoté to 18 months for a noble *Grand Cru*.

Success in turning grapes into wine depends upon an amalgam of details and finely balanced judgements. Among the Côte's top producers, who meet, taste and discuss together, these are being constantly refined. In the end, quality depends as much upon the determination to excel as upon technical competence or access to cutting-edge technology. In Burgundy, winemaking reflects history, tradition and a sense of place to all of which technical considerations play a subsidiary role. It also demands considerable humility and constant self-questioning. The belief that science alone is sufficient to make top-class wine, that once the science has been mastered, the art will somehow take care of itself, is the very opposite of the truth: from the fact of saying everything about the one, nothing whatever may be concluded about the other.

Tasting young Chardonnay

PART 4

MODERN CHALLENGES

CHAPTER 12
TASTING BURGUNDY

Examining the colour of Pinot Noir Grand Cru in a tastevin

asting is an emotive subject. On the one hand, there is a need for a mechanism to convey an impression of a wine's character and quality where the goal is objectivity; on the other, human individuality makes this an impossible expectation; what one judge, however experienced, regards as fine another may consider indifferent. The difficulties are obvious and as tasting is a human activity one must recognise the inherent limitations, not least of which is the existence of significant individual differences in taste thresholds for many common chemical compounds: substances which appear strongly present to one taster may be undetectable to another. *Ex cathedra* statements on balance and quality are therefore a risky business.

It would be easy to settle on Hugh Johnson's criterion of fine wine as wine worth talking about, but that would not help anyone trying to convey the relative merits of thousands of wines from a single Burgundy vintage. The best that may be expected is an ability to put aside personal preferences and assess wine against some accepted yardstick of quality. For this, experience alone is insufficient and must be supplemented with some knowledge of how wine is put together and of the parameters of quality; these, to a great extent, may be learned. What is also essential, but largely unteachable, is good taste – an almost instinctual feel for what is fine and well-made and what is merely ordinary. Judgement is all too easily influenced by circumstance but quality is no respecter of official classification, price or reputation; in the wider world of wine one often encounters expensive, *soi disant* 'fine' wine which is dull, mediocre, contrived stuff, and 'little' wines with genuine quality and interest. Too often pretension masquerades as class and the widespread inability to distinguish the one from the other partly explains why we have so much of it both in wine and elsewhere. Where wine is concerned everyone has their opinion; discernment is in much shorter supply.

Tasting has a cultural dimension. Palates are formed by experience which conditions perception. Someone accustomed to the ripe, sweet fruit of the Barossa will have difficulty finding quality (let alone pleasure) in an angular young Pinot or austere, minerally Chardonnay. On a broader front, culture intervenes in determining what is considered good; here, fashion, marketing and peer pressure are powerful forces for conformity rather than individuality. Tasting Burgundy involves culture in a third sense in that one is not just drinking wine but in a sense participating in the culture which produced it. If not, *terroir* has little relevance.

The ability to taste well is therefore a complex amalgam of experience, learning and instinct. What, fortunately, is not necessary is a degree in chemistry. Just as computer use does not require an acquaintance with program language, deep study of the science of wine chemistry, though helpful is not essential to a sound palate. The basics of tasting skill are largely non-technical.

This chapter is about tasting in general and Burgundy in particular. Its primary focus is not the mechanics of tasting, which are well-documented elsewhere, but quality assessment, which is not. Experience of top-class wine, of whatever provenance, is the surest foundation for developing a good palate. Being an insightful taster is as much an art as a science; food technologists rarely make great chefs.

Tasting Passe-tout-grains from cask

WORDS, KNOWLEDGE & EXPECTATIONS

Wine appreciation is not immune from today's culture of impatience and exaggeration. Words, especially hyperbole, are cheap and a ready flow of exotic verbiage is accepted in many quarters as evidence of connoisseurship. While a varied vocabulary is certainly useful, it does not justify the belief that a comprehensive description of a wine's every nuance equates to good judgement. On the contrary, an obsession with descriptors – trying to find that elusive aroma of 'peony' or taste of 'pomegranate' that someone else has noted – is superficial play and too often masks a lack

A 15th century burgundian vaulted cellar

of genuine appreciation. Sensations are what matter and these are easily camouflaged by words. Language treads the fine line between precision and pretension but is meaningless when divorced from such deeper understanding.

The indispensable background for tasting Burgundy is a good knowledge of appellations and *terroirs* – some geography, topography and the broad characteristics of individual communes plus an appreciation of what differentiates *Grand* from *Premier Cru* from *Village*. In Burgundy wine is not just varietal expression but above all a marker of place; the further up the qualitative hierarchy the more this influence is amplified. Typicity is tied to *terroir* expression and both are intimately allied to subtle differences between one patch of land and another, so tasting without this background removes a critical reference. It also helps to experience wines as they age. Young Burgundy is not always instantly attractive and 'reading' it accurately requires understanding the transformation of wine as it goes through cellar maturation and evolution in bottle. It is also to be noted that wines from such northerly regions tend to be more vegetal in character, lacking the richness of those produced in warmer, sunnier regions.

Perception is coloured by the complex amalgam of knowledge and experience which form our expectations. With wine, as much else, distorted expectations lead to flawed judgement. Young Burgundy is often misunderstood by those who equate quality with extremes. Consumers now routinely expect opulence, and in increasing doses, as they ascend the quality scale. The prevailing perception among many who buy the finest wines is that receipts should match expenditure; the better the wine the bigger should be the fruit bomb, the louder the taste explosion. The expectation includes instant gratification; the idea of waiting a decade or longer for a wine to be ready to drink is anathema. As well as patience, understanding great wine demands intellectual exertion, something also incompatible with the requirement of immediacy. Wine is unusual in this particular respect: the über-wealthy accept the need to make some kind of effort to fathom the obscurities of the depressingly nihilistic art with which they adorn their homes and offices, but expect the quality of their Château Latour or Chambertin to be self-revelatory; tannin and acidity merely spoil the fun. Burgundy delivers greatest satisfaction to those who understand its arrangements and appreciate its subtleties. Indeed, on the Côte anything approaching exuberance in wine is regarded as rather vulgar.

GROWERS' STYLES

To burgundian *vignerons* any conscious thought of house style comes a distant second to delivering typicity. Nonetheless, winemakers do have preferred styles and grape juice, being essentially neutral, gives them a variety of options for self-expression. As a result, a distinctive winemaking signature runs through the range of many Domaines: some are more obviously oaky than others, some richer and more approachable, others more restrained or elegant. There being no single valid expression of any particular site, within limits such stylistic variation is entirely compatible with faithful *terroir* definition. In musical terms, the notes remain constant but the interpretation varies. Some have subtly changed style in acknowledgement of the preferences of high-profile opinion-formers but Burgundy has by and large proved immune from this influence.

Slow, cool, maturation brings out the best in any great wine.

EXAGGERATED STYLES

In many minds, increasing quality is defined by increasing concentration. Fortunately, neither Pinot Noir nor Chardonnay lends themselves to this fashionable style which relies for much of its undoubted appeal on 'hedonistic' immediacy. The populist 100 point formula combines super-ripe fruit, heavy extract and alcohol and as much new oak as the fruit will take, more if you can manage it, into an explosive mixture which stifles subtlety, simplifies flavour and limits *terroir* expression. Superficially impressive but tiring to drink, these 'everything' wines consume you before you have the chance to consume them. Such crude obviousness represents the very antithesis of the burgundian ideal. While the guiding principle appears to be 'more, and more obvious equals better', the unspoken reality is that 'more, and more obvious equals less effort for the consumer'. This materialistic claptrap has no relevance to *Grand Vin* and is nothing more than a dishonest attempt to redefine the concept of quality.

THE GOLDEN RULES

There are few rules, but two are fundamental: first, if a wine has star quality this will be evident throughout its life; second, any early imbalance is likely to remain or intensify. The implications are clear: anyone who tells you that 'someday this wine will be great' is talking through their hat; and no amount of bottle ageing will transform indifferent young wine into fine old wine. This is not to say that minor imbalances cannot be adjusted or that age will not smooth rough edges, rather that quality should be evident from the outset and imbalances are rarely self-rectifying.

THE MECHANICS OF TASTING

There is no 'masonic' secret to the mechanics of tasting. The routine is straightforward and available to anyone not handicapped by blocked sinuses, anosmia or other neurophysiological taste defects. The process comprises two separate operations: the first, analysis, requires 'reading' the wine, identifying its components by sight, smell and taste; the second, synthesis, involves organising and evaluating these impressions. The conclusion may be as simple as 'buy' or 'avoid', 'like' or 'dislike' or as complex as an identification of *climat*, producer and vintage. The essential is to establish a routine and then stick to it. The precepts of biodynamic viticulture have reached the tasting room: many believe that a wine's taste qualities vary with the lunar cycle, tasting differently on 'flower', 'leaf', 'fruit' or 'root days'. Growers often bottle on a waning moon to avoid adverse effects of changes in atmospheric pressure and gravitational pull, so there is no reason not to take notice of such influences to determine the best time to open a treasured *Grand Cru*, even if this might make for a few more abstinent days at home.

GOOD TASTE AND DISCRIMINATION
'Good taste' is involved in two different senses. The first stage requires it as a greater level of sensory discrimination. The more elaborate one's category bank, the more perceptive one's judgement. Consider mountain guides and Inuits who have many different terms for snow whereas most of us only have a few (snow, slush, sleet); skiers may add a few more (powder, mashed potato, breakable crust, hard-pan, boiler-plate, etc). The Inuit's snow doesn't differ from anyone else's, merely his ability to read and classify it for his own purposes. The same applies to wine drinkers: most are content with a few simple descriptors (acidic, fruity, dry, bitter, mellow, etc) but these won't get you far in a burgundian cellar. Discrimination is greatly amplified by some background knowledge of winemaking and viticulture which contribute a much wider range of analytical possibilities, particularly those relating to faults or deficiencies. In the second stage, 'good taste' matters in the aesthetic sense of refined judgement – developing personal standards against which wine can be compared – and a discriminating feel for quality. These skills are largely instinctive but can, to a limited extent, be cultivated. Here, exposure to top-class wine is essential, particularly for winemakers who have no other yardstick to guide them. Many lack that experience and it shows in their wines.

Unlike a machine which analyses a liquid by computing its chemical or physical composition, human wine analysis is strongly interactive. Tasters bring mood, palate, knowledge, experience and expectations to the party. It helps to understand the ethos of the Domaine whose wine you taste – what the winemaker

Tasting is a universal language - not quite!

is trying to achieve. (This is a strong argument against tasting everything blind.) The more background information you have the more you are likely to find. The remainder of this chapter sets out the more important quality markers; first though, a brief recap of the fundamental processes:

APPEARANCE

First impressions are important. In the glass, wine should be bright and lively not turbid or flat. A wine's robe and intensity give an indication of its quality and vitality. In general, the finer the wine the more brilliant and attractive should this be, limpid, yet translucent, with a vigorous tone. Vibrancy of colour correlates with acidity in both colours and is a useful indicator of the quality of the vintage. Brilliance suggests quality while a dull, matt aspect indicates a softer more subdued wine. Colour intensity reveals a wine's constitution; a deep sustained colour suggests a fleshy, complex wine – a light tone a gentler, lighter wine. In general, a young red *Grand Cru* should appear intense and brilliant; the finest often display a lustrous velvet or satin-like sheen. One myth that needs knocking on the head relates to a wine's 'tears' or 'legs' visible running down the sides of the glass after the contents have been swirled. These are often wrongly said to be evidence of glycerine and that their presence indicates quality. They are in fact the result of differential surface tension between alcohol and water; the alcohol (lower surface tension) evaporates more rapidly sculpting the 'legs' on the glass. The phenomenon is known as the Gibbs–Marangoni effect. The higher the alcohol the more pronounced the effect, which can be suppressed altogether by covering the glass to prevent evaporation.

Genetically, Pinot Noir contains less, and particularly less purple, colour pigment than other major red grapes; it holds half its colour in blue-red waveband so is naturally less deeply coloured than other red varieties. Unless the wine comes from very old vines, a dark, heavy, opaque Burgundy should trigger concern. An orange tint in a young red wine or hints of brown in white are equally disturbing: as with many fruits early browning indicates incomplete ripeness and presages premature ageing.

Hue provides useful information about maturity: young reds are more or less purple at the rim shading to brown with increasing age; whites are neutral or lightish tinged with gold or green deepening and becoming yellower over time. Premature oxidation of white wines, evidenced by a flat tone, deep colour and sherry-like aroma, has been a serious and much-discussed problem in Burgundy and tasters should be aware of this possibility. A gentle controlled oxidation is what the cork and bottle age should bring, resulting in a normal colour progression. New wood and botrytis add a dimension of deep yellow but this is bright and vibrant; a dark,

The French police don't just fine errant motorists

dull, yellowing young wine should ring alarm bells.

As a broad generalisation, red wines from the Côte de Beaune tend to lighter hues and less intensity than those from the Côte de Nuits where a higher proportion of iron in the soil produces more deeply coloured and backward wines. Communes differ – Pommard's soils are more iron-bearing so its wines tend to be darker than those of neighbouring Volnay; and Cortons are often relatively dark for similar reasons. Conversely, CdB whites have a vibrancy and intensity that one rarely finds in CdN whites. A fine young white Burgundy should be lightish (some are even watery) and bright with perhaps the merest hint of green-gold lustre. Whites are less marked by colour gradation than reds, but one often finds a luminosity and brilliance above the green-gold glints in the great CdB *Grands Crus* which are rarely encountered elsewhere.

AROMA

In bottle, aromas are the single most important source of information for the taster of Burgundy as these provide the keenest markers of *terroir*. There are two routes to sensing aroma: directly via the nose and indirectly via the mouth. The latter provides a passage through the upper palate to the primary olfactory organ – the olfactory bulb. It is by this so-called retro-olfaction or 'palate aroma' that the aromatic complexity of a wine reveals itself. Its importance in 'taste' is easily demonstrated by sipping a wine while holding one's nose – the taste sensation is muted and the aromatics disappear altogether. To crystallise this distinction, direct smell is technically referred to as 'odour' and indirect sensation as 'aroma'. A useful tip with tasting young wine is to smell the glass that has been empty for a minute or so; this offers an artificial glimpse of how it might develop in bottle.

Aromas come both directly from the grape and also from subtle chemical interactions of constituents as wine develops. In particular alcohols and acids react to give tiny quantities of highly aromatic compounds, principally esters. Different grape varieties contain different constituents: Chardonnay, for example, is particularly high in flavour and aroma 'precursors' – substances which are not themselves tasteable but which fermentation transforms into ones which are – whereas Muscat grapes have similar taste qualities to Muscat wine. Significantly, recent research in the Côte d'Or confirms that different vineyards produce consistent differences in grape composition. As these are likely to translate through to wine, this suggests a possible route for tracing *terroir* typicity from site to glass. It should be remembered that aromas are susceptible to condition, especially temperature – subtleties are muted by cold (reversible) and blown off by warmth (irreversible) making wine taste flat.

Wine undergoes an aromatic progression. Typically young red or white wine starts life showing primary fruit and floral qualities; on the nose it should be fresh and appetising. Acidity, although not itself directly smellable especially influences aromatic strength and character, so the progression from fermentation through acid-reducing malolactic fermentation can produce significant aromatic change. Over time these primary qualities transform into mature secondary and tertiary aromatics. In bottle, both Pinot and Chardonnay have an incomparable array of aromas. These are broadly divisible into those deriving from the grape or *terroir* and those from processing.

Pinot's varietal/*terroir* aromas include:

Fruit: strawberry, raspberry, red cherry, black cherry, griotte

Concentrating on concentration

cherry, cranberry, blackcurrant, redcurrant, myrtleberry, plum, tomato (green and ripe), and even grapefruit. Fruit components are common to both burgundian and other origin Pinot, but at the top level the Côte (as yet) delivers more aromatic nuance and complexity than wines from elsewhere.

Floral: lilac and lily, rose petal and violet are all noted in Pinot. Some claim that floral aromas, especially violets, distinguish great Burgundy from the merely good and from New World Pinots; however, it is possible that such aromas are a factor of climate rather than *terroir*.

Earth/*terroir*: earthiness, mushroom, farmyard, liquorice, barnyard, truffle, viscera and leather.

Vegetal: Pinot can smell of beetroot, moss and olive and in Burgundy is often overlaid with a non-descript but characteristic vegetal component. The most likely source is grape stems which can give a strongly herbaceous nose and flavour which is offputting above a certain concentration although this character can also appear in 100% destemmed wines.

Animal: A rare occurrence is a plague of ladybirds; this happened in 2004 with the result that many of the reds from that vintage have a strong, individual odour.

Processing: aromas and flavours include those derived from oak: vanilla, mocha coffee, coconut and spiciness (particularly cinnamon and clove); heavily charred casks impart distinctive elements with a burnt character (smokiness, tarriness and toastiness and roast coffee bean), and cellar operations: deprived of oxygen wine in cask becomes 'reduced' resulting in a flat taste and rubbery or vegetal smell; in this state it needs racking off its lees into a fresh barrel; with young wine in bottle this should blow off given a few hours decanting; if not, suspect stems; oversulphuring produces pungent, sometimes eggy, smells and flattens taste; clumsily filtered wine tastes cardboardy.

Young burgundian Chardonnay is often deceptively neutral in aroma. While New World versions may show more obvious fruitiness – grapefruit, peach, even tropical fruit types (banana, pineapple, mango, etc) the Côte's whites tend to more temperate climate aromas: floral (acacia, borage and hawthorn) and fruity – apple, lemon, gooseberry and so on. Processing often imparts a creaminess and spiciness from oak; wine whose lees have been stirred (*bâtonnage*) excessively may smell and taste yeasty or 'leesy'. Age reveals Chardonnay's true character as it loses its youthful fruitiness and florality to a complex raft of aromas, of which nuts, butter, acacia honey, fig, prune and spiciness are but a few.

In general, aromas should be attractive not blowsy. A wine's appearance and aroma are its calling cards; if these are unappealing the impulse is to back off. At no stage should any single constituent dominate, certainly not new wood which easily marks both Pinot Noir and Chardonnay.

TASTE

The fact that much 'aroma' is sensed via the palate means that taste per se is intimately bound up with aroma per se. Flavours subtly related to aromas enhance flavour and allow the appreciation of a wine's structure and equilibrium. All are bound up with site and season as temperature plays a critical role in flavour-development: exposure of bunches to the sun increases time-release 'bound' flavours at the expense of immediately tasteable 'free' flavours (acids break the bonds which release bound flavours). This is one mechanism by which vintage and vineyard location influence what ends up in the glass.

Physiologists recognise four 'true' tastes: sweetness, salt, acid and bitterness and it is these that supply the basic material upon which assessments are built. To these should perhaps be added a fifth – *umami*, a Japanese term related to savouriness and describing the flavour component shared by meat stock, mushroom and cheese. This, best construed as a kind of 'deliciousness', probably has greater resonance for eastern than western palates. Molecules in the wine simulate taste sensors (papillae) on the tongue both by physical and chemical contact. The information this provides is relatively limited and one needs to look beyond to a second level of taste-sensations. These are subtler impressions rather than clear sensory signals, parameters which serve to differentiate good wine from fine wine from the ultimate accolade of *Grand Vin*.

YOUNG WINE

Tasting young wine is a special skill. Cold, damp and badly lit cellars distort balance, accentuate tannin and acidity and mask fruit. Unless a wine is destined for early consumption, tasting at this stage is not concerned with precise aroma and flavour descriptors as these change significantly both in intensity and character in the weeks and months before bottling. From birth up to around three or so years the important indicators relate mainly to tannins, alcohol, acids, concentration and ripeness of fruit, texture and balance – the building blocks which define balance and presage a graceful (or awkward) evolution. Aroma and flavour play a distinctly secondary role to structural components. What is sought is a good concentration of fruit, ripe – better slightly under- than overripe – but not bitter, tannins, ripe acidity (a fresh zing, not lemony or harsh) and moderate alcohol, fused together by an harmonious texture and natural balance. It is easy to be misled by superficial qualities – soft fruitness with no hard edges and a layer of sweetening alcohol – but top-class Burgundy is often somewhat diffuse and even mean at the outset. *Grands Crus*, being the slowest to develop, are generally the least expressive in a range and least likely to deliver immediate appeal. Much of what is written about young wine involves elaborate descriptions of essentially transient aromas and flavours when what is required is a brief analysis of the main structural elements. For this reason such output has very limited value.

Interactions & Absolutes

Having 'read' a wine's components the taster must then make an assessment of its quality. Here experience and personal taste are major factors. For most people, pleasure is the sole aim of drinking wine and this at a level where consistency matters more than difference. Preferring Muscadet to Montrachet is neither wrong nor a crime but putting the one above the other in absolute quality indicates a lack of taste. In discussing fine wine, where difference matters more than year-on-year similarity, gross personal preferences defer to an acceptance of universals of quality. Nowhere are these brought into sharper relief than in Burgundy. The rest of this chapter looks at the more important indirect markers of quality.

TYPICITY

The entire *terroir* philosophy is based on the premise that individual vineyards have their own wine personalities. Inherent finesse gives Chardonnay and Pinot Noir an extraordinary ability to translate the subtleties of *terroir* into wine and to reveal them in tasting. *Terroir* markers are relatively sensitive, enhanced by lower yields and cooler temperatures but blurred by adverse vintage conditions. Differences between one vineyard and another often come down to subtle nuances rather than gross personality traits. In general, the grander the *terroir* the more distinctive is its wine irrespective of prevailing vintage conditions.

For the taster, identifying atypicity is generally easier than the reverse. There is no shame whatever in confusing Romanée-St-Vivant with Musigny and it would be foolhardy to claim the ability to identify even the *Grands Crus* with unwavering accuracy. One might therefore expect a degree of humility which, unfortunately, is not always forthcoming: 'if in tasting you sense the soft rays of early morning sun or the discrete aromas of some box wood, or again the scent of stone dust warming up, you are in Les Perrières (Meursault) and certainly not in the Charmes du Bas' (Jean-Claude Mitanchey, in *Le Terroir et le Vigneron*, Jacky Rigaux, 2006). It is just such pretentious rubbish that makes wine appreciation an easy target for ridicule.

It is clear that there exists no simple relationship between principal soil elements and taste qualities – limestone does not give 'limey' flavours, clay a 'clayey' taste or minerals minerality. It is often suggested that the primacy of limestone accounts for the roundness and richness of wines while clay develops tightness

and structure and sand power and finesse. Undoubtedly soil character and composition influences overall wine quality, but any more specific pronouncements are insecure. Knowing something of the *terroir* from which a wine comes gives some idea of what sort of structural qualities to expect. Côte d'Or Burgundy comes from limestone soils which are distinguished by an impression of flavour developing from the back to the front of the palate. In contrast, many New World Pinots and Chardonnays whose character derives principally from fruit grown on non-limestone soils, develop flavour in the opposite direction. Limestone can also give a slight sense of saltiness on the tongue.

Minerality is a quality noted approvingly at every level in Burgundy and elsewhere. The concept is not well defined but indicates a taste impression suggestive of freshness and stoniness, though not related to any particular mineral. Unattractively high acidity magically becomes something infinitely more desirable when re-classified as 'minerality' – which it is not. Lees stirring white wine (*bâtonnage*) can impart minerality but excess can render it heavy. Many consider minerality an essential component of all fine wine but until a worthwhile definition comes along it remains subjective and hard to pin down.

LENGTH AND PERSISTENCE

These are hallmarks of all genuinely great wine. Tasters distinguish two separate indices: length of finish (how far along the mouth flavours travel) and persistence (how long they remain after swallowing). Although neurophysiologists admit no taste papillae beyond the back of the tongue, some wines have flavour which unquestionably continues down the throat (for example, the famous Romanée-Conti peacock's tail). Persistence is a measure of tenacity and relates to a wine's constitution rather than simply to its tannic power or alcoholic strength. A wine's density and intensity in the mid-palate are particular quality markers; whatever its pedigree hollowness here indicates a less than great wine. As Michael Schuster notes, 'With the finest wines you exhaust the liquid on your palate before you exhaust its possibilities' (Schuster, 2004). With lesser wines, you exhaust the possibilities before you exhaust the liquid.

Tasting in a burgundian cellar - make sure the samples are fresh

TEXTURE AND MOUTHFEEL

A refined texture is absolutely critical to wine quality, particularly in reds. No genuinely fine wine lacks it. As with food, it is not flavour alone that matters, but also mouthfeel (think of a slimy, gelatinous piece of fish or meat). This sensuous aspect delights or jars on the palate. The finest Burgundies combine liveliness with a supreme silkiness and opulence of mouthfeel and it is the fusion of these with an exceptional intensity and purity of fruit that distinguishes top-class red Burgundy from almost any other great wine.

BALANCE

It is in the nature of things to notice an imbalance and ignore balance itself. Balance is arguably the most important single element of a wine's quality. It is to be understood not as a passive equilibrium but a vibrant, dynamic force: the energy-charged poise of the ballet dancer *sur pointes* as opposed to the couch-potato's catatonic stupor. It is defined in terms of wine's ingredients – principally alcohol, fruit, acid and tannin in reds, the same less tannin in whites. Age accentuates imbalances so wine should be broadly in balance from the start. Acidity is an essential component of balance in both red and white wines; often attensive, even biting, at first it is progressively absorbed releasing a raft of subtle aromas. A shade too much (think of top German Rieslings) is preferable to a deficiency. Tannins may sometimes appear overdone but provided they are fruit- not oak-based generally integrate given time. What is important is that both are ripe; unripe tannins are harsh and often bitter; unripe acidity pierces and puckers. Balance is easily destroyed by excess: too many modern pretenders to greatness are over-ambitious – too rich, alcoholic and strident; hard work to taste or drink with pleasure and of limited lifespan. In contrast, balanced wines enjoy a more even evolution. Truly great wine should appear seamless: a balanced amalgam of constituents in perfectly controlled, effortless poise.

COMPLEXITY AND DEPTH

In wine, increasing quality correlates with increasing complexity, increasing information-richness. Depth denotes an amalgam of fruit density and taste profundity and contrasts with 'shallowness' – wine that is light in fruit and simpler in structure. Slippery concepts perhaps but readily demonstrable by tasting *Village* Beaujolais and Côte de Nuits *Grand Cru* side by side. There is another sense to complexity, in which it refers to something in the taste of a wine which is not directly apparent – a hidden element hinted at but not obvious.

CLASS

This, the most intractable of qualities, defies definition. A wine from a fine *terroir* can be excellent or mediocre but class is an attribute apart. Whereas many super-size offerings contrive to compensate a lack of class with opulence and impact – 'flash cash' rather than old money – real class prefers understatement. Here one is invited to read between the lines rather than having the message screamed out in 60-point headline type. Class allows no half measures: it is either there or not and if you have to look for it, it probably isn't.

ELEGANCE, SUBTLETY, FINESSE … AND POWER

Great wine is characterised by subtlety, each sip revealing a different facet. In a culture of impact and immediacy the more restrained tones of finesse and elegance are often dismissed as dilution. Conversely, dilution is too easily finessed as 'elegance'. It is all too easy to consider elegant what is in fact washed out. It is mistaken to think that finesse, subtlety and elegance are incompatible with intensity. On the contrary, the power of a message comes from its authority, not its volume.

ENERGY

A wine quality may be indefinable but nonetheless have significance for the drinker. Foremost among these is 'energy' which is found to a greater or lesser extent in every wine. With *Grand Cru* one looks for a core of vitality which is not found to the same degree in lesser appellations. This bears no relation to alcoholic strength, fruit concentration or extract, but is rather a species of internal energy: the finer the wine the stronger its energy current. In Burgundy, great *terroir* does not transmit as force and extract but as energy often concealed beneath disarming delicacy. Plant physiologists struggle with the concept of power but some who speak the biodynamic language have allied it to vibrant energy in the soil's minerality which the vine transmits to its wine. As with human aristocrats who have crusted up, some *Grand Cru* bottlings, despite their pedigree, lack dynamic energy and thus interest.

PURITY

With Burgundy, one seeks precision of flavour, luminosity, definition; clean lines unclouded by artifice or muddied by

Decanting old Burgundy

insensitive oaking, vegetal flavours or contrived extraction. Purity doesn't mean one-dimensionality – on the contrary, one expects it even in a well-made *Village* wine. It is clarity, definition, sharpness of line and balance which produce the most authentic *terroir* expression. The analogy with literature is compelling: expressiveness is not compromised by economy of language where each word is essential, none gratuitous – qualities one seeks in *Grand Cru* wine as much as in great writing.

STRUCTURE

A wine's structure defines its constitution and determines its evolution and ultimately its quality. As with a building, presence and authority are determined by its architecture; this is not solely a matter of aesthetics but of structural engineering. A wine's foundations, pediments and roofing come as tannins, acids, fruit and alcohol with texture and balance as important adjuncts. Like buildings, wine can be lopsided or ungainly. Tannins form the structural backbone of red wine, within a spectrum from aggressive and tight to soft and silky. Fruit varies from simple to complex, overripe to underripe, dense to light, fleshy to lean. Texture may be grainy or supple, heavy or lean and so on. The structure of a fine wine should derive mainly from fruit, not from excessive use of wood or contrived manipulation. White wine structure is formed round acidity, which must be clean, natural and ripe – fresh tasting rather than soft or flabby. Lesser wines tend to be simpler, more obviously fruit-dominated often with structures that owe more to processing than to fruit character. None the worse for that: not all Burgundies are *vins de terroir* or *vins de garde*.

COMPONENT SOURCES

Evaluating wine ultimately requires the ability to relate taste attributes to their origins, especially where defects are concerned. What one seeks are character, depth and purity that derive principally from fruit. In Burgundy, the demands of *terroir* expression make this a prime consideration.

WOOD

This is a complicated technical subject, but there are some basic facts of which tasters should be aware. New oak easily marks both Pinot and Chardonnay especially if the casks are heavily charred. (For good reason, new oak is banned in parts of Italy, Germany and Alsace). In Burgundy, French oak is preferred and the proportion of new to old wood in the total cask population and how long a given wine spends in it will determine its taste impact. After too long in cask a wine dries out – its fruit attenuates and it loses freshness. New wood is used both to ensure perfect hygiene and to add flavour and palate structure to wines – in particular, promoting fat and silkiness. Older casks give an altogether gentler, less oxidative aspect to wine maturation. Wood tannin is progressively leached into the wine from new casks but is not of the same character or flavour impact

as tannin derived from fruit. In particular, oak tannins are more durable and tend to remain in wine long after fruit tannins have integrated. In short, wine whose structure originates from fruit tannins is likely to evolve more harmoniously than wine whose tannins are mainly wood-derived. As a general rule, new wood should not be detectable either on the nose or palate after a few months in bottle. If it is, then a wine's evolution is suspect.

ACIDITY

In wine, organic acids – mainly malic, tartaric and lactic – are an essential part of its structure and flavour. Malolactic fermentation changes acid composition converting malic (apple) acid to softer lactic (milk) acid and significantly modifies aromas – hence the undesirability of judging a wine before malo is complete. Acidity adds an element of balance and grip and provides freshness to both reds and whites but its character varies: dominating harsh, bright acidity indicates an imbalance, while a refreshing weight of ripe acid is a positive sign. An excess is preferable to a deficiency, especially in white wines which have negligible compensating tannin to provide the structure for longevity. Tasters should be on the lookout for added acid, used

Firing casks. How this is done can markedly affect the quality of the wine matured in them

in hot climates and vintages to correct deficiencies, and be aware of its characteristic hard line of flavour which integrates poorly. This is more obvious in white wine and generally unattractive.

TANNINS AND PHENOLICS

Phenolics (of which tannins are a sub-group) come from a variety of sources including grape skins, seeds, stems and oak casks and differ in type, quality and flavour impact depending on the source. Tannins shape a red wine's perceived structure, contributing to both texture and balance across the palate; being strongly antioxidant, they also influence evolution in bottle, protecting against premature oxidation. Although without direct influence on aromatics, subtle variations in fruit-derived tannin between one vineyard and another are considered instrumental in transmitting *terroir* identity. Tannins also stabilise colour in red wine; those lacking adequate tannins shed colour more rapidly.

Tannins constitute the backbone of red wines. They are felt on the underside of the tongue as tactile sensations of tightness, sometimes astringency (bitterness is evident at the top and back of the tongue) and can be aggressive and harsh, bitter or soft as the case may be. Winemakers take care to avoid stem and pip tannins which are bitter and unyielding. Active tannins, which come principally from fruit, not oak, suppress the perception of fruit, which makes tannic wines of both colours appear less appealing and more reticent when young. It is received wisdom that, over time tannins combine (polymerise) into longer chain molecules and become less potent; this process releases the repressed fruit flavours so wines appear to fatten and flesh out as they mature and their structure softens; colour depth is lost, hue changes and sediments form. The first part of this process in now in doubt as research has revealed that while the impact of tannins may lessen as wines age their measurable concentration does not necessarily decrease. Moreover, it has been found that longer-chain tannins taste more, not less, astringent than shorter ones, which blurs the neat picture of tannins combining over time into longer, less harsh tasting forms (Cheynier et al., 2006; Vidal et al., 2003).

What is true is that wines with more or harder tannins evolve more slowly than those with fewer or softer tannins making it essential to peer beneath a wine's outer shell to assess whether there is enough fruit to balance its structure. Vintages which appear unpleasantly tannic early on are not necessarily devoid of quality. The 1988 and 1993 red Burgundies are excellent examples of initial tannicity integrating to allow softer more attractive aspects to emerge after a decade or two in bottle. Pinot Noir is unusual among red varieties in having a relatively low concentration of grape tannins, tempting winemakers to overwork inherently weak fruit or use excessive new oak to obtain adequate structure. 'Beating up' fruit results in undue tightness and aggressivity on the palate giving an impression of artificial rather than natural structure; too much oak imparts an overtly woody smell coupled with a dry-textured mouthfeel and attenuated fruit. Rather like garlic in food, tannin should support not mask natural flavour. The taster therefore needs to consider both the level and style of a wine's tannins and to be aware that wood and fruit tannins differ in character and influence. In the majority of Côte d'Or vintages there is more than enough natural tannin for reasonable life expectancy, so refined quality is the aim not maximum quantity. It is often the case that a wine's complexity or simplicity correlates with the quality of its tannins – although both are likely products of *terroir* rather than any inherent causal relationship. The greatest red Burgundies have a tannin silkiness which manages to merge seamlessly with the fruit, alcohol and acid in perfect textural harmony.

Tasters need also to be aware that tannins are highly temperature-sensitive, tightening up if cooled; so the temperature at which a wine is drunk will influence its perceived overall taste balance. Tannins also tend to firm up at high acid levels distorting balance and masking fruit. It is also worth remembering that a fresh phenolic feel can easily be mistaken for acidity – which it is not. The amount and style of tannins varies with vintage: hotter years produce riper rounder tannins, cooler years tighter firmer tannins. Although tannin concentration decreases as berries grow and ripen, riper fruit results in more seed tannin, not less as conventional wisdom has it.

Phenolics play a less obvious role in white wines. Tannins are present to a significant degree in many white wines – though finer and in lesser concentration than in reds; in excess, they can suppress fruitiness and leave an impression of leanness. Most lack noticeable tannin but those made with prolonged skin contact or harshly pressed may show a tasteable phenolic component. Modern presses are designed to avoid this happening, so there is no excuse for heavily phenolic whites.

The 'dodine' - a stainless steel instrument used for bâtonnage

PHENOLIC RIPENESS

A long-standing problem for grape growers in climatically marginal wine regions such as the Côte is that sugars and phenolics (seeds, skins, stems) do not invariably reach optimum ripeness at the same time (see Chapter 10). In Burgundy phenolics tend to ripen first, in warmer regions sugars first, so picking when sugar levels are correct often means underripe phenolics. Leaving fruit on the vine until the phenolics ripen fully produces undesirably high sugar levels resulting in excessive alcohol. Tasters need to be alert to the phenomenon of unbalanced physiological ripeness which shows either as underripe, green tannins at acceptable alcohol levels or else ripe tannins accompanied by high alcohol and overripe fruit characters (jamminess/portiness). This is emphatically not to say that mediocre ripeness invariably signifies mediocre quality – many vintages age gracefully in spite of (or perhaps even because of) incomplete phenolic ripeness – rather than it is often the cause of poor balance and harsh flavour components.

FRUIT AND QUALITY

The style of fruit in a wine says much about its origin and production. Without doubt, the greatest varietal (that is single variety) wines are made in regions where grapes struggle to ripen but then only when the fruit is near maximum ripeness. These conditions generally pertain in Burgundy although in some vintages achieving full ripeness is a problem. In general, cooler conditions tend to emphasise freshness and minerality while warmth accentuates fruitiness. Proper ripening conditions develop a flavour progression in grapes which is essential to a wine's character and evolution. Drought and excessive heat show up in tight, firm, dense tannins from unusually thick skins and consequent high solid-to-juice ratios. Water-stress later on produces wines which seem overripe from increased sugar concentration as the grapes effectively dry out. In contrast, heavy rain near harvest time encourages thirsty grapes to pump water which brings dilution. A different aspect of fruit quality is evident where wine is made with whole bunches (that is without removing stems) in closed vats (carbonic maceration). This technique, pioneered in the Beaujolais, produces soft, fleshy fruit characters with gentle, round tannins. Some of the Côte's finest Domaines also work with 100% whole bunches but these are traditionally vinified and have traditional structures with no 'carbonic maceration' qualities. Finally, it must be re-emphasised that if a wine does not start out with good fruit, it will never develop it!

CONCENTRATION VS. EXTRACTION

To the question of how to distinguish themselves in the world, many winemakers have two popular responses: first, put an animal on the label, which apparently doubles sales; second, pump up your wine to pneumatic proportions with more oak, more concentrated (preferably overripe) fruit and extract and hope that no-one who matters will see through the artifice.

Within limits, extract is beneficial, in that wines with higher extract contain more natural preservatives and therefore evolve more slowly. In white wines high extract can give an impression of richness, but countervailing minerality and freshness are essential for balance. Historically, the best Burgundy vintages were those with the ripest grapes; today, almost every vintage is picked at levels of ripeness that previous generations would have regarded as exceptional. Nonetheless, given today's vogue for big wines, the competent taster needs to develop a fine feel for the distinction between natural concentration and contrived extraction. Concentration *per se* is no recommendation; one needs also to answer the further question: what is being concentrated?

LEES AND STIRRING (BÂTONNAGE)

The practice of stirring white wine lees to add richness has a long history on the Côte. Provided the lees are clean and the frequency of the operation not immoderate, the results can be beneficial in enriching leaner wines; excess makes for undue fatness. But, look out for any pronounced 'leesy', yeasty character, which is indicative of excess *bâtonnage*.

SUGAR AND ALCOHOL

High alcohol (>14%) characterises many cult super-*cuvées* but in general, and certainly in Burgundy, is an enemy of wine quality. It masks *terroir*, gives a false impression of sweetness and is unpleasant. Even at moderate levels it is detectable as a raw, burning sensation at the back of the mouth (think of brandy) and is often the result of using commercial yeasts in fermentation. For fine Pinot Noir and Chardonnay desirable alcohol levels lie between 12–13.5% for *Village* to *Grand Cru*. Given reasonable extract, these levels are entirely compatible with maximum expression of aromatics and with good texture. In ripe vintages natural alcohols may exceed the ideal but, given decent viticulture, the wines should still be in balance although typicity is not assured. In unripe vintages sugar may be added at fermentation to increase alcohol within prescribed limits. Excessive chaptalisation is undesirable as it renders wine flat and heavy. Some winemakers deliberately leave a small quantity of natural sugar in their wines to add palate appeal, especially in whites, but this mutes purity and typicity. Tasters should be sensitive to residual sugar and masking alcohol and be suspicious when they detect them. In general, a wine's texture should cover its alcohol, not be swamped by it.

OXIDATION

Oxygen plays a seminal role in the evolution of wine in bottle. Here one must distinguish oxidation, which is a slow, gentle oxygenation, from oxidisation which is a rapid transformation due to contact with air. Even the small amount of oxygen in a sealed bottle affects its contents by slowly changing the wine's state of oxidation. This change is cyclical, as the wine gradually passes from a state of oxidation, where it tastes more open and appealing, to a state of reduction where aromas and fruit are subdued and the impression of structure enhanced making it appear lean and unforthcoming, often with a transient 'off' odour. This is particularly noticeable in the months after bottling ('bottle shock') or transport. The rate of change from oxidative to reductive is affected by temperature, slowed by cold and accelerated by warmth; so cellar temperature is an important determinant of a wine's state. This topic is gracefully elucidated by Dr Neil McCallum in his 'Dry River Jottings'.

There has been much debate, especially on blogs and websites, devoted to the phenomenon known as 'premature oxidation'. Although not widely recognised as an abnormality or acknowledged by producers until about 2004, this damaged white Burgundies in particular since the mid-1990s. There is no pattern – 'premox' attacks randomly – top Domaines were as much affected as lesser ones and *Grands Crus* as much as *Régionales*; some bottles in a case were fine, others oxidised to a greater or lesser extent with incidence reported as varying between zero and 100%. After

Ideal cellar conditions. This mould - racodium cellare - keeps insects from the uncapsuled corks but is under threat from excessive hygiene

a few years in bottle, when they should be approaching optimum drinkability, wines became yellow/brown in colour, flat, caramelly or sherry-like on the nose and palate. Many contributory causes have been cited, including reduced antioxidant phenols in cleaner juice from gentler presses and greater oxygen ingress from increased bâtonnage, but it is likely that the phenomenon largely results from an unfortunate combination of two factors: the use of hydrogen peroxide in cork manufacture and the trend to lower sulphur dioxide use (the phenomenon is not observed pre-bottling). The peroxide spontaneously degrades into oxygen and water, releasing destructive free oxygen into the bottle; less free sulphur reduces wine's ability to absorb and neutralise this, hence the problem. The presence of peroxide has been attributed to incomplete washing of residue off the corks after peroxide treatment. It has also been suggested that the methods used to introduce sulphur tend to protect wine unevenly: in some parts of the vat/tank SO_2 is amalgamated well, in others not. If true, this would account for premox's apparently random distribution. With no clear cause, there is no identifiable solution. However, producers are now awake: sulphur dioxide is on the increase and although the incidence remains worryingly high, premox is now firmly on producers' radar, if not yet in terminal decline.

OTHER FAULTS

Wine faults are legion. A handful of the most common are:

Corkiness: This manifests itself as a musty, mushroom-like aroma and a drying on the palate from the contact of wine with the molecule tri-chloro-anisole (TCA). It infects corks indiscriminately; however expensive or thoroughly pretreated they may be, the risk of cork taint remains. Exposure and tasting are the only means of acquainting oneself with these and other common spoilage organisms.

Brettanomyces: Detecting 'brett' has become almost a cult way of demonstrating tasting expertise. Unfortunately, research suggests that even among winemakers there are many false positives, where another substance is misidentified as brett or it is absent altogether. In fact, in low doses, brett can enhance quality so the almost Pavlovian dislike of it among New World winemakers has shut them off from much that is fine and enjoyable. What is brett? Technically, it originates with yeasts naturally present in vineyards and wineries; these do not themselves produce

spoilage but are precursors of substances which do. There are three responsible molecules; in order of sensory impact these are: 4-ethyl-phenol (sticking plaster, farmyard and horsey aromas), isovaleric acid (cheesy, rancid, sweaty saddles) and 4-ethyl-guiacol (spice, clove, smoke, bacon). Brett-tainted wine loses primary fruit characters, fleshiness is muted which brings acidity to the fore; tannins appear attenuated and somewhat rustic. It is widely believed that brett reflects poor cellar hygiene; in fact it affects good and bad alike, although there appears to be a correlation with the use of oak. Although individual threshold sensitivity to these substances varies, their general character is well recognised and tasters should be on the lookout for them.

Sulphur and sulphides: Sulphur, usually in the form of sulphur dioxide gas, is an effective and widely used antiseptic, antioxidant and preservative. Once in contact with grapes or wine it reacts to produce a multitude of compounds, some volatile and thus smellable, others only tasteable. High sulphur levels produce an aggressive pungency in young wine with aromas redolent of matchsticks and burnt rubber, and cardboard flavours (sulphites) in older bottles. Sulphides, especially hydrogen sulphide (bad eggs), are highly aromatic but generally only occur in wine in low concentrations. Hydrogen sulphide reacts with alcohol in particular to produce mercaptans which smell of burnt rubber or wilted onion. Excess sulphur provides an element of insurance against wine spoilage but damages colour, aroma, flavour and texture and compromises purity. Systematic overuse suggests that vinification and *élevage* are not all they should be. Sensitivity to sulphur compounds varies from person to person; many respond badly to excess and allergic reactions are not uncommon; these effects are probably related to histamine levels.

Botrytis and rot: It takes only a few grey-rot-damaged grapes to taint an entire batch of wine. When this occurs (for example, in the hail and rot struck 1983 Burgundy vintage) wine smells musty and tastes sour and attenuated. Noble rot (*Botrytis cinerea*) is a desirable fungal infection in areas producing sweet wines and indeed, a small proportion of botrytis can enrich a cuvée of Chardonnay. It manifests as an element of unctuousness on the nose and added palate richness and appears sporadically in white Burgundy vintages. However, botrytis overlays true character and masks typicity so is discouraged on the Côte.

THE IMPORTANCE OF TIME

A wine's evolution and life expectancy are determined by its constitution. This, in turn is the product of grape variety, *terroir* and climate with contributory elements from winemaking. In general, growers don't set out with the intention of making twenty-year wines, but viticultural refinement has produced better ripeness, more and riper tannins and acids; wines with more balanced constitutions simply take longer to unpack. The hallmark of fine wine is not just its capacity to age, to endure without falling apart, but to do so in a manner that is both attractive and interesting. In this regard, the taster needs to be aware of two phenomena: first, that Pinots (and to a lesser extent Chardonnays) tend to close up at some time after bottling – may be months or a year later – and remain closed for an indeterminate period. This process is normal but unpredictable; the closed phase may last months or years or not happen at all. So what seems ethereal in cask may taste somewhat less expressive a few months later and it takes faith to believe that the wine will ultimately deliver. Second, the greater the wine, in general the more difficult it is to taste young and the slower its progress towards maturity. This means digging deeper and looking more searchingly at youthful *Grands Crus* than at *Villages* or *Premiers Crus*. Thus it may be that in one cellar, at their outset lesser wines taste better than greater.

Much fine Burgundy is drunk too young – at every level, *Village* as well as *Grand Cru*. Premature consumption means losing much of the wine's elegance, complexity and expressiveness. A young *Grand Cru* may be oaky and attractive in a fruity sort of way but that is incidental; consume it too soon and that is all you are likely to get. As to optimum drinking, there are no rules. As with any fine wine, the drinking window can be maddeningly unpredictable. What is certain is that it makes no sense to buy five-star wines and expect them to deliver after two or three years; they may, but in general you risk catching them in a closed phase and being disappointed. As a general guideline, *Villages* and lesser *Premiers Crus* are best left for 3–5 years while *Grands Crus* in the best vintages require 10 years plus. Of course, when you drink a wine also depends on how you like it: young and more obviously fruity, or older and more expressive.

Both varieties tend to lose their identifying varietal markers with age; a 20-year-old Puligny can smell like an old white Hermitage, and an aged Pinot Noir like an old southern Rhône Grenache or mature St-Emilion. The smells and flavours of mature Pinot (game, *sous-bois*, etc) and Chardonnay (nuts, butter, honey, acacia, etc) are an acquired taste and actually disliked by many, who understandably wonder what all the fuss (and expense) is about. They would be much better off buying a good *Village* wine and using the money saved on some wine education.

Obscure hieroglyphics on a stack of Latricières-Chambertin

HALLMARKS OF GRAND CRU

The universals of wine quality being only to a limited extent specifiable, much depends on opinion. A wine may come from a *Grand Cru* vineyard but not attain *Grand Cru* quality. The true hallmark of Côte d'Or *Grand Cru* is probably its sheer sensuality, its ability to thrill; this is inadequately conveyed by descriptors or definable qualities, however cleverly expressed. Drinking a glass of great Burgundy resembles listening to a great orchestra where the overall impression transcends the contributions of the elements that produced it. Each component is there but none dominant. The extra dimension arises from their fusion into something special and uplifting. *Grand Cru* is not mind-blasting disco-din, rather, subtler music where the silences between Mozart's bars are also Mozart though no music is heard. Fine Burgundy possesses an internal, almost spiritual, energy which transcends description.

As well as exciting the senses *Grand Cru* should stimulate the imagination and challenge the intellect. Like any wine, it must also give pleasure. This is the one true fundamental: from saying everything exhaustively analytical about a wine nothing can be concluded about pleasure. This is the only way to account a preference for a young, fruity Beaujolais over a tight, tannic *Grand Cru* and has nothing whatever to do with intrinsic quality. Appreciating Burgundy also demands understanding that one is tasting *terroir* above grape. *Terroir* may be seen as a message put into the bottle by the producer for the consumer; the more complex it is and profound the greater the pleasure in its deciphering. If these are the criteria, then even a Bourgogne Rouge or Blanc may qualify along with the finest Musigny or Montrachet.

Many who regularly drink the world's great wines have little idea of what has gone into the contents of their glass – a calamitous waste of an open bottle on a closed mind. Developing a palate offers a new dimension of pleasure and affords an insight into the greater secrets of wine – something upon which a deep wallet has absolutely no bearing. Such secrets are the essence of Burgundy.

All is clarity

CHAPTER 13
BUYING BURGUNDY INTELLIGENTLY

How does one set about buying Burgundy in a marketplace where many who venture end up disappointed? The facile answer is 'buy the best', but not only is this is not a strategy open to most but drinking *Grand Cru* every day would soon pall, pleasurable as it might seem to try. For those prepared to develop a palate for Burgundy there is value, interest and enjoyment to be found at every level and for those who have already taken the plunge, the real fascination lies in the differences between vintages, estates and vineyards. A well-balanced cellar should represent a range of styles and qualities on the Pinot Noir/Chardonnay theme.

The message of *The Great Domaines of Burgundy* is that the secure route to good Burgundy is through the most dependable Domaines. At this level, the name of the producer is more important than the name of the vineyard. This remains true. As most producers offer a variety of wines the trick for the astute buyer is to target estates whose style you enjoy and then buy the best available at whatever level fits the budget. Expense is no guarantee of quality: you will fare far better with a Bourgogne *tout court* from a top source than with a *Premier* or *Grand Cru* from a third-rater; indeed, it is much more fun to discover attraction in a modest wine than to pay a fortune and be disillusioned. In Burgundy there is plenty of interest to be found in well-made generics which often come close to their *Village* counterparts. For example, Fred and Michel Lafarge's Bourgogne Rouge is Volnay in all but name, and it would be a blinkered idiot who did not prefer Anne-Claude Leflaive's Bourgogne Blanc to many *Village* Pulignys. In culinary terms – better a grilled chicken from a three-star chef

Direct sales are an important part of many Domaines' economy. No ostentation here - just a simple sign

than a clumsily executed *Coq au Chambertin truffé, aux cinq épices avec purée de fenouil, pied de porc et concassé de fruits rouges* from an incompetent.

For those 'converting' from Bordeaux to Burgundy, the best advice is to start with the simpler wines – *Régionales, Villages* and those from the Côte Chalonnaise and the Mâconnais and work up to the Côte d'Or *Premiers* and *Grands Crus*. There is little point starting at the expensive end without a good feel for the lower rungs of the ladder. Enjoying a few lesser wines will put the finer bottles into perspective, especially when tasted side by side.

Since the first edition of *Great Domaines* in 1992 buying Burgundy has become considerably easier with the emergence of an international network of fine specialist importers. For the most part these businesses are staffed by people passionate about the region who work hard to find value from lesser-known producers as well as listing wines at the grander end of the spectrum. Tap their enthusiasm and knowledge and if you like what they sell you trust them for the more expensive bottlings. Many have branched out into New World Pinots and Chardonnays and with careful selection there is much of real interest to be found here.

Burgundies are inevitably expensive. The contributory costs of producing a bottle have been estimated at: labour 40%, equipment, buildings and depreciation 18%, marketing 15%, planting and vineyards 12%, insurance etc 8%, finance costs and other expenses 7%. Making fine wine is highly labour intensive and France has among the highest labour and social costs per man hour of any viticultural region. This breakdown excludes the cost of land; difficult to estimate but an indication comes from the sale in 2006 of the Vosne-Romanée Domaine René Engel to François Pinault, owner of Château Latour, for 2 million euros (= US$2.5 million) per planted hectare. The moral: expect to pay a premium for *Premier* and *Grand Cru* and for top-class producers. A wine priced significantly below that of its peers is unlikely to enthral. Equally, there is no reason to accept that a premium-priced limited-release will invariably outpace the same grower's regular bottling. Fortunately, Burgundy's small scale has largely safeguarded it from the '*super cuvée*' phenomenon which has infected much of the wine world. Old vines, often the source of premium bottlings, are recognised as a valuable asset in any blend, whether in a generic Bourgogne or as a component of a *Grand Cru assemblage*. Given the small scale of burgundian production extracting their

Buying Burgundy sur place is an attractive but often expensive option

produce for a separate bottling inevitably detracts from the totality. Expense does not necessarily mean value, nor the converse. In fact, Burgundy delivers excellent value provided you look for it. The shrewd buyer will not overlook the lesser regions of Burgundy outside the Côte d'Or where there is much of worth to be found. The Mâconnais is particularly exciting, especially for whites, and the Côte Chalonnaise offers good, if relatively simpler, reds. In particular, Pouillys and Mâcons (white) and Mercureys (red and white) are offered by a slew of quality-conscious producers and well worth seeking out. These are not cheap in absolute terms but offer abundantly good value in comparison to their cousins on the Côte. The interest shown by top Côte d'Or Domaines in the wines of the Mâconnais and Côte Chalonnaise have given these areas a leg-up and brought their wares onto the radar of buyers looking for that elusive combination of quality and value. Try the Bouzeron wines of Romanée-Conti's Aubert de Villaine, Faiveley's Mercureys or Leflaive's and Lafon's Mâcons. You get first-division winemaking for less than first-division prices.

If you must stick to the Côte, then mine the secondary villages for quality and value – Fixin, Marsannay, Chorey, Savigny, Pernand-Vergelesses, Monthélie, Auxey-Duresses, St-Aubin, Santenay, Maranges – and the Hautes Côtes where one often finds winemakers from top Côte estates doing their own thing in both colours. But bear in mind that, in more difficult vintages these villages tend to fare markedly less well. In particular, ripeness in west-facing vineyards can be marginal and the wines consequently ungenerous, lacking the flesh to balance their skeletal structures.

Finally, and for the canny buyer most importantly, look for value in second-division vintages. These 'lesser' years often give the deepest insight into the intricacies of the Côte's vineyards and can provide excellent quality at an affordable price; they should be in cellar of every true connoisseur. These days, with modern viticultural know-how, severe *triage* and sensitive vinification, fine, concentrated wine can be produced in climatically difficult conditions. Indeed, there are many remarkable surprises to be had from such vintages. Unfortunately, the rush to taste early on has led to many inaccurate assessments with vintages written off prematurely (one thinks particularly of 1991 and 2001). This presents those interested in buying quality rather than ratings with an opportunity as prices are often discounted. This is certainly the case in the major international salerooms where

Buying direct from the producer - here in Gevrey-Chambertin -

adds a personal dimension to the transaction

many a bargain is to be found among unfashionable vintages as the 'smart' money chases what is perceived as the 'must-haves'. In consequence, those lacking the critics' *imprimatur* of excellence are less sought-after. It is also true that when a new 'great' vintage comes along, its predecessors tend to get left behind, as it were. At the time of writing one can pick up first-rate 1993s, 1996s, 1999s, 2001s, 2002s, 2003s and 2004s for a fraction of the price of the equivalent 2005s. Top growers will not bottle unworthy or poor wine, so trust the reputation of the Domaine for typicity and interest. Disappointments with 'great' wines from 'great' vintages are more than matched by pleasant surprises from 'lesser' wines from 'lesser' vintages. Try it!

Obviously, any serious cellar will contain some great bottles of *Premiers* and *Grands Crus* from top estates. It is essential to remember that these are made on a much smaller scale than in Bordeaux. In a good vintage, Château Lafite produces on average 20,000+ cases, La Romanée-Conti vineyard just 460. Scarcity therefore is an important determinant of both price and availability. The best wines from top estates are sold on allocation to overseas importers. Demand for these treasures routinely exceeds supply, so if you want them then register an interest early on and be prepared to pay whatever is asked. In this respect, Burgundy is unlike Bordeaux where *en primeur* prices have rarely kept pace with inflation and where plentiful supply ensures that most wines can be found approaching maturity at an inflation-adjusted discount to the original offer. Except for a few *garagistes*, the case for buying Bordeaux *en primeur* is tenuous at best; in Burgundy, which has as yet no *en primeur* campaign, the case for buying on release is unanswerable. The best estates have waiting lists of prospective importers hopeful of getting on the ladder with a small allocation and the importers themselves have a similar client pecking order. As Henri Jayer helpfully advised, the only way to get on the list is probably to kill those above you! In Burgundy, once sold, the top wines vanish into private cellars and thereafter become increasingly difficult to find.

To summarise, there are several strategies for establishing a varied and interesting Burgundy cellar: buy lesser wines from top producers; work with a dedicated Burgundy specialist; mine outside the Côte d'Or and within it look for value and quality from secondary villages or unfashionable vintages. Good Burgundy is expensive, but no more so in absolute terms than wine from any other comparable fine wine region and there is always value and interest to be found without undue compromise on quality.

CHAPTER 14
BURGUNDY & FOOD

Regular wine consumption has long symbolised the attainment of a certain personal and social refinement. Indeed, one might consider it a vector of civilisation. In this respect, it is closely allied to the arts of the table progressively adopted by most developed societies and is justly considered as marking a stage in the evolution of taste and discernment. In modern times, this process has been sustained by a relatively small caucus of *vignerons* dedicated to *terroir*, tradition and excellence, supported by like-minded sommeliers and restaurateurs.

Most wines, particularly the finest reds, are made to be enjoyed with food. Sadly, the dramatic rise in the price of top Burgundy now means that much is sniffed, sipped and spat in tasting-size pours rather than in decent measure around a well-provisioned table. This analytical approach to wine has leached into the restaurant business where the rise and accessibility of 'fine dining' has spawned an industry devoted to the subject of 'wine and food pairing'. This false gastronomy dissects aromas, flavours and textures on both sides of that equation with the apparent object of arriving at ideal combinations of wine and food and vice versa. Its high priests talk in exaggerated language of 'the limitations of dramatic structure' and the 'dynamic range' of menus and of meals as 'compositions' which 'might easily open with savage ferocity before moving to a conclusion of gentle serenity'. (From a noted fine wine magazine, July 2009. I will spare the author by not further identifying the source of this pretentious drivel which does nothing for the cause of civilised eating and drinking.)

Such projects take little account of reality. People tend to drink what they enjoy and can afford (especially in restaurants) and wine selection often takes second place to that of food. We eat what we like and drink what we like – often together – generally with little regard to the niceties of compatibility. These foodenistas also disregard the personal aspect of drinking whereby individual preferences and occasion powerfully affect perception. A light, floral rosé or a simple Riesling drunk on a warm, sunlit deck after a beautiful walk, a few sets of tennis, a round of golf or a pitch of untracked powder can easily trump the greatest Pétrus, Hermitage or Chevalier-Montrachet broached to smooth over a monumental matrimonial. Wine selection is influenced by mood, perception, the season, the weather and a multiplicity of extraneous circumstances which cannot be mapped onto the objective landscape of 'pairings'. Unless the purpose of the meal revolves around wine, it is generally the ambience and attendant circumstances rather than wine itself that defines the experience. Reducing such pleasures to a set of

rules is pseudo-science at its most absurd and should not be given mind-space by anyone with an ounce of good sense.

The only rule is that you must drink what suits the mood and the moment. If you have a special bottle it makes obvious sense to give it the best chance to show itself to good account. Where food is concerned, this means avoiding competing flavours. Known incompatibilities for most fine wine include chocolate, eggs, highly smoked food and for some obscure reason, ham. Oily fish also presents difficulties as do heavily spiced and most curried dishes. These incompatibilities apart, the world is your oyster – or perhaps not as oysters are too salty for most wines, Chablis and Champagne excepted.

In selecting food for wine, a good rule of thumb is that the greater the wine the more refined should be the food. Simple dishes – meaning simple in flavour or robustness rather than culinary simplicity – are best enjoyed with younger or lesser wines; hearty fare with hearty, uncomplicated wine. However, the concepts of simplicity and complexity have become confused. A grilled piece of noble fish is, in essence, a simple dish but its very delicacy and richness of flavour provide an ideal foil for a top-notch Chardonnay (or dry Riesling, Sémillon or Pinot Gris). Conversely the notion of culinary refinement is all too often misinterpreted by chefs who understand it as requiring the maximum number of different flavours on one plate and a minimum of twenty words on the menu. Deprived of several lines of dish description, customers in high-end establishments seem to feel themselves short-changed. At the production end, an exaggerated zeal for fusion generally results in little more edifying than con-fusion. As the late food critic Egon Ronay pithily sums it up, in most cases this is 'nothing more than ridiculous and pointless eccentricity'. Subtlety in wine demands subtlety in the kitchen which rarely works with an exaggerated palette of ingredients; in any case, good quality raw materials don't require elaborate disguise – more than three different principal flavours in a dish and you are probably overdoing it. Provided one's fish or meat is of fine quality – the sole requirement is to retain its flavour and texture onto the plate, unsullied by overfussy accompaniments. Sauces complement (a much overworked word) textures and subtle spice and seasoning can enhance (another one!) flavour and add aromatic interest. Too often, unfortunately, the whole enterprise founders on the unholy alliance of unsubtlety and exaggerated culinary ambition.

First-rate ingredients simply cooked - the finest accompaniment to great Burgundy

In deciding on food for Burgundy 'quality' comes into play in two senses: first the quality level – a simple Bourgogne will go better with most rustic regional dishes – in Burgundy the likes of *pot-au-feu, coq-au-vin, jambon persillé, oeufs en meurette;* as one ascends the quality scale from *Régional* through *Village* to *Premier* and *Grand Cru* the demands on the kitchen change as the need becomes one of allowing the wine primacy over the food. To compromise the elegance and complexity of Montrachet or the majesty of Chambertin with elaborate saucing or exotic spice is a serious act of vandalism. In choosing wine there is a natural progression: where food takes pride of place, wine is secondary and simpler; then both food and wine come on equal terms; finally one arrives at a cut-off point at which the wine should take precedence.

A corollary of this is that it is senseless to order great wine in grand restaurants, where one is paying for the skill of a chef to demonstrate culinary pyrotechnics which generally involve assemblages of diverse ingredients – often experimental, at times outrageous – which are unlikely to preserve the subtleties of fine wine.

One has also to consider 'quality' in a second sense which relates it to the individual taste qualities of a given vineyard or producer. A relatively robust Clos de Vougeot or Chambertin will taste differently with a given dish to Crus which emphasise delicacy, such as Volnay or Chambolle-Musigny. There is also the matter of maturity: in general, younger wines, of whatever provenance, with their fruitier flavour profile and firmer tannins can take stronger food than more mature wines which do better with subtler fare. The splendid exception is the marriage of mature wine – northern Rhône Syrah and Côte de Nuits Burgundy in particular – with well-hung winged game, where pronounced flavours on both sides are synergistic rather than competing.

Cheese is particularly difficult. Wine and cheese fight spectacularly and more often end up as mutual wreckers than felicitous companions. Poor wine, however, is well served by strong cheese which masks its imperfections. An old London winetrade adage 'buy on an apple, sell on cheese' makes the point succinctly. The chalkiness of young cheese – especially goat which tends to high natural acidity – sees off most wines comprehensively; at the other end of the maturity cycle, the wonderful nitrogenous pungency of the great French creamy rind cheeses (Brie, Camembert, Epoisses, Pont l'Evêque, Vacherin, Munster and the rest), mature cheddars, Roquefort, Stilton and other strong blues, fight tooth and nail with wine of any sort – a decidedly one-sided

Un embarras de choix!

heat which the cheese invariably wins; even the much vaunted Sauternes:Roquefort combination is far from the harmonious marriage which it is generally portrayed. Best advice: enjoy the cheese, have a biscuit or piece of bread, then tackle the wine. If you must pair Burgundy and cheese, go for the mildest – a young Cîteaux or similar – and avoid anything redolent of the farmyard. Otherwise, save your *Grand Cru* and bring out a mature tangy Madeira or old Oloroso or Palo Cortado Sherry, all greatly underrated and perfect accompaniments to pungent cheeses.

With most generic Bourgognes and simpler *Village* wine you can eat more or less what you like. When one reaches the level of *Premier* or *Grand Cru* some care is needed if you are to get the best from the wine. This is not university degree stuff, merely an appreciation that great wine can be spoiled by inappropriate food. It can also be comprehensively wrecked by bad storage, being served too warm or too cold, and by cheap glasses, in which case the food scarcely matters.

There is no Burgundy producer I know who is not interested in eating or not well aware of what gastronomy is all about. Apart from regular visits to the starred restaurants they supply, many travel to visit their principal markets around the world. This gives them the opportunity to taste and compare different cuisines and to reflect on the diversity of dishes offered to partner their wines. Many also cook superbly and are fascinated by the interplay of food and wine. Their abundant enjoyment of fine food is, however, unclouded by nit-picking dissection of what goes with what. The reality is that wine is designed for and best enjoyed with food but finding that elusive perfect combination is rare. Searching for compatibilities should be fun but not the stuff of nervous breakdowns or literary pretension.

In short, there is no necessity – unless you have nothing better to do – to understand either the physiology of taste or the complexities of wine composition and chemistry and certainly no need to get involved in the intricacies of food science or textural analysis to enjoy to the maximum wine with food. It is enough to appreciate that food changes the taste of wine and vice versa and to be aware of basic incompatibilities, grape characteristics and the sort of flavours and aromas to be expected as wine matures. Beyond this, common sense prevails – drink what you enjoy with food you enjoy. If you are fortunate enough to have some great Burgundy then treat it with respect and allow it the space and the fare to express its true magnificence. Choosing suitable companions to share it is probably far more challenging than choosing the food or fretting over menu 'dynamics'.

CHAPTER 15
BURGUNDY & THE MEDIA

Burgundy has 'enjoyed' a rocky relationship with the media. Unlike Bordeaux where favoured scribes are treated like visiting dignitaries, burgundian *vignerons* have trod a more cautious path and, with a few notable exceptions, kept journalists at arm's length. This approach is the product of natural reticence, a strong independent streak and a fair measure of distrust. As with much else it takes little irresponsible comment to make people clam up and a deal of effort to prise them open again.

Fortunately, Pinot Noir and Chardonnay are grapes which do not lend themselves readily to be turned into *vin des journalistes*. Pneumatic body enhancement, which has done such a power of good for the likes of Syrah, Merlot and Cabernet, is largely inimical to burgundian varieties – both to Pinot Noir and Chardonnay, even given the overoaked, high alcohol styles which characterised the immediate post-war decades in the New World. While most in the media understand this, some continue to view Burgundy through Cabernet spectacles and, not surprisingly, find it wanting. The unappealing leanness they see in many Burgundies elicits unfavourable comparison with the fruity sensuousness they have come to expect from other 'fine' wine. Many, blinded by exposure to new wood, merciless extraction and the vinous equivalent of cosmetic surgery, have difficulty distinguishing contrived concentration from the natural depth that comes from well-managed, low-yielding vineyards. Young Pinot Noir, especially, seems to present particular difficulty for some critics.

This perspective is more than balanced by a caucus of specialist Burgundy commentators. Dedicated and knowledgeable, these people comb the region regularly and work diligently to give consumers and the trade up-to-date information. They chronicle the passage of each vintage with commendable independence identifying those who, in their opinion, are worth watching as well as the underperformers. Nowadays, a grower can no longer expect to coast along on his reputation before being fingered should the standard of his wines decline. Outside this inner circle floats an amorphous journalistic jelly; scribes whose knowledge varies from modest to barely rudimentary with wine appreciation skills to match. Despite the fact that journalists, however competent, are not 'on the ground' day-to-day, some affect to take the place of the *vigneron* and have the temerity to give specific advice on winemaking and maturation. Such infections of hubristic claptrap deserve short shrift.

All is not, however, sunlit. In recent years problems arose because journalists sought, for their own convenience, to operate in Burgundy as they do in Bordeaux via a one-stop shop in the form of a broker who collected samples from many properties which could then be tasted in one place without the inconvenience of multiple visits which were seen as waste of time. *Vignerons* were expected to consign barrel or bottle samples to one central point and these were then taken off for tasting heaven knows where (hotel room), heaven knows when (late at night) and heaven knows how (100 samples an hour, blind or not, and so on), none of which is conducive to sound judgement. This approach is doubly unreliable as cask samples rarely reflect what ends up in the bottle. Domaines felt that this was not doing justice either to them or their wines and sought to change the arrangements and retake control.

They insisted (rightly) that journalists taste at the Domaine where only wines which were in fit condition (which generally means post malo in the spring following the vintage) would be offered in an appropriate order and where, if necessary, a selection of casks of one wine could be shown to give a more representative picture of the final product. This way of working also gave producers the opportunity to assess their competence as much as the reverse and exclude the incompetent and to those interested only in foisting ill-informed opinions on the public. Most importantly, the *vigneron* had the opportunity to interact face-to-face with visitors, not so much to influence judgement as to explain nuances – *terroir*, vine age, harvesting dates, vintage conditions etc – which bear upon a wine's character and prognosis.

Having observed Burgundy for many years, I find the restraint and patience of the Côte's *vignerons* truly saintly, given some of the less savoury rubbish to which they have been subjected – often, sadly, from people who ought to know better and, worse, in some cases clearly designed to further personal agendas. A proportion of this was manifest nonsense from the less-reputable end of the journalistic spectrum but some ill-informed copy emanated from reputable sources and caused much distress. For example, some time ago a high-profile critic in a well-known magazine described a recently released *Grand Cru* from a five-star estate as 'not worth a $10 varietal'. The wine duly blossomed into a worthy ambassador for its origin and status. Neither a retraction nor the courtesy of apology was forthcoming. Such episodes merely serve to heighten producers' distrust of the media. Fortunately, Burgundy's new-found self-confidence means those at the top end are not beholden to critical approbation to promote their wares and can be selective as to which wine-writers they receive. A few of the worst offenders have justifiably been shown the door; the best now visit on terms of mutual respect. Wine journalism demands humility as well as intelligent understanding; ego-trips are ill-advised and profoundly unattractive.

The fact that young Burgundy is barely fit to sample until spring following the vintage has not prevented the annual rush of journalists anxious to scoop the important 'first impressions of the vintage' for an impatient market seeking information before it really makes sense to give it. Too many assessments are undertaken early, often in November when wines are unfinished; what is tasted then is unlikely to reflect accurately what ends up in bottle. Growers will understandably show their best lots and, even if they wanted to, cannot possibly offer a representative sample of say twenty casks of a single wine, even in the unlikely event that they have decided on the final assemblage. The best time to taste before bottling is immediately before or preferably just after malo. At this stage of a wine's evolution the most useful indicators relate to structure and texture rather than to transient aromas and flavours which have no place in descriptions until much later. At this stage one can only expect a glimpse of a wine's true character. In some vintages (for example 1985, 1991, 1994 and 2001) early guidance proved misguided – either too optimistic (1985) or the reverse. Responsible writers revised their evaluations; most did not bother. The ideal time for judgement is when the wines have settled down in bottle. Even if today's market conditions make this impractical, pre-bottling assessments have limited value as definitive appraisals.

The time-consuming deluge of individual visits faced by Domaines, especially at the top end, has to some extent been alleviated by the Grands Jours de Bourgogne, a triennial week-long festival started in 1986 and designed to showcase recent (but usually not the latest) vintages to the trade and important consumers. This is conducted in a village-by-village wine-fair format where estates gather to show their wares. Some villages put on special tastings – *Premiers* and *Grands Crus* perhaps in Morey-St-Denis, a Clos de Vougeot horizontal at the Château, or a *terroir*-themed tasting in Chassagne-Montrachet. These are well-organised events where tasters can move at their own pace, sample what interests them and then perhaps follow up with selective Domaine visits. This works to everyone's advantage.

For years there has been concern about the manner in which wines are tasted. Henri Jayer described the proceedings of some so-called professional tasters as 'scandalous'. 'They manage to judge 150 wines in the morning, as many during the afternoon and sometimes even another series after dinner. They make their choice and one finds the results in a revue several months later. Who is capable of objectivity with the 50th or 60th wine tasted when the palate is saturated with tannins and alcohol … They cannot underpin a serious evaluation of Burgundy's wines' (quoted in Rigaux, op. cit., 1997). Jayer makes two important points: first, the number of wines tasted is far beyond what the palate can reasonably cope with; second, that the speed needed to taste so many samples is incompatible with good judgement. Both are entirely fair: after a time even the best-trained palate succumbs to distortion and fatigue which then tends to exaggerate the influence of high-impact elements, and it really is impossible to make any kind of credible assessment on a wine with a few seconds exposure as flavours need time to develop on the palate. These are matters of neurophysiology not opinion and unlikely to be the subject of significant individual variance. The message is clear: be very wary of assessments from such sources. Of course writers have only so much to devote to each visit; nonetheless, the demands of credibility and integrity require that they work at a sensible pace.

The tasting notes by mean of which much of this endeavour reaches the public offer little more than a lexicon of exotic adjectives and purple prose. Depicting any wine, especially Burgundy, as the produce of a variegated fruit and vegetable stall is of questionable value for the simple reason that aromas and flavours change dramatically during *élevage* and again in the months after bottling. Whether a wine evokes blueberry, blackberry, cranberry, bilberry, loganberry, wimberry, wortleberry, boysenberry, gooseberry, tayberry, rocket, pocket or docket is irrelevant as this week's liquorice and lavender can all too easily turn into next week's gammon and spinach. The only value in filling page upon page with language of such villaous ugliness is to sell magazines. Indeed, one is often tempted to enquire, while ploughing through these interminable vegetarian smorgasbords, what happened to the varietal fruit; submerged, presumably, beneath the general weight of horticulture or perhaps lost in action altogether.

Then there is the controversial matter of scoring. Many find this practice objectionable, not just because of the inherent implausibility of reducing wine to numbers but also because scoring systems always seem to bunch near the top of whatever scale is chosen. If 10/20 or 50/100 denotes undrinkable or faulty

then why bother with 1–10 or 1–50? At the other end, does it really make sense to mark one wine 16.5 and another 17.0 – what does this half point difference mean in tasting reality? Not much probably, but it may dramatically affect a wine's saleability. In any event, superimposing further categories seems to destroy the point of what is supposed to be an ordinal scale. For many consumers a score of 19 out of 20 or above means 'must buy' while one of sub-17 means 'leave alone'. The absurdity of this hardly needs pointing out.

This is not to say that numerical scores, tasting notes and the rest have no place in wine writing. One can see the attraction of quantifying the inherently unquantifiable, but must also recognise the pitfalls. Sensation is not science, nor pleasure readily mapped on to taste qualities. A score provides a rough guide but is no substitute for understanding what contributes to the character of a wine or help in assessing its evolution or capacity to delight. Nor are numbers, however sophisticatedly crunched, the slightest indication of the enjoyment to be had from a well-made bottle from a junior vintage, smaller appellation or lesser-known producer. Informed descriptions and scores can be a useful resource and the ability to produce them matters to those whose job is communication; but such are all too often cheap copy and their value has been greatly overplayed. Einstein's epigram encapsulates the difficulty: 'Not everything that can be counted counts; not everything that counts can be counted.'

A more immediate consequence of attempts at quantification is a skewed market as buyers chase the 90+ pointers and avoid the also-rans. Genuine connoisseurship does not consist in having a deep enough pocket to buy what someone else has scored highly but in developing a profound understanding and appreciation of the factors that contribute to wine quality and refining one's palate to reflect that understanding. In the quest for drinking pleasure discernment definitely trumps dollars.

Today's wine-writing panjandrums make or break reputations. If you have the power to destroy livelihoods and influence expensive buying decisions, consumers of your output have the right to expect integrity, independence and, above all, competence. Evaluating young wine, especially Burgundy, requires training and expertise; endless practice is not enough. One only has to look at any skilled activity – for instance recreational skiers or golfers – to appreciate that doing something

Previous page: Line-up of valuable Burgundy wines

for years is no guarantee of mastery. It is therefore entirely reasonable to expect those who set themselves up as pundits to demonstrate their competence with a reputable qualification such as the British-run Master of Wine or a wine evaluation Diploma from a recognised authority. The fact that these are openly derided in some quarters – usually by those who might have difficulty obtaining them – makes the value of such people's recommendations questionable.

There is a continuing debate as to whether or not wines should be judged blind. The case for the former rests largely on the fact that blind tasting removes influence from preconception. There is an equally compelling argument for tasting 'sighted' (the only option in a grower's cellar) particularly in a group where discussion and background help to eliminate personal idiosyncrasies. However, smoothing 'highs' and 'lows' in this way tends to produce a neutral consensus.

The media are understandably inordinately fond of blind tastings which pit Burgundy against the New World. In general these heats are short ones, as classically styled wines are poorly rewarded in comparative tastings compared with those from regions producing wines with strong primary fruit characters. The position is reversed once the wines age, when Burgundies reveal the mature complexities for which the New World has, as yet, no ready response. Ageability is the single greatest criterion of great Pinot Noir and Chardonnay and while it is easy to understand the relish of an undiscovered New World producer beating a top-class Burgundy Domaine, such triumphs reflect a false comparison. The New World has come relatively recently to both Pinot and Chardonnay and it makes no sense whatever to taste these technologically precise young wines against great Burgundies. In any event, reducing Burgundy to mere varietal wines, such beauty contests completely disregard its ethos and culture.

With a wide variation in journalistic quality, cutting out the middleman seems a sensible policy. *Vignerons* now increasingly choose to communicate directly with their markets via the internet and many Domaines have excellent multilingual websites. What is noteworthy is that winemakers rarely post definitive evaluations of wines or vintages until some time has elapsed and even then tend towards caution. If producers steeped in years of experience are reticent in making such assessments what qualifies outsiders to second guess them?

Minor cavils apart, the market is well-served by the best of today's media. Their reportage is fair and honest and access to the internet has enabled them to bring a wealth of resources to anyone seeking to stock their cellar with good Burgundy: progress all round which should be widely welcomed. What remains of concern is the almost impregnable status of the modern guru; gurus are guides not gods and it is to be hoped that their influence will be radically reassessed as the market becomes more sophisticated. Meanwhile, each consumer must make his own terms with the undoubted fact that journalists' assessments inevitably reflect the preferences and personalities of those who make them and that accepting someone else's opinion is to abrogate to a greater or lesser extent one's own distinctive ability to judge according to individual taste and culture.

Tasting notes - an invaluable aide-memoire

It is perfectly reasonable to ask whether Burgundy is the best place to make Pinot Noir and Chardonnay. This is not the same, however, as asking where the best Pinot or Chardonnay is made. Producers outside the Côte ask both questions and to neither is the answer as straightforward as one might suppose.

Undoubtedly, when it comes to *vin de terroir,* Burgundy is presently unchallenged. Along with Germany, Piedmont and the northern Rhône, it turns out the most compelling examples of site-specific wine to be found anywhere. Although, in spite of highly promising site discoveries (such as Central Otago, Mornington Peninsula or the Willamette Valley), Burgundy is likely to remain supreme in this respect for the foreseeable future, there is no *a priori* reason why this should be so: the book

of great *terroir* is not finite. Indeed, *terroir* wine is not the only valid expression of either Pinot Noir or Chardonnay. When it comes to *vin de cépage* the contest is less clear with delicious, finely crafted examples of both varieties from as far afield as New Zealand, Australia, South Africa and the USA. Most come from young vines and it is therefore entirely conceivable that when these plantings mature their wines could have the depth and presence to rival those of the Côte, albeit as different individual expressions of the varieties. By then producers will have mastered their vineyards and their focus will have shifted from producing varietal to *terroir*-driven wine. It is therefore worthwhile casting an eye over the similarities and differences between Burgundy and its would-be rivals.

Autumn vines in South Africa's stunning cape winelands

Producers outside the Côte need a clearly defined route map. At present there is understandably much heart-searching over style. Experimentation and uncertainty throws up Pinots spanning a spectrum from dense, extracty, Syrah-deep body-builders to strawberry-elegant ballerinas, and Chardonnays ranging from light, floral and unwooded, to the super-charged, canary yellow and exotically fruity. In contrast to France where grapes are the medium not the message, elsewhere the variety, not the land, is the star of the show. Put crudely, this approach emphasises fruit flavours whereas the Old World aims to subdue fruit flavours to transmit a sense of place.

Where large volumes are involved, building a brand involves developing a style which is saleable and likely to attract international attention; in this, stylistic considerations usually trump the quest for absolute quality. At the top end, those with self-confidence eschew the need for competitive success or guru ratings and rely for reputation on the judgement of their clientele. If making elegant wines, fine and light of touch, is the aim you follow this route leaving those needing the prop of public plaudits to go their way and follow market fashion. There is no reason why this perspective should alter but if it does it is likely only do so in response to the recognition and development of site-specificity.

A significant increase in Burgundy exports has made it possible for winemakers to study five-star *terroir* wines at first hand. This is a two-edged sword. While such exposure provides a valuable yardstick, many either make the mistake of trying to shoe-horn their products into a predetermined style with little regard for suitability or drop into the bad habit of picking one idea or practice from a favoured producer and applying it without regard to its place in a cohesive methodology. Using burgundian techniques doesn't make the results Burgundy!

The tendency to draw conclusions too quickly from limited experience is a recurring problem. In general it is not until a vineyard is around twenty years old that it makes sense to attempt any definitive assessment of the character of its wine; in Burgundy, twenty-year-old vines are still considered young. The temptation to compensate for the natural deficiencies of young vines has led to overworking fruit. Treating Pinot Noir like Cabernet or Syrah is a recipe for disaster.

Even with good sites, the problem, in most cases, is not delivering fruit but delivering fruit of a purity matched with a sound structure and sophisticated texture. Here there is no substitute for vine age and close working experience of a

Fine stemware makes all the difference to wine appreciation

vineyard. Structure, power and minerality characterise the best Côte d'Or reds and whites and these derive principally from specific soil-types which are not replicated elsewhere. This is a fact that the New World must live with until it discovers its most propitious sites and develops individual expressions of origin. In this context, it must be remembered that New Zealand's first commercially productive Pinot Noir vine was planted by Larry McKenna at Martinborough Vineyards in 1988, Oregon's by David Lett in 1965 and South Africa's in the 1980s. The development of direction requires careful thought; at present it remains work in progress.

The lesson from Burgundy is that not all vineyards are capable of greatness; there is a pecking order in the qualitative hierarchy which sets the ceiling on quality potential of any given site. Thus a producer in the Mâconnais or Côte Chalonnaise, aware of the limitations of his land, will never claim to aspire to produce great white Burgundy, merely great Mâcon or Pouilly. In contrast, New World producers vie for primacy, setting out to make the greatest Pinot Noir or Chardonnay on earth. A powerful message here in the human sphere for today's egalitarians!

MARGINALITY

Anyone attempting to make Pinot Noir or Chardonnay in the classic burgundian style faces the problem of marginality. If success is defined by classicism, part of Burgundy's allure is the sense of its being made at the limit. Appropriate siting is therefore of paramount importance and key is the realisation that sites with the potential to deliver interesting character are most likely located in cooler areas, away from destructive heat. Both varieties perform best given a longish, cool ripening season. As it is, too much Pinot and Chardonnay are planted in inappropriate places – too hot, poorly drained, heavy clays, excess vigour-promoting nitrogen, and so forth. Vineyards planted in warm climates, on fertile soils and with disease-free clones tend to become galloping sugar factories; conversely, fertility is affected by unduly cool temperatures, so tracking ever higher altitudes to achieve a longer ripening season tends to produce lean, ungenerous wine.

Marginality is assisted, paradoxically, by an element of disease, as the viruses (notably leaf-roll) which attack both Pinot Noir and Chardonnay compensate for excess vigour or heat by reducing yields. It is therefore possible to produce excellent, elegant, European style wine in areas that are significantly warmer than European latitudes provided one accepts the low yields that go with disease and low-vigour soils. The balance is easily destroyed: Pinot's thin skins protect poorly against extremes so it mustn't ripen too slowly or rapidly. Another important consideration is the energy input reaching vines. Due to orbital differences and a localised ozone layer anomaly, the southern hemisphere has 7% more radiation input than the northern hemisphere. As light in the ultra-violet (B) and infra-red ends of the spectrum are critical for ripening tannin, this is a major factor in determining the potential for any particular site. The viticulturalist Richard Smart suggests that the hole in the ozone layer over parts of Australia and New Zealand accounts for the quality of Pinot Noir fruit produced there.

A good case can be made for the importance of diurnal temperature variation. It is no coincidence that the finest Pinots and Chardonnays come from sites where nights are cool, which allows the accumulation of flavour and aroma compounds and preserves acidity, all of which are destroyed by heat. A clue to the mechanisms involved comes from the observation that the synthesis of anthocyanins is temperature dependent: 17–26°C being the optimum. Therefore the proportion of daily temperature that falls within this range is significant. In warmer climates, it is around 20%; in cooler areas (including Burgundy) it reaches 80%. So, in warmer sites, grapes are likely to develop sugar ripeness without anthocyanin accumulation. This has clear implications for site selection.

Defining the most suitable soil-types for Pinot and Chardonnay is bedevilled by the lack of consensus on which factors are essential and which merely tangential, and on the relative contributions to quality of a soil's physical and chemical aspects. The importance of limestone to the structure and minerality of Burgundy is taken as conventional wisdom, but it is doubtful that this is a defining element. The unshakeable belief that it is may simply reflect that this is what Burgundy has. Claude Bourguignon asserts that it is internal surface area of clay that correlates most strongly with vineyard potential rather than any chemical attribute, so limestone may not be the philosopher's stone many take it for. Its chief virtue, high porosity, is equally evident on, for example, the deep gravel beds of Martinborough or Gimblett Road and what limestone there is in New Zealand comes in the form of solid rock rather than age-eroded soil. It has also been suggested that the minerality often associated with limestone has less to do with chemical composition and more to do with high porosity which puts vines under greater water-stress.

Many geologists (Prof. Jake Hancock and Gérard Seguin, for example) have posited physical structure as the critical factors determining quality potential; necessary perhaps but not convincingly sufficient. If pronouncements on the importance of limestone to quality in burgundian varieties are premature, the gadarene rush to find and plant it may be misdirected.

Experience demonstrates unequivocally that clay is essential to both Pinot Noir and Chardonnay; wines grown on it have a taut, austere structural element which those from slate or sandstone lack. Where geologically suitable sites can be found in the New World, the fact of having a mild continental climate without the autumnal rain risks of the Côte together with the freedom of choice in viticulture and winemaking that non-appellation regions enjoy is an inestimable advantage which should be turned to good account. If these factors coalesce there is no reason whatever why *Grand Vin* should not be the result. Meanwhile, it is inadvisable to jump to conclusions until experience shows how much of the quality of a specific site is attributable to climate rather than soil.

Unscientific as 'sense of place' undoubtedly is, the reality is that both varieties – Pinot especially – are very choosy as to sites where they will give that extra dimension of quality which

Young Pinot Noir vines in stony soil at Ata Rangi vineyard, Martinborough, New Zealand

turns 'good' into something special. The New World tends to focus on *terroir*, clone and technical winemaking competence, often forgetting that planting in the wrong place eliminates all prospect of achieving quality before you've harvested the first bunch. Too often the result of great expense and effort are either fruit bombs or else thin, insipid varietal wines with poor structure and simple flavours. Only in a very few sites internationally will burgundian varieties go that extra yard which turns them into something exceptional. This is not to cast gloom on the New World Pinot and Chardonnay industry, rather to emphasise the absolute primacy of site selection. If you have to manipulate your wine to achieve balance on a regular basis then the inescapable conclusion must either be that you have the wrong grapes planted or else that the site is inappropriate.

WHAT TO PLANT

Phylloxera-affected vines, Marlborough, New Zealand

Until relatively recently the lack of virus-free and virus-resistant clones has unquestionably hampered the production of quality burgundian varieties outside France. Badly virused or otherwise poor plant material – for instance the degenerate BK5 Champagne clone – were, for many, the sole available choices. Gradually these vineyards are being replanted with clean, small-berried clones and better adapted rootstock which will, of themselves, improve overall quality and ageability.

Different clones have different growing habits and taste characteristics. As in Burgundy, the debate is whether to plant a single clone or a multiple selection. Many prefer a mix both for health insurance and flavour diversity, a strategy which works well in places with existing productive plantings. In New Zealand, for example, the combination of modern, rich-textured Dijon clones provides a balancing foil for the earthiness and savoury character of the local Abel clone. Some (notably in the USA) have gone further and are experimenting with field blends of different clones on different rootstocks co-fermented, rather than blocks of single clones vinified separately and blended later. The quality of rootstock is as important as that of the scion and the fact that some of the mother blocks may carry disease make this a further quality-limiting factor. Rootstocks 161/49 and 3309 are preferences on the Côte, but the essential consideration is adaptation to soil conditions particularly in respect of active limestone and vine vigour. There are few plantings on own roots (without grafting onto phylloxera-resistant rootstock) but this is risky as phylloxera spreads easily; for example, it has recently reached Martinborough which doubtless terrifies those with ungrafted vines.

Plant density is on the increase with much experimentation at densities comparable to those in Burgundy (up to 12,000 vines per hectare although 4,000–8,000 is the norm). This is felt to promote root competition and thus deeper-rooted, more water-independent vines which better reflect *terroir*. Josh Jensen, who makes fine Pinots and Chardonnays at Calera in southern California, attributes increased wine quality with vine age to deeper root systems and reports that this has allowed him to reduce finings from 3–4 egg whites per cask to just one (the reason for this is unclear). In many places density is constrained by considerations of practicability or economics: decreasing row spacing limits access for machinery to work soils and collect fruit, while increased labour costs make higher densities uneconomic.

CLIMATE & VITICULTURE

Viticulture is a prime determinant of success or failure at building wines with great structure and texture and this, as much an intellectual as a technical process, requires sensitive adaptation to the prevailing conditions, especially those of soil and climate. The main considerations are water management, crop level, matching vine vigour to site and optimising fruit maturity. In particular, careful management of the foliage canopy, the vine's 'engine', through control of both bunch exposure by shading or deleafing and yield by shoot spacing and lateral growth, is an indispensable element of quality fruit production, especially for young vines which tend to high natural vigour. It also gives an element of control over the effects of heat to ensure full ripeness without tipping into overripeness. While great heat and high levels of UV cause problems of sunburn and overripeness, cooler conditions promote reproductive growth in vines (seeds and berries) rather than vegetative growth (leaves and stems).

Canopy management is an effective tool for mitigating the adverse effects of inappropriate siting but becomes complicated in places that are less than ideal. These days, as Richard Smart has commented (interview in www.grape.co.za 2002), it is all too often used to remedy defects rather than a proactive practice to deliver quality fruit. An over-efficient canopy is undesirable as it proliferates foliage and super-charges sugar accumulation at the expense of tannin and pigment development. The challenge is to develop and ripen sufficient fruit tannin as this transmits site character which oak tannin does not. Fruit tannin is at the forefront of any great wine and develops increasing prominence as vines age – another good reason not to expect too much from young vineyards. Exposing bunches and flowers to direct sunlight by deleafing ripens tannin and fruit wood, provides aeration and ensures bunches remain free from shading but is not recommended when vines are stressed. Fine-tuning the balance between skin tannin and overall tannin (stems, seeds, etc) can also be managed in the vineyard: low vigour sites give a greater percentage of skin tannin and overall tannin, but the latter is not because of the vigour per se but because of exposure to sunlight and heat. The clear lesson is that there are significant benefits from establishing a better balance between leaf and fruit; the danger is that a mix of viticultural technology, productive disease-free clones and perfect canopies simply turn out high alcohol, fruity, varietal wines – precisely not what is sought.

Texture is also hugely important. Paul Draper at Ridge Vineyards, the most articulate exponent of the need for fine texture, having studied its manifestations with many, often very old vines (mainly Zinfandel), is convinced that texture is primarily vineyard derived and that where it is present there is no need to blend or manipulate to obtain it. He concludes that no matter what was done, many vineyards did not give wines that show sufficient bonding between tannins and anthocyanins to give the desired richness of texture. In general, texture is best worked on in the vineyard rather than in the cellar. New vineyards must therefore be planted and managed on sound information, mindful of the fact that the contribution of site to wine is far more complex than simple statements of climate or soil-type might suggest. There are likely to be considerable advances in thinking on this particular subject.

Small-berried Californian Pinot Noir

HEAT, WATER & STRESS

Most organisms, including vines, benefit from an element of stress. Stress comes through excess heat or drought and matters because it disrupts mechanisms of grape development. Vines need water to work properly but do best where supply is correct rather than excessive or deficient. In Burgundy this means rainfall; elsewhere water arrives both as rain and through irrigation systems. Limiting availability to avoid grapes pumping water and diluting flavour is achieved naturally by well- (but not too well-) drained soils. Deep roots tapping into more stable subterranean water and moderate clay content in soils evens out supply and protects vines from extreme drought and heat spikes. Indeed, the mantra of deep roots as the only route to *terroir* expression may simply reflect their role in protecting vines from water stress. Both heat and lack of water will produce the other main stress factor, dehydration, which is especially destructive of fruit quality. With Pinot Noir heat dehydration promotes shrivelling, which produces dry, jammy flavours; with Chardonnay it results in an overripe, exotic character which enriches flavour in small doses but otherwise becomes overpowering and masks *terroir*. In extreme conditions the vine will shut down without a balanced supply of water to keep ripening and sugar accumulation going. Physiological ripeness issues (see page 222) often relate to the stress levels on vines – so a measure of control to avoid having to accept shrivelling to achieve tannin and flavour ripeness is obviously welcome. In general, irrigation helps reduce stress and deliver decent physiological ripeness at 13–14% alcohol; the disadvantage is that irrigated vines tend to ripen later than non-irrigated ones. Irrigation makes sense provided it is used with quality rather than volume in mind.

Shrivelled fruit - the result of sunburn or dehydration

YIELD & HARVESTING

What is beyond dispute, wherever your vineyard, is that low yields are a critical key to quality. This is not a complicated matter: crop Pinot Noir much above 40–45 hl/ha (many in Burgundy would put 35 hl/ha as an absolute maximum) or Chardonnay over 50 hl/ha and you have blown your chances of making decent wine. A vine can only ripen so much fruit, so increasing yield generally means flavour dilution, deficient texture and lack of depth; winemakers are then tempted to compensate with over-extraction or excessive wood, which blurs purity and compromises balance. Managing yields is a matter of skill – and courage. If you prune short for low yields there is no fall back if frost or hail strike; cordon training helps devigorate young vines, gives more even ripening and bud burst and is cost-effective, but produces slightly larger berries, so many avoid it. Such considerations exercise minds and illustrate policies. With Pinot Noir, reduced yields and increased vine age mean more of the deeper, savoury qualities which fuse the seemingly contrary aspects of delicacy and depth. The process can't be hurried, so those with young vines must adapt to what they have.

When to pick is one of any *vigneron*'s most quality-critical decisions. Properly ripe fruit will deliver its qualities with

Pinot Noir vines at Yarra Yering, Yarra Valley, Victoria, Australia

relatively straightforward winemaking; if not, the winemaker has a hard job and the pitfalls are many. Until relatively recently fruit was harvested when it reached more or less balanced ripeness. Now many, driven by the style preferences of high-profile public palates, deliberately lengthen hang-time for super-ripe flavours and high extract. A few hours or days in autumn heat will increase natural concentration by evaporation and push fruit towards raisining. Extended hang-time is a choice that many find abhorrent and unequivocally disastrous for both Pinot Noir and Chardonnay. As Jim Clendenen of Au Bon Climat in California comments, 'Of course wines have more flavour that way, but is it a better flavour? It's the question of whether you like fresh, just-picked raspberries or stewed, cooked raspberry coulis or raspberry candy. What you taste in those wines is simply more sweetness and less acidity … (they) don't go well with food, and they don't age' (*Los Angeles Times,* 15 September 2004).

For those more concerned with real rather than crowd-pleasing quality, harvesting for balanced fruit is a complicated decision, especially on sites prone to over- or underripeness. Ideally, each constituent of the fruit should be optimally ripe at the moment of harvest – but this is rarely the case, so compromise is generally called for. Does one pick for maximum colour when flavours are likely to be overripe, for acids when flavours are underripe, for flavour and sacrifice colour; or for structure and perhaps sacrifice both? The window of opportunity is narrow, especially with Pinot where grapes can pass from just ripe to overripe in a matter of hours without attaining that elusive ideal balance. Picking Pinot Noir early gives less concentrated wines, lighter in style with a flavour emphasis on the red fruit and floral end of the spectrum. Early harvested Chardonnays can be green and raw in character but the grape rapidly sheds acidity and accumulates sugar, demanding vigilance and risk to harvest at ideal balance. Selectively picking, block by block, row by row or even one side of a row before the other, pays dividends but means manual harvesting which is uneconomic for many. Machines are incompatible with top quality as they only harvest berries, thus liberating juice which starts fermentation sooner than ideally desirable and increasing skin contact, both of which have a negative impact on flavour.

The problem of assessing fruit maturity and thus of deciding when to harvest has been made more complex by the realisation that physiological maturity is largely unrelated to sugars. It used to be thought that grapes were ripe when they reached a predetermined sugar level. Indeed, in the 1970s grapegrowers in California were paid, in part, on harvest sugars – the higher the better. Now the decision is more sophisticated as it is has become clear that ripe sugars do not necessarily mean ripe everything else, especially flavours. Sugar levels may be fine yet tannins remain hard and green. This is the problem of 'physiological ripeness', a loosely used concept for which there is, as yet, no industry accepted definition. The general idea is illustrated by imagining four ripening clocks, one each for sugars, phenolics, acids and flavours. These track the ripeness of each component and run concurrently but at different rates depending on site, climate etc. The trick is to coax them to arrive simultaneously at the optimum value.

While much can be done during the growing season to promote even development, picking is still often based on gut-feel rather than any precise, science-driven criteria. Some pick on taste, some on analysis; others use a combination of both. In Burgundy, more often than not, adequate phenolic (tannin) ripeness is attained before adequate sugars – making chaptalisation necessary. Elsewhere – in warmer Oregon and parts of South Africa, for example – the reverse is true. In general, a marginal sugar deficiency (which can be corrected) is preferable to excess, and attaining full colour of less importance than preserving elegance and maximising flavour ripeness. Indeed, growers often report that fruit aromatics are more intense at lower ripeness levels.

The desirability of trading off colour density for flavour needs to be more widely accepted. One option is to harvest some clones for optimum fruit flavour, leaving others to ripen fully; the eventual balance is likely to improve on any individual component. How you characterise the problem often dictates the solution: for some, the concern is how to devigorate sugar production to allow phenolics to catch up; another formulation has it that leaf-fall often occurs before the fruit is fully ripe, so whilst further hang-time may achieve concentration of flavours it does not necessarily produce development of flavours. Here the solution is to try and keep leaves on the vines to delay autumn senescence. It is an unfortunate fact that whereas in the past one picked ripe for phenolics, modern perspectives mean that you now often pick ripe for style. For producers seriously intent on quality, the lessons are clear: know your vineyards intimately and be prepared to accept the risks to achieve proper fruit maturity. This is the new frontier.

A sea of virused vines near Stellenbosch, South Africa

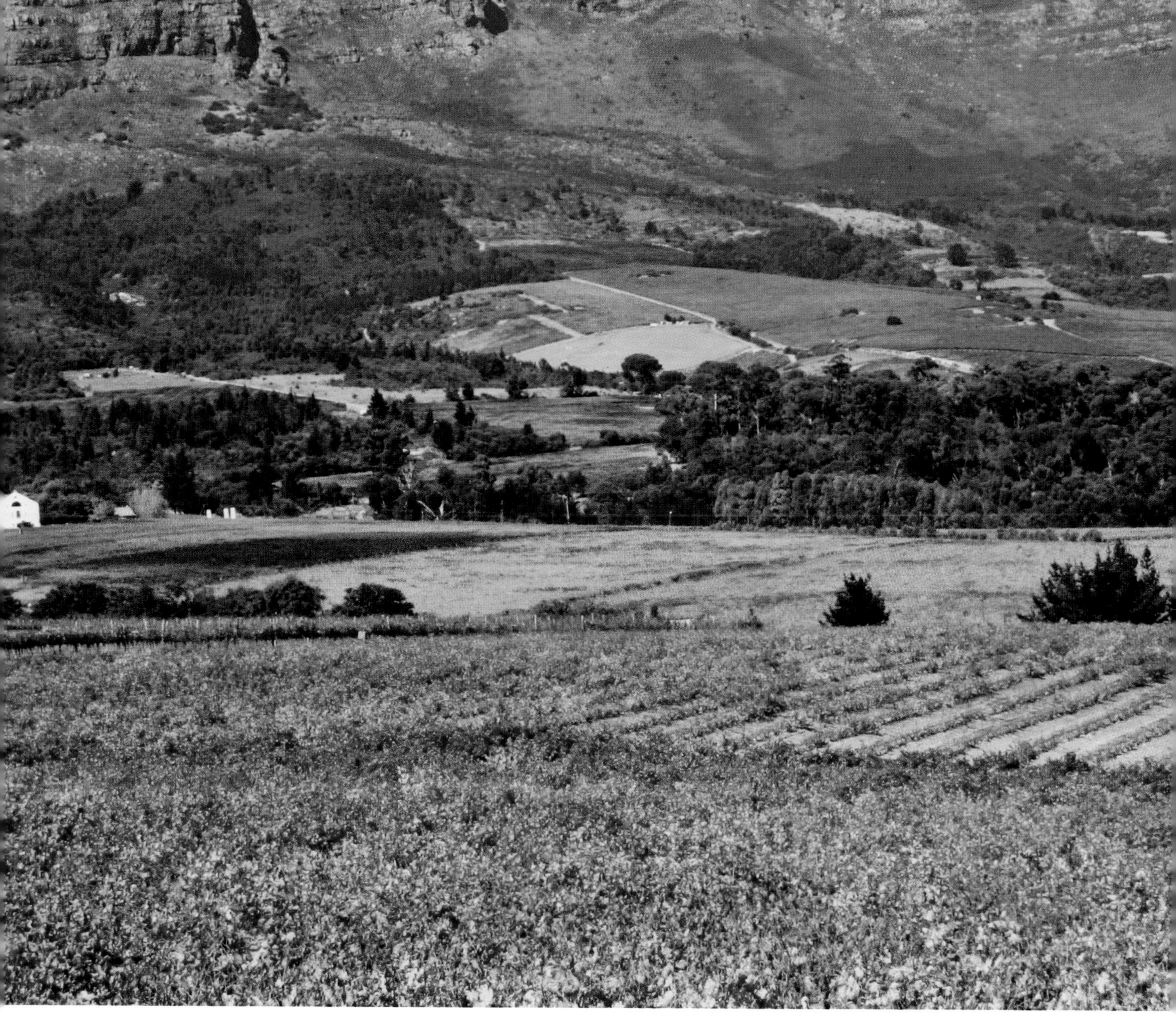

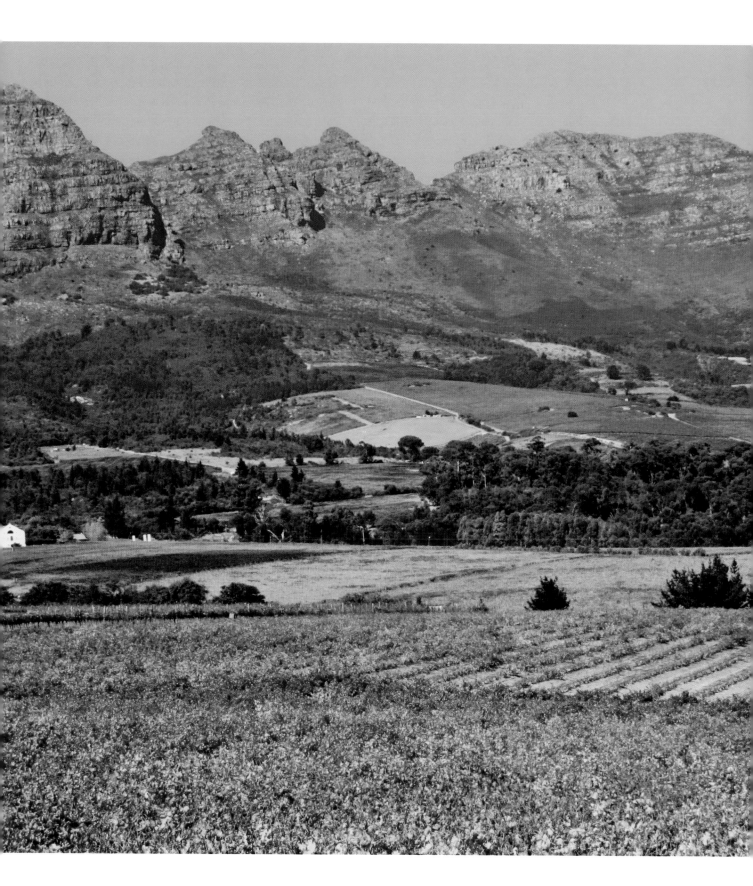

VINIFICATION

It is worth restating that successful wine production is an amalgam of three fundamental stages: growing maximum character into grapes; extracting this into wine; and preserving it into bottle. In this, excess is definitely the enemy of the good. *Terroir* makes a convenient excuse for poor winemaking: 'it's the *terroir* talking' can often be translated as 'our winemaker isn't up to it', so it is essential to find out what works on a particular site.

Pinot Noir is less forgiving than Chardonnay although both are compatible with wide stylistic variation and a variety of vinifications. What is evident is that on many sites, especially those with young vines, delivering fruit is much easier than delivering structure. While abundant fruit is a deliberate style element in wines for early drinking, a sound structure is indispensable for those intended to develop in bottle. This is best coming from fruit tannins, but all too often derives instead from high levels of new wood. Refinements in barrelmaking enable winemakers to emphasise certain flavours and promote a desired palate structure but such recipes give wines with superficial appeal that lack distinctive individuality and the qualities for graceful long-term development. Delicacy is also easily destroyed by excessive new wood. Some winemakers report, curiously, that French-coopered American oak is altogether gentler and somewhat spicier imparting less obvious vanilla character than American oak coopered in the US. In addition, US oak used in larger casks (usually 500 litres) seems to integrate wine and wood

better than traditional-sized barrels; however, this may be an effect of volume as much as of oak origin. If they haven't done so already, perhaps someone might try casks made from both American and French oak. In warmer regions, wines have naturally higher extract and can take more oak; but what is being added? Power should properly come from a wine's inner energy not from alcohol or artificial structure. The aim should be to encourage oak to 'dance' with the wine, not to crush it to pieces. As Steve Smith MW, a talented New Zealand winemaker, put it: 'we almost put our white winemaking cap on when making Pinot Noir'. Making Pinot as if it were Riesling is rather an insightful approach.

In warmer regions, acid balance is a particular problem. Not only do different places give different acid compositions – for example, New Zealand tends to produce more malic acid than Burgundy – but winemaker education turns out graduates filled with Pavlovian terror of bottling anything with the slightest acid deficiency. This may make sense for bulk wine but is less relevant to the production of fine wine. Such inflexibility means that acid is adjusted in many wines which don't need it. Chardonnay, which lacks structural tannin to any significant degree, reacts to acid deficiency both in terms of taste balance and of reduced longevity, so a decent level of natural, ripe acidity is therefore essential. Added acid is rarely a quality improver. 'Rely on natural acidity where possible' should be emblazoned above every winery door.

Alcohol and texture are also critical to overall balance and appeal; any wine aspiring to greatness should leave a sensation of cohesion and seamlessness in the mouth. Both alcohol (ethanol) and new wood enhance the impression of 'sweetness' and mask deficiencies, particularly raw tannins and acidity, but an excess of either is unpleasant. Fruit and flavour are relatively easy to deliver – texture is the hard bit, especially with Pinot Noir which often lacks integration and fine mouthfeel. *Grand Vin* has an almost unobtrusive structure – 'silkiness' is not far off – which allows the fruit and underlying complexity to emerge.

Much destruction of balance comes through using artificial rather than natural yeasts in fermentations. There are strong opinions on both sides of this debate, but experience suggests that those who rely on commercial yeasts buy their reassurance that every gram of sugar will be scavenged out and fermented to alcohol at the expense of elegance. Another ruse is to leave residual sugar in both Pinot and Chardonnay; this gives superficial market appeal but is not a quality marker.

Young vines in a climate-controlled propagation fridge

APPELLATIONS

After a few years of production the temptation to declare certain sites or regions as of special qualitative significance may become hard to resist. The arguments for not delimiting are strong unless there are distinct soil types (as in New Zealand's Gimblett Road or Australia's Coonawarra terra rossa) clearly related to quality and with indisputable geographical boundaries. Even here there are pitfalls – think of the dissent over Chablis Kimmeridgian clays (*Le vrais Chablis et les autres*) or the fall-out over boundaries in Coonawarra. Politics apart, it seems prudent to defer delimitation until the evidence is incontestable. It may well be that quality is more accurately correlated with elevation, exposition or climate than with specific soil types and these are inherently harder to map.

New vineyard planting at Craggy Range, Martinborough, New Zealand

WHERE NEXT?

Although much excellent wine has been made and strenuous efforts continue to find suitable sites, New World experience with burgundian grapes is still in its infancy. The passion for them from an increasingly sophisticated consumer base has more than been matched by the coterie of producers prepared to requite it. It is tempting, but mistaken, to believe that without any generally accepted style guidelines 'anything goes'.

There is much that still needs to be ingrained by those seeking to produce high-quality Pinot Noir and Chardonnay. In particular, there is a need for better acquaintance with top-class examples – not to mimic Burgundy but to develop a more finely tuned idea of first-divison quality. More thought also needs to be given to wine selection. While there is a strong trend towards premium individual vineyard bottlings it is far from evident that this is the wisest direction. New vineyards will take time – generations possibly – to reveal their character and potential, and without clear indications that a site is exceptional, it would make more sense in the meantime to use cask selection to define premium bottlings. On a broader canvas, regional 'specialities' rather than vineyard identity are the most logical marketing peg and should be the first step on the route to promoting quality.

One reason why many areas have failed to make significant headway with burgundian varieties is a lack of focus. Specialisation is required at both producer and regional level. Producers must make a commitment to these as flagship wines rather than just other products in their range, and regions promote them more actively. This means accepting that Pinot Noir, in particular, is a long-term project requiring significant human and financial resources, not just something that industrial volumes of Sauvignon Blanc or Cabernet allow you to play with. A producer with a couple of blocks of Pinot in a larger range will never achieve top class. Not the least in this approach must be a strong measure of critical self-honesty, to admit that a wine is ordinary and above all not to release indifferent wine at exaggerated prices. Bland, poorly made commercial Pinot and Chardonnay row the consumer in the wrong direction – away from the individuality and interest these varieties are capable of, even at entry level. Fighting the market-dominance of Sauvignon Blanc, Cabernet, Merlot and Syrah will require a sustained effort to communicate the individuality, food-friendliness and age-worthiness of burgundian varieties and to convince consumers that light-coloured reds and minerally whites can be truly classy. This means a collective effort, funds and regional marketing. The fact of a caucus of producers all doing much the same thing gives Burgundy a powerful marketing edge. What the New World can deliver, and does so in abundance, is value, putting neophytes on the path of discovery which, with the finest Burgundies at least, would otherwise be out of range.

Is Burgundy the best place to make Pinot Noir and Chardonnay? With a relatively short growing season and the attendant risks of spring frost, hail and prolonged autumn downpours, its climate is certainly far from ideal. Indeed, it has even been suggested that Burgundy succeeds despite its climate. Yet, notwithstanding many excellent non-burgundian wines at, as it were, *Village* and *Premier Cru* level and tantalising, if occasional, glimpses of greatness, nothing has yet emerged which approaches the finesse, complexity and class which define *Grand Vin*. It is also important in a universe where elegance is king that producers and their critics factor leanness and austerity into a mindset that too often equates quality with opulence.

Dr Neil McCallum has argued persuasively in his newsletter

Vineyard at Calera, a top Californian Pinot producer

The strong south-easterly wind - the 'Cape Doctor' - retards ripening but helps keep the vineyards free of airborne pests and diseases

'Dry River Jottings' (www.dryriver.co.nz, 2001) that 'overall … the Burgundian *terroir* presents a very narrow vision of what Pinot Noir is capable of, for climatic, viticultural and winemaking reasons'. As he sees it, Burgundy's climate and winemaking practices, restrictive by law and tradition, work against the optimisation of 'flavour and colour possibilities presented to the winemaker in the grapes, although [they are] sufficiently formalised to help provide a *terroir* statement'. In particular, he cites sulphur dioxide regimes which damage colour, flavour and texture for the sake of the popular goals of hygiene and microbiological security: 'Nowadays there are other ways of achieving these safety goals and one wonders what the results might be if the traditions in question had not been so slow to change.' The thrust of an eloquent argument is two-fold: first, it is not that Burgundy is not the best place to make Pinot and Chardonnay rather that with less restrictive practices and a looser hold on 'tradition' it could do better; second, that it will take time for New World styles to become detached from the apron strings of Burgundy and thereby to find acceptance in their own right. The former presents as much a challenge to the Old World as to the New.

Burgundy's perspective is that while the New World depicts itself as passionate for *terroir*, it continues to turn out *vins technologiques*, wines essentially fashioned by taste-choice in response to consumer demand. Whatever the merits of this opinion, *terroir* is not a monopoly of the Côte d'Or and there should be absolutely no doubt that fine sites are waiting to be discovered and exploited. This is the long-term challenge for today's neo-Burgundians.

The immediately pressing task is to introduce hardened Cabernet, Merlot and Sauvignon Blanc drinkers to fine Pinot and Chardonnay, bringing them the best available at every price-point. There is also the need to transmit the Old World's aesthetic to consumers in the New to feed the developing interest in more classically styled wines. As tastes migrate away from primary fruit to the deeper pleasures of aged flavours and subtle structures, thoughts of both producers and consumers will inevitably turn to *terroir* and the development of regional and local identities. In the meantime producers strive to attain the same sensory and emotional response from their wines as one has from benchmark Burgundy even if this ends up as a different expression of the given variety. Fine Pinot Noirs from New Zealand, Russian River or Oregon and Chardonnays from California, Australia or South Africa can hold their heads high, not because they resemble Burgundy but because they exemplify attractive, if different, varietal expressions. The late Len Evans, Australian wine's most outspoken advocate, suggested that the hallmark of a great wine producer is constant dissatisfaction. This is not a bad precept for anyone anywhere aspiring to offer great Pinot Noir or Chardonnay.

POSTSCRIPT

While this book is principally about quality it is also, as it must be, about pleasure. Where wine is concerned people are by and large like domestic cats – they do what they want to do. The vast majority drink what gives them pleasure and suits the mood irrespective of what anyone else tells them is worthy. From this perspective, considerations of absolute quality play no obvious role and it is easy to see why the consumer's preferred red wine formula – sweet fruit, alcohol, soft tannin and unobtrusive acid – has been so enthusiastically embraced and emulated. Considerable fire-power has been brought to bear to support this particular style which, albeit in superior form and at greatly inflated price, has now come in many minds to define excellence. In this respect, much of the wine world is now driven by fashion which prefers a few, clearly delineated style attributes to the subtleties of grace, individuality and definition. This conveniently overlooks the fact that high-impact, super-concentration plus absence of defects does not equate to quality however slick the presentation or universal the appeal. It also creates obvious difficulty for Burgundy's hierarchical system where quality is closely allied to site identity, with styles favouring subtlety and diversity to which the 'sweet 'n' sexy' model is profoundly ill-suited. In such a market, driven largely by conformity, Burgundy's abiding challenge is to educate consumers as much to what it is not as to what it is and that its appeal lies as much in originality as in any intrinsic attributes of quality.

Burgundy's classically structured styles clash with expectations of immediacy and obviousness and much is lost when the rich traditions of its wine culture are subjected to the superficial perspectives of contemporary taste. Fortunately, exposure to genuinely fine wine continues to lead many away from the crude attractions of exaggerated flavour to an appreciation of individuality, restraint and elegance. As consumers become more confident and adventurous they are increasingly prepared to take on the challenge Burgundy presents and delight in the discovery of subtlety this brings.

Where does pleasure fit in to all this? We can, I think, often answer every conceivable question about a wine yet have no idea how to answer a question about pleasure. Whatever the wine panjandrums may say, pleasure, being defined by a unique relationship between wine and consumer, is inherently unquantifiable. This highlights the absurdity of 'wine by numbers' – the idea that a 90 pointer is necessarily more enjoyable than 85. Wine critics will no doubt say that they are deliberately taking pleasure out of the reckoning for the sake of objectivity; drinkers will riposte that pleasure is the sole reason for their drinking in the first place. Beyond any derivative delight to be had from the 'privilege' of drinking a highly scored wine, ratings are no reference for pleasure potential. As consumers establish the confidence to detach themselves from guru apron-strings, they will increasingly realise that numbers are poor indicators of pleasure and that they are perfectly capable of deciding for themselves what they value and enjoy.

A further problem for Burgundy is that its deeper delights are as much intellectual as they are sensual and thus by no means destined for everyone. Indeed, much of what connoisseur circles consider fine many find unappealing. Elitist as it may seem, there are indeed absolutes of quality but these have no obvious pleasure connotation, tending to reflect tastes acquired and refined by experience. Just as Plato abhorred the possibility that certain ideas should fall into the wrong hands – those considered incapable of proper understanding – so the rarest and most precious of Burgundies risk much the same fate of finding their way onto uncomprehending palates.

Fine Burgundy exemplifies the subtlety and finely crafted individuality which epitomises cultivated standards of taste. The need for deeper understanding confronts the modern consumerist ethic which emphasises hedonism and promotes leisure as an unenriching compound of maximum expenditure and minimum effort in a market where items of equal price are perceived as equally tasteful. This is reinforced by arrangements which put income, and thus purchasing power, into the hands of people with no longstanding wine culture, who have never had the opportunity to cultivate taste: an ideal platform for commercial and social exploitation.

In such circumstances it is not surprising that red Burgundy continues to divide opinion like no other wine, apart perhaps from the whites of Alsace and Germany, with many knowledgeable palates failing to see either the quality or the attraction. Those bitten by the bug have an almost obsessive devotion to the region and its producers and happily immerse themselves in its diversity with a passion, often backed by formidable knowledge. Indifference is not an option: those who dislike Burgundy do so with equal fervour – but fervour which often appears to conceal a lack of understanding rather than any aversion to the wines themselves. It is difficult to understand

Early spring pruning in Bâtard-Montrachet

how any genuine, intelligent wine lover could possibly dislike La Tâche or Musigny.

Burgundy seeks to take you on a journey to discover vineyards and producers through their wines. Embarking on this requires a level of commitment which is a step too far for many, in today's impatient and superficial culture. This requires acceptance of the proposition that quality is related to site identity and furthermore that this is optimally expressed through natural concentration from low-yielding old vines. It also recognises the seminal influence of transmitted history and tradition, both in farming practices and in the heritage of plant material. Appreciating Burgundy is, above all, an activity where reward is related to effort so it is not surprising that its fragmented pattern of production and undoubted inconsistency proves an unappetising conundrum. Politically incorrect as the sentiment may be, *terroir* wines fare best in the hands of dedicated amateurs.

While the idea of *terroir* itself continues to be hotly debated, no-one has questioned the excellence of burgundian *Grand Cru.* Nor has anyone come close to supplying a credible alternative explanation for its supremacy or for the fact that humbler appellations, however skilfully worked, have proved incapable of producing anything remotely comparable. The robustness of Burgundy's hierarchy is powerful evidence of the influence of non-human factors on quality. It remains the touchstone for *terroir* advocates and the nemesis of *terroir* sceptics.

Meanwhile, modern Burgundy exudes solidary confidence. Not since the latter decades of the *siècle du soleil* and the zenith of négociant power at the end of the 19th century has the region glowed so brightly. This comes not simply from the power of restricted supply over insatiable demand but from confidence in the ability to deliver consistently fine quality at every level. International interest in the region has now mushroomed to a point at which surging demand, especially from the Far East, threatens value; this is a market force with which consumers must live. With the New World increasingly offering affordable alternatives and exciting quality this pressure should ease.

This is not necessarily to say that the tally of truly exciting wines has increased dramatically. Technological advance and better understanding of viticultural and winemaking processes have undoubtedly raised the bar and improved consistency, but these alone will not produce great wine. The art of the *vigneron,*

his sureness of touch and his feel for quality, are what ultimately matter. These, inseparable concomitants of all the finest Domaines both in Burgundy and beyond, remain in remarkably short supply.

Overcoming Burgundy's stylistic non-conformity requires producers and consumers to take a stand for individuality. This task is not made easier by the fact that wine appreciation has a strong cultural dimension. It is much harder for a palate educated on ripe, sweet fruit to see quality in a raw young Burgundy than for a palate accustomed to this style of wine. Indeed, if anecdotes of the finest being mixed with Coca-Cola or Sprite are to be believed, the taste is deeply unpleasant to some cultures. Money from all corners of the world now chases fine wine as much for being a desirable collectible as for its drinking pleasure. This turns *Grand Vin* into a totem of social status rather than something to be savoured for itself, a role it shares with many other rare artefacts. True wine appreciation is more than just liking or disliking a taste coupled with an idea of where the wine comes from; it exemplifies a unique and stimulating interaction which depends as much on what the consumer brings to the wine as the reverse.

Wine is life-enhancing and part of the art of good living. It stimulates the intellect, refines the palate, enlivens food and energises company. Appreciating Burgundy goes further: it invites one to taste *terroir* while imbuing oneself with a culture – a perspective which is increasingly out of tune with the zeitgeist and far removed from the ethos of contemporary values and discourse. Here, Pinot Noir and Chardonnay express nuances and typicity of site, bringing a compelling extra dimension to the pleasure of drinking which is so conspicuously lacking in many modern 'cult' wines. On the Côte d'Or 'Grand Vin' is not the perfect tasting note; it is also the added profundity which comes from a sense of place.

Burgundy is a friendly, welcoming place, animated by skilled, dedicated *vignerons*; a region that should enthral anyone genuinely interested in fine wine. It is my hope that those who already love these people and their wines will have discovered something new and interesting in these pages and that those tempted to explore the region further will be stimulated to do so. If this book furthers that project it will have achieved its principal aim.

A wild orchid growing in an ancient Pinot Noir vine stem

Appendices
Measures

Measures of capacity

In continental Europe, the litre is the unit of liquid measure; in the UK and USA the gallon is used, as well as fluid ounces for bottle sizes. However, UK and US gallons and fluid ounces differ (see below).

0.75 litres = 75 centilitres = 1 standard bottle

1.50 litres = 150 centilitres = 1 magnum

3.00 litres = 300 centilitres = 1 double-magnum

9.00 litres = 900 centilitres = 12 standard bottles = 1 case

100 litres = 1 hectolitre = 133 standard bottles = 11 cases of 12 bottles + 1 bottle = 26.42 US gallons

1 UK gallon = 4.55 litres

1 US gallon = 3.78 litres

1 UK fluid ounce = 28.4 millilitres

1 US fluid ounce = 29.6 millilitres

1 standard bottle (75 centilitres) contains 25.36 UK fluid ounces

1 UK pint = 0.5568 litres

1 US pint = 0.473 litres

Casks:

1 'barrique' = 1 'pièce' = 228 litres in Burgundy (225 litres in Bordeaux), the standard cask size

1 'feuillette' = 1/2 a standard cask

1 'quarteau' = 1/4 a standard cask

1 'demi-muid' = 600 litres; however 'demi-muid' is often used to refer to casks of larger size

The capacity of fermentation or storage vats is usually expressed in hectolitres or gallons according to country convention.

Measures of yield

Yields are expressed in hectolitres per hectare (Europe), tonnes per acre (US, Australia and New Zealand), or tonnes per hectare (South Africa). These are metric tonnes (= 100 kilos = 2,204 pounds weight). 1 tonne per acre = 14 hectolitres per hectare.

Note: 1 UK ton = 2,240 pounds. 1 US short ton = 2000 pounds. 1 US long ton = 2,240 pounds.

1 hectolitre per hectare (hl/ha) = 100 litres per hectare = 133.3 bottles per hectare = 11.1 cases per hectare

1 hl/ha = 53.9 bottles/acre = 4.5 cases per acre

40 hl/ha = 5,332 bottles per hectare = 444 cases per hectare

40 hl/ha = 2,158 bottles per acre = 180 cases per acre

1 standard pièce per hectare = 2.28 hl/ha

15 standard pièces per hectare = 34.2 hl/ha

Units of area and yield

Europe uses hectares and hectolitres per hectare; the USA and Australia/NZ use acres and tonnes per acre; South Africa uses hectares and tonnes/hectare.

Yields and planting density

It takes approximately 130 kilograms of grapes to produce 1 hectolitre of wine.

At a planting density of 10,000 vines per hectare a yield of 40 hl/ha equates to about half a bottle of wine per vine. At 40 hl/ha, 1 hectare will yield 17.8 standard casks (i.e. 17.8 x 225 litres = 444 cases).

A planting density of 11,000 vines per hectare and 8 bunches per vine is approximately equivalent to a yield of 55 hl/ha. This is also equivalent to 1 pièce (cask) per ouvrée = 24 pièces per hectare. This amounts to some 650 grams of grapes, or half a litre of wine, per vine.

A yield of 100 hl/ha requires 13–16,000 kg/ha (13–16 ton/ha) = 5.3–6.5 ton/acre.

1 ton/acre = 2,471 kg/ha equates to around 19 hl/ha

Measures of distance (linear) and area (square)

Metric systems work in kilometres, metres, centimetres and millimetres; imperials in miles, yards, feet and inches.

1 kilometre = 1,000 metres = 0.621 miles

1 metre = 100 centimetres = 1,000 millimetres = 1.094 yards = 3.281 feet

1 mile = 1,760 yards = 1.609 kilometres

1 hectare = 2.471 acres = 100 ares = 10,000 square metres

1 are = 100 square metres

1 journal = 8 ouvrées = 1/3 hectares (i.e. 3 journaux = 1 hectare)

BIBLIOGRAPHY

Raymond Blanc
A Taste of My Life (Bantam, 2008).

Henri Cannard
Balades en Bourgogne (Broché, 1983).

Véronique Cheynier et al.,
'Structure and properties of wine pigments and tannins',
American Jnl of Enology and Viticulture, 2006 (57).

Rolande Gadille
Le Vignoble de la Côte Bourguignonne (Belles Lettres, 1967).

Stephen Gwynn
Burgundy (Constable, 1934).

André Jullien [1728]
Topographie de Tous les Vignobles Connus, translated as *The Topography of All the Known Vineyards* (G. & W.B. Whittaker, 1824).

Matt Kramer
Making Sense of Burgundy (William Morrow, 1990).

Marie-Hélène Landrieu-Lussigny
Les Lieux-Dits dans le Vignoble Bourguignon (Jeanne Laffitte, 1983, Marseille).

Jean Lavalle
Histoire et statistique de la vigne et des grands vins de la Côte d'Or (1855).

Neil McCallum
'Dry River Jottings' *(Little Things Mean a Lot, 2007)*
dryriver.co.nz/index/Home/Jottings

Richard Olney
Romanée-Conti (Rizzoli, 1995).

Pierre Poupon and Gabriel Lioger d'Ardhuy
En Bourgogne, Cabottes et Meurgers (privately published, 1990).

Jacky Rigaux
Le Terroir et le Vigneron (Terre en Vues, 2006).

Jacky Rigaux
Ode aux Grands Vins de Bourgogne (Editions de l'Armançon, 1997).

André Jullien
Topographie de tous les vignobles connus (1824).

Michael Schuster
'*What do We Mean by Quality in Wine Today?*', paper delivered to the Académie Internationale du Vin, London, 2004.

S. Vidal et al. 'The mouth-feel properties of grape and apple proanthocyanidins in a wine-like medium', *Journal of the Science of Food and Agriculture*, 2003, 83 (6).

Acknowledgements

My thanks are due to many who gave freely of their time and expertise. In particular, I should mention the saintly patience of Françoise Vannier-Petit from the University of Dijon who spent hours walking the vineyards explaining the nuances of geology and siting and then more hours correcting the many errors in the manuscript. She also kindly supplied photographs illustrating the Côte's geology. Our shared concern was to publish only information known to be correct. Without Françoise's expertise this book would contain numerous inaccuracies. Needless to say, any that remain are my own.

I also benefited greatly from the expert help of Nancy Sweet, specialist researcher at UC Davis, whose input on US clones was invaluable, from Zelma Long and Phil Freese who took time from busy schedules to make invaluable comments on the grape and viticulture chapters and from Jeremy Seysses for the same on vinification. My sincere thanks to them all.

Special thanks are due to my wife Geraldine, who, as well as contributing many photographs to this book, was unfailingly supportive.

The map of Clos de Vougeot on page 81 is published with the kind permission of *Bourgogne Aujourd'hui* magazine (number 92, February 2010).

The publishing team at Kyle Cathie were both helpful and supportive: Kyle herself, Sophie Allen (editor), Stephanie Evans (copy editor) and Geoff Hayes (designer) all worked hard to produce the best possible result. Eugene Fleury was responsible for the map text design which greatly enhances the value of this book.

This book draws on many sources. Many are acknowledged but if there are ideas or arguments that should have attributions but do not, their authors will rightly feel aggrieved. I trust they will accept my profound apologies and put the lapses down to weak memory or failure to keep proper notes.

A chance conversation with Etienne de Montille one memorable musical evening at Clos de Vougeot sparked the idea for this book, so he deserves special mention. Aubert de Villaine's encouragement both for the new edition of *Great Domaines* and *Grand Cru* has meant much; his agreement to contribute a foreword is a signal mark of favour which is particularly appreciated.

Finally, but by no means least, my very special thanks to all the *vignerons* and producers both in Burgundy and internationally who put up with endless probing into their methods and ideas. These charming and remarkable people work hard to produce the bottles we all cherish and enjoy. Those of us who love Burgundy and its noble grapes would find our world greatly impoverished without their skill and dedication.

Overleaf: Nature's art: close-planted old vines in a snowy landscape